D1715693

Human Behavior and Wall Street

Human Behavior and Wall Street

JOHN L. KING

THE SWALLOW PRESS INC.
CHICAGO

First Edition
First Printing

Published by
The Swallow Press Incorporated
1139 South Wabash Avenue
Chicago, Illinois 60605

LIBRARY OF CONGRESS CATALOG NO. 71-189196
ISBN 0-8040-0560-1

To my Mother and Father
Lillian and William David King

The best-kept secret in the American economy is how it works.

Robert L. Heilbroner

Contents

Tables and Charts

Human Behavior and Wall Street

CHART 1

NATIONAL INCOME AND PRODUCT ACCOUNTS 1971

Relation of the four major measures of production and income flows:

GROSS NATIONAL PRODUCT is the market value of the output of services and goods produced by the nation's economy.

NATIONAL INCOME is the total earnings of labor and property from the production of services and goods.

PERSONAL INCOME is the total income received by persons from all sources.

DISPOSABLE PERSONAL INCOME is the income remaining to persons after payment of personal taxes.

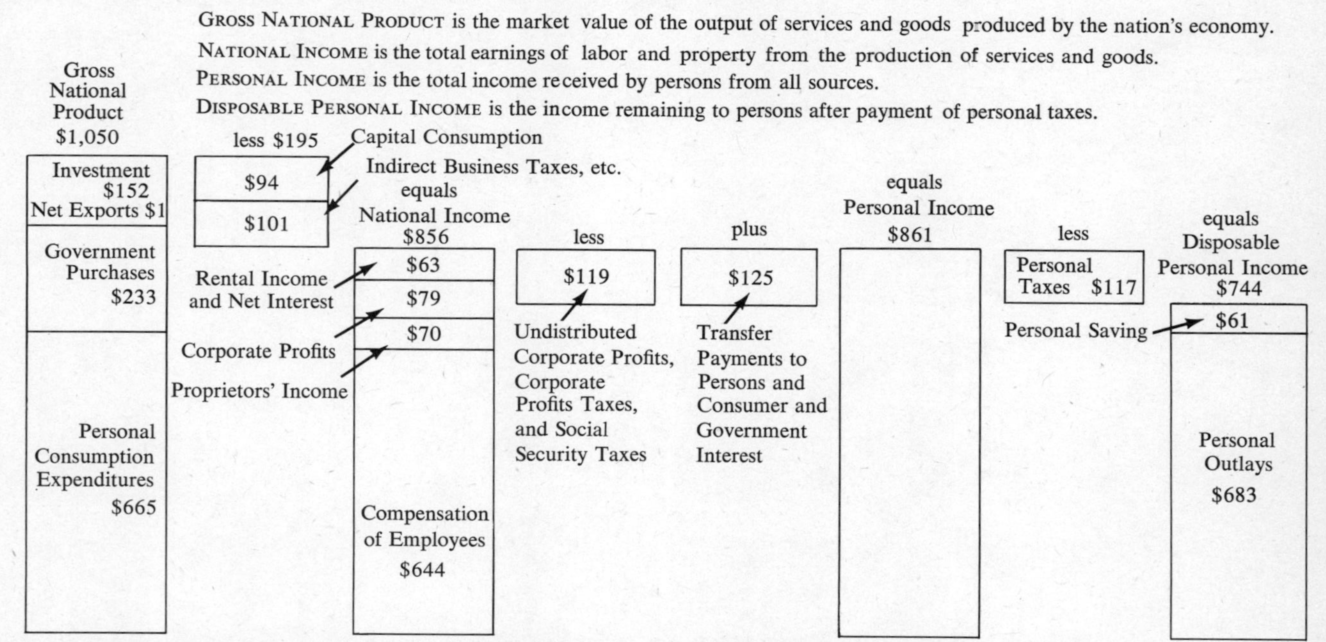

SOURCE: *Survey of Current Business*, U.S. Department of Commerce, Bureau of Economic Analysis, July 1972, p. 13.

Introduction

> Cause and effect run from the economy to the stock market, never the reverse.
>
> *John Kenneth Galbraith*

"What did the Dow do today?"

This question is asked thousands of times each day, and it is reflected in the evening news on TV and in the daily neswpapers.

When we ask the question, it is just another wording for, "How did stock prices *behave* today?"

The effort in this book is to throw some light on the fact that the behavior of consumers determines stock prices. *Cause and effect run from the consuming masses through the economy to the stock market, never the reverse.*

That this area has been little explored is both mysterious and understandable. Economists have long been concerned with hard statistics (tons of steel, thousands of autos, dollars of loans and bank deposits) and mathematics (econometrics, game theory), and one would have expected the "science" of economics to develop a sophisticated behavioral economics. But it has not. Perhaps this is because many in financial circles do not believe that human economic behavior can be properly quantified, that not enough people behave the same economically. Money Managers on Wall Street have too often paid attention to exceptional behavior, because it stands out. The focus of concentration should be on common behavior, even though it is less observable—akin to watching oneself grow old or being aware of fingernail growth.

Human behavior is by and large, to put it simply, common. If we did not behave in most areas in a consistent and uniform way, human groupings would soon come unglued and society would cease to function. Common human behavior, while the source of contention among persons, is still the cement that binds us all together. Even small groups, as small as a married couple, for example, could not function without accepted (whether consciously or not) behavioral patterns and rules of conduct. Behavior is all there is, and patterns permeate behavior. Both experience and research indicate that behavior patterns are remarkably uniform and predictable. For instance, in the field of economics we can say that in an inflationary period the consumer moves rapidly to control the *only* prices *he* can control, to reduce his expenses in an effort to bring his personal budget into balance:

1. He switches from premium to regular gasoline for his car, despite engine pings and preconditioned response generated by the gasoline companies and the automobile companies to use only the more expensive type gasoline.
2. He goes to fewer movies.
3. He "brown bags" lunch instead of eating out.
4. He takes the cheapest form of vacation and abandons air travel.

It is of course not true that the American consumer's economic behavior patterns have been ignored by American business. Actually the American consumer is the most extensively and expensively researched person alive. We know about his eye movements in supermarkets, we know his color preferences for a hundred products, we know which name he will like for a new auto from Detroit, and on and on. But this is marketing knowledge. Sophisticated techniques, based on patterned human behavior, have been developed to sell breakfast foods and deodorants. Marketing men know how to move the vast quantity of goods the factories produce. But this sophistication and interest about human behavior patterns in economic life have not been transferred to Wall Street and its army of Money

Managers throughout the country. Or if transferred, the significance is usually stood on its head, thus producing gross misunderstanding of the forces actually at work. This unfortunate reversal is illustrated clearly in a recent *Monthly Economic Letter* of New York's First National City Bank:

> The pessimistic view [toward consumer behavior] does not fully recognize the overriding importance of the strengthening in the financial position of the consumer that has occurred since mid-1970 in response to moderate money growth. At some point this will lead to increased demand for goods and services . . . when *money supply growth steps up sharply, consumers find that they are accumulating larger cash balances than they desire to hold.* Consequently, they shift excess money balances into income-earning assets. This shift is reflected in rising prices of securities and falling interest rates. When yields on financial assets slide, consumers step up their spending for real assets—cars, houses, home furnishings, refrigerators, and some nondurables such as clothing and shoes.[1]

What the First National City Bank's money men do not fully recognize is the overriding importance of the consumer in initiating economic trends. *Cause and effect run from the consuming masses through the economy to the stock market, never the reverse.*

Consider another illustration. *Saturday Review* selected Fred Borch, head of General Electric, as its "Businessman of the Year" for 1970. Mr. Borch said:

> Although unemployment is at its highest in seven years and prices are up while profits are down, *the public mood appears to be more pessimistic than the business recession warrants.* Industrial output for 1970 was less than half of 1 per cent below 1969, a record year. On the other hand, personal income in 1970 set a new all-time record, rising more than 7 per cent, and corporate profits were down a bit, but even during the worst period of the year they were only 10 per cent below the 1966 high-water mark.[2]

Here again a switch of the actual cause-effect relationship is seen. Mr. Borch assumes productivity is the key to consumer behavior, rather than the reverse. He correctly attributes importance to the psychology of the consumers, but he unjustifiably blames them for not responding properly to the statistics. Mr. Borch and his financial colleagues must come to give prime consideration not to production figures, profits, earnings per share, etc., but to consumer attitudes, expectations, and behavior. In 1970 people were moody and economically despondent. Unemployment was high and getting higher; prices were rising higher and higher, and real income, despite wage increases since 1965, was losing ground dramatically. People were scared; they lacked confidence in the machine's ability to correct itself. They responded by saving, thus making the recession deeper and almost impossible to turn around by the end of 1970.

The economists and the politicians could have better judged the situation by taking account of consumer attitudes, instead of relying upon conventional wisdom which read the production figures. By late 1970 it was announced that the U.S. economy had "bottomed out" from its recession. Presumably the consumer did not hear the announcement. Three months later he had his own quiet announcement: Continued lack of confidence. In March of 1971 the Gallup Poll reported:

> Further evidence of the pinch on many family pocketbooks is seen. . . . All persons were asked to appraise the state of business in their own communities. The percentage of people who say that local business conditions are "very good" or "good" has dropped from 54% in August to 44% in late February.[3]

The people had endured the brunt of the economic onslaught in growing unemployment, rising prices, and shrinking purchasing power. They rebelled: They saved and compounded an already grievous problem. This unfamiliar pattern was lamented, even chastised, by governmental and financial experts: The people should "know better" (translate "spend") because the Status Quo has said "business conditions are improving." In March of 1971 Herbert Stein, a member of the President's Council of Economic Advisors, said:

> Lack of confidence has now come back to the center of the stage as an explanation of the claiming limit on the ability of monetary policy to generate the target GNP.[2]
>
> Have we reached such a state of confidence that increases in the money stock do not cause the purchase of other assets, including stocks and bonds, increasing the value of wealth owned by households, reducing the cost of borrow-

> ing, stimulating expenditures for housing and state and local facilities, and in turn and in time also stimulating expenditures for consumers' durable goods and business investment? There is no evidence that we are in such a condition and much evidence to the contrary.[4]

Again, as in the case of GE's Fred Borch cited earlier, Mr. Stein reversed the cause-effect relationship. He reasoned that increasing the amount of money would of itself stimulate people into buying. Money, however, was not the problem, since savings and personal incomes were at all time highs. The money was available, but the people were not spending it—and would not spend it, regardless of what their political leaders *told* them and regardless of how many consumer goods industry *produced.*

In April of 1971 there appeared a ray of official recognition about the role of the consumer in economic affairs. Arthur Burns, chairman of the Federal Reserve Board, said:

> The fact stands out that the impact of business cycles on consumption has recently diminished, while the effects of consumption on the business cycle have become more decisive.[5]

This book, then, is an investigation into mass human economic behavior.

Surface considerations will not suffice. Persons involved in the securities markets, for instance, often assume that there is a "psychology" in the market, a psychology they generally define as "confidence" or "lack of confidence." But this is too simple. What is *behind* the confidence or lack of confidence? What factors account for people's confident economic behavior? This is the question. Answers do not come easily, though facile talk about "consumer confidence" occurs at many levels. For example, two weeks after President Richard Nixon's historic economic message in August 1971, a Gallup Poll indicated that 73% of the American people had responded favorably to Nixon's proposals. This reaction was construed as saying, "I am willing to spend now," whereas in fact the consumer seemed simply to be saying that he was happy something was being done. Consumer confidence is keyed *not* to the theme, "Is the country better off now?" or "Is business better off now?", but "Am *I* better off now?"[6]

1

Consumer Sovereignty

For the most part we do not first see, and then define, we define first and then see.

Walter Lippmann

Why should the consumer and his behavior loom so large now? After all, he has always been there. Economists have taken account of him, have even spoken of "consumer sovereignty" in the marketplace. Corporations have always produced their products for him. Television and the advertising industry have lived off him. Why his increased importance now? Has he not always been important? Yes, but his power and his visibility are now greater.

In an industrial and technological age, with its penchant for production statistics, the consumer maintained his importance but often was more invisible than his significance justified. Sometimes, though touted as important, he is still ignored; somehow he is not "seen." He cites his preference for compact autos, but Detroit responds with amazing sluggishness. She cites her preference for miniskirts, but New York cuts them midi anyway. Nevertheless, the consumer prevails—and today is more powerfully and visibly prevailing. Wall Street would do well to heed.

One economic fact of life which has crept up on us is that we now live in a Service Society or a Software Society. The majority of workers no longer directly produce goods. America is today a country where most people work and earn their incomes in service industries—servicing other people or servicing the hard goods produced by the minority of workers. When we add together all the federal and state government employees, public school teachers, hospital workers, firemen, airline stewardesses, policemen, auto mechanics, bank tellers, social workers, bus drivers, lobbyists, garbage men, TV repairmen, stock market brokers, bartenders, supermarket checkout clerks, plumbers, doctors, secretaries, insurance salesmen, lawyers, Disneyland guides, etc., we can understand that two out of every three American workers has a service-oriented job and that these jobs account for well over half the total national employee compensation.[1] The world of the baker and the candlestick maker are gone in more ways than one.

But wait. Perhaps it may soon be more accurate to say that that world is gone in only one way, the symbolic way. To the extent that the baker and candlestick maker represent a predominately production-oriented society, yes, that world is gone. However, literally they may be returning. The sweeping industrialization that followed the Civil War in America marked the turning from smaller, individual proprietorships to larger corporations. Now we see a trend returning us to smaller units. "Bigness = goodness" is a formula brought under sharp scrutiny and skepticism. The Club of Rome, an international organization of scientists and industrialists, publishes *The Limits to Growth,* calling for zero population and economic growth. In Washington, many sport buttons urging: "Think Small, Lesser Seattle." In the Southwest, the New Mexico Undevelopment Commission has emerged to fight population and economic growth in the state. In November 1972, the majority of Colorado residents voted against the 1976 Winter Olympics being held there. On grounds of ecology, aesthetics, and the quality of life, growth and bigness seem false gods to many. On economic grounds alone, size is now a matter of debate. The growth of conglomerates or large corporations (e.g., Penn Central, LTV, Lockheed) no longer appears inevitable. The demise of the family neighborhood grocery no longer seems fated.

In terms of we *can* and we *desire,* there are new possibilities and new values. Economic and social developments are permitting, in some cases demanding, new directions. As Robert Theobald urges us to recognize, we are saying goodbye to the industrial age; we are entering a post-industrial era, a cybernation era, in which learning, leisure, crafts, service will play a significantly larger role. The goal of full employment, the linking of job and income, the acceptance of poverty—all will become obsolete. This is no utopian notion; it is beginning to happen now. In a production society, *with the bulk of the consumers* drawing their incomes from the large manufacturers, we have experienced a strong tendency toward pre-set prices, corporation-dictated "choices" for the consumer, higher prices without commensurate quality, business laws with a focus on *caveat emptor* rather than "let the seller be fair." Now, however, *a service economy generates its own income and spends most of it back on services.*

Today the consumer *is* sovereign. More than 40% of American families have an annual income between $9,000 and $15,000, and, despite the inroads of inflation and taxes, families are in a position to make expenditures beyond what are necessities. They have extra money to save or invest, and most are in a position to borrow or to use credit through installment buying. Thus, an American family can spend more than their income in a given year, or they can reduce their spending and save money. Their spending patterns have changed. They have excess funds to buy stocks, bonds, mutual funds, and the like. The sheer size of their disposable personal income dwarfs the business and government income sectors. What the consumer decides to buy is what sooner or later will be made and indicates where corporate profits will be made. Since stock prices are closely related to corporate profits, it is important to understand what makes the consumer tick, and what the nature and thrust of his spending will be in the years ahead.

As the consumer is less dependent on production as the source of his income, he becomes a more critical consumer. Better income and more stable savings back up spending decisions and the consumer is freer economically. A program of guaranteed income (including Theobald's "committed spending" for the "middle class poor" dispossessed of their traditional white collar and management jobs in a post-industrial era) helps provide this economic stability for the consumer. As Theobald concludes:

> The decision to introduce both the guaranteed income and committed spending will permit the market to be allowed far freer play than at present, for it will act to reinforce the

wishes of people. . . .[2]

"The wishes of people"—they are a-changin'. The consumer's new values are another major factor in explaining why the consumer and his behavior loom so large today.

> Man's specific tool for adaptation and survival is . . . the evolution of values. That which works in helping us survive becomes a "value." Values gradually are integrated into complex adaptations we call value systems. Value systems develop momentum of their own and then enhance or impair our ability to adapt to new conditions.
>
> Up to now the rate of change in our lives has been slow enough to permit the processes of evolution of values to remain automatic and therefore largely unconscious. Today the rate of change we now produce in the conditions of our lives is too swift for the processes of spontaneous evolution of values to keep up. For the first time in 2 million years we must learn to exercise a new freedom—the freedom to *choose* our values *consciously*.[3]

One new value choice appears to be a lessening of the acquisitive drive. For many consumers, especially those under thirty-five, there is a preference to owe rather than own. The value-change root of altered behavior on the part of young adults seems to be invisible to conventional wisdom in the business community. Take housing, for example. Between 1950 and 1970, during a period when population and incomes and standards of living rose in the U.S.A., expenditures for new private housing units dropped from 5.5% of the GNP to 2.2%. This reflected a new behavioral attitude toward home ownership. Many factors contributed to this new value: Couples had fewer children and delayed those they did have (made easier by the Pill and other contraceptive devices), making apartment living feasible for longer. Families were more mobile than a generation before, and renting became more logical. And ownership of material goods per se (including houses), a traditional Americanism, became a slightly tarnished goal. The less acquisitive life style of the young is, says the Status Quo, a passing fad. Maybe. Maybe not.

In any case, let us look more closely at the housing market and how it has been talked about the past few years. In the spring of 1971 *U.S. News and World Report* carried a cover story on "New

Big Boom in Housing." The article concluded:

> The sharp increase in sales in most sections of the U.S. underscores a long-term trend in this country toward home ownership. In 1940, only 44 per cent of American families owned their own homes. Today, the proportion is 63 per cent.
>
> Actually, the trend slowed down considerably in the past decade, a period marked by two intervals of very tight money which threw the home-building industry into depression—in 1966-67 and again in 1969-70. Now easier credit and the shift to smaller, cheaper houses are once again giving the American public an opportunity to satisfy its hankering for real property.[4]

Actually, who are these present home owners, these 63%? The "new" owners are middle-aged people (those with the bulk of the cash), the parents of the youth. The "sharp increase in sales," the article had said, were in houses that catered to the upper-income classes and were in high rental units ("$195 per month, one bedroom"). The houses bought were expensive custom-built homes, not mass-produced homes. Boom in housing? The mass market for broad home ownership nationally in the 1970s may be a fantasy. Even President Nixon's new economic program, with its surge in housing, resulted, for the first time in our country's history, in more *apartments* being constructed annually than single-family dwellings. To buy housing-based securities indiscriminately, then, predicated on an optimistic projection of "American home ownership" may be to commit financial hari kari. Economists must also take account of this value change at a basic level. Housing construction figures have always been a mainstay in their prediction bag. And speaking of value change, who would have thought a few years ago that today mobile homes would account for 90% or more of housing units being built for under $15,000?

Many consumers still feel powerless in the economic jungle (and with cause, especially when individually confronting a picky but important problem, like trying to get an error corrected on one's bill with a large department store's computerized service), but Ralph Nader probably felt somewhat powerless when he wrote *Unsafe At Any Speed.*

What if all 77 million wage and salary workers and their families gave up drinking Coca Cola for one month? or eating Planters Peanuts? Or what if no one bought a Chevrolet for one season? "What if's" are academic. Boycotts have demonstrated the economic power of the consumer. Overseas in 1970 Japanese housewives boycotted buying TV sets when they learned the same sets were being sold cheaper in the U.S. than in Japan. It took one month for the Japanese manufacturers to get the message and make price adjustments. In America examples abound.

In 1970 students in California set fire to a branch of the Bank of America to dramatize their disapproval of the bank and its practices. (We can skip the moral question involved in burning a bank; our point is made aside from that.) The bank quickly replaced the destroyed branch, but made few changes acceptable to the students. In 1971 the students organized their own credit union in the Isle Vista community. They use this institution as a bank: They keep their savings there, make loans, pay half the profits out to members, retain the other half for operating expenses, and manage the bank themselves (There is an abundance of talent in modern management techniques, computer operation, etc.).

Also in 1970 the National Austerity Council of San Francisco began circulating pledges which read:

> Until the President has announced total and immediate U.S. withdrawal from Southeast Asia I pledge myself to buy nothing but essential food items; to cash in all U.S. Government bonds I hold and to withdraw all savings I have in banks, savings and loan associations and credit unions; to attend no paid entertainment and drive as little as possible, sharing transportation to the maximum extent; to persuade as many friends and neighbors to join this dollar boycott. I acknowledge that through my continuing support of the U.S. economy I have been contributing to the horror. I will now disassociate myself from this madness by minimizing my participation in the economy that supports it.

Another sort of boycott illustrates a facet of the value changes we mentioned ealier. And the underlying issue is at the heart of the value conflicts we are witnessing. Workers at the General Motors Vega plant in Lordstown, Ohio have displayed an inexplicable (inexplicable to the Detroit top brass) disdain for meaningless work. This GM plant sports the world's fastest and most modern assembly line (one car down the line every 36 seconds versus the more traditional speed of one about every 60 seconds). Of course, there is nothing new about assembly-line work being fast and boring; that has been true for years. But exchanging rapid, deadening work for good pay may be coming to the end of the line. Earning $6.87 an hour (base plus benefits), the Lordstown Vega worker went out on strike in the spring of 1972 over "work standards, job discipline, and worker layoff," issues which fundamentally focused around the speed of the assembly line and the dullness of the job. Values are changing; the standards by which jobs are judged are altered. As Gary Bryner, president of the UAW Local 1112 at the Lordstown plant, said: "Job monotony? Five years ago the union didn't even discuss it." Things are different in the old production sector. GM and other large corporations will likely respond by automating even further, eliminating workers and reinforcing the trend toward doing more with less.

All of this is the more visible portion of the value changes and of the consumerism revolution of the past decade. William Longgood's pioneering and hard-hitting book, *The Poisons in Your Food,* made little lasting impact when it appeared in 1960. In 1972, his most recent book on the larger ecological crisis, *The Darkening Land,* came as almost a surfeit on the book market. During this period Nader became a household word. Truth-in-lending and packaging-and-labeling legislation emerged from Washington, D.C. Robert Choate, Jr. attacked non-nutritional breakfast cereals. Alice Tepper created the Council on Economic Priorities to keep a "social balance sheet" on major corporations. Consumer protective agencies came into their own; in 1971 alone twelve states, eleven counties, and forty-two cities established such offices—so reported Virginia H. Knauer, Special Assistant to the President for Consumer Affairs (an office created only as recently as 1969).

Boycotts and strikes are more direct and more dramatic, but the effects of the consumers' value changes, while sometimes less visible, are perhaps more significant. These are the changes which will have sustained and long-range effects. Analogous to but quieter than the Lordstown Vega incident is a phenomenon *Newsweek* noted in early 1970:

> A growing number of Americans . . . are walking away from their middle-class status, goals, professions and jobs, in fields from engineering to nuclear physics, to learn a craft and make it their vocation. . . . These new craftsmen are dropouts of all ages from the worlds of the student, the housewife and the executive, and in an affluent but increasingly impersonal society they want most to use their hands on leather, metal, wood, glass or clay.[5]

Robert Theobald might elaborate this observation and suggest a result of our social adoption of his proposals:

> It will encourage those receiving the guaranteed income and committed spending to join together in consentives to do what they want to do. Consentives will be groups of people with a purpose which binds them together; this purpose can be social or productive. If it is the latter, success in the consentive would lead its members back into the market should this be their wish. The goods produced by these consentives would not compete with mass-produced projects available from cybernated productive organizations; the consentive would produce the "custom-designed" goods and services which have been vanishing within the present economy [cf. baker and candlestick maker].
>
> This type of productive unit would continue far into the future, for the use of a man's hands is one of the most satisfying ways of spending time. The proportion of the population spending most of their time in this kind of production would decline, nevertheless, as other activities seem more challenging and education in its fullest sense takes an ever more central position.[6]

What about value changes which affect our behavior toward war spending and toward the funding of social consumption (e.g., cleaning up polluted lakes, keeping the air clean from industrial waste)? Does our concern in these areas still reflect the fundamental motif, "Am *I* better off now"? Basically, yes. The concern is with the question whether there will be a world or a country left to be better off in.

If one takes seriously the consumer's importance to Wall Street, are there means at hand to translate his attitudes, behavior, wages, bank account, and debt into useful tools of prediction? The answer of this book is Yes. The consumer's values and plans can be got at meaningfully.

The University of Michigan Survey Research Center, under the original direction of George Katona, developed many years ago "anticipation approaches" or "consumer sentiment indexes" for consumer spending. That is, they reasoned that consumers do in fact plan ahead with their personal financial expenditures, notwithstanding the fact that impulse spending is always going on at the same time. Since this happens, consumers are surveyed every three months under the Michigan program and asked a variety of carefully phrased questions as to what they plan to do within the next six-month period regarding spending. Their willingness to spend must of course be reinforced with the ability to spend. Consumers, all of us, do plan in a general way whether we will buy a new car or a washing machine or a color TV. Now, at the time of the interview when the consumer is asked questions about these plans, the consumer quickly runs through his mind all he is aware of: the monthly food bill, his savings balance, how much he owes, his job stability, his personal feelings about inflation, and a score of other variables. The central focus is price; then, in response to the question, he says Yes or No.

He has accepted or rejected the market offering *then* in his plans for tomorrow. Now, he can, and often does, change his mind when the six-month period is up, but his economic behavior in areas where he can control prices by himself will indicate the follow-through, that is, whether he will or will not do what he said he was going to do six months earlier. This book outlines the methods by which one can plot this "follow-through." Thus, before the first reading matures (that is, six months from questioning) it is possible to find in the interim spending patterns of the consumer whether or not he will make final his original Yes or No.

The simple reading of the Michigan surveys will not *alone* provide the answer, but definitive answers can be found, as the author has successfully demonstrated, to second-guess Wall Street. Despite concrete proof, the editor of *Barron's,* one of Wall Street's widely read media, wrote the author that "empirical evidence indicates consumer surveys to be unreliable."

It is difficult to change habits of thought, even more difficult to admit that there may be something "out there" cruciallly important that heretofore has been "invisible." As Walter Lippmann reminds us:

> In the great blooming, buzzing confusion of the outer world we pick out what our culture has already defined for us, and we tend to perceive that which we have picked out in the form stereotyped for us by our culture.[7]

One form of stereotype or definitional lens through which we see the world is the framework of business indicators used and supported by Wall Street, Money Managers, and the mass media. Great faith is put in "leading," "lagging," and "coincident" indicators.

It is assumed, especially with the "leading" indicators, that the data are "fresh," but much such data are three to six months dated —hardly "leading." It is further assumed that "leading" indicators portend the future because in the past they have sometimes done so. But in the past there was a U.S. which was devoted to making goods as the mainstay of economic growth and progress. However, now, in the 1970s the manufacturing sector is overshadowed by the service sector. Yet leading indicators data are drawn largely from the manufacturing sector. Therefore, of what value are leading indicators that indicate business activity in a sector that no longer leads, that is becoming increasingly less important to total economic activity in general in the U.S.?

Another stereotype on Wall Street is the way the average consumer is perceived by the Money Managers. He has long been fleeced by the Street and is seen as a lamb to be taken. He is considered not very bright. Donald T. Regan, chairman of Merrill Lynch, put it this way in a recent book, *A View From The Street:*

> One must agree with the sage who said that "a foolish consistency is the hobgoblin of little minds." For the taxpayer who was crying for social improvements and environmental protection was at the same time crying for tax relief.[8]

Mr. Regan failed to note that this taxpayer was perhaps really crying for his tax dollars not to be misspent to support wars and other things alien to his family and his personal welfare.

The average consumer is not stupid. His life style, his thoughts, his attitudes are quite different from the way Wall Streeters perceive them. He is no boob. He even has the sense to play shy of stocks; the average consumer had not been in Wall Street for a generation, until he began to succumb to the mutual funds. However, when he got a chance in the early 1970s to bail out of mutual funds and recoup some of his losses, he did just that.

Tracing the consumer along the path from his first response to "consumer sentiment" questions to his subsequent purchase or non-purchase can be done and can provide knowledge that Wall Street analysts can put to good use. This data will not provide the final answer, but it can provide excellent guidance in marking general directions; it should cause more attention to be paid to the little guy 'way out there somewhere who, in a Service Society, is free to call economic shots of great dollar magnitude and, thereby, tremendously influence which of the corporate stocks listed on the stock exchanges will rise, which will fall, and what the overall *trend* of the stock market will be.

A consumer in a Service Society is not the same kind of consumer that the Production Society produced. He has more money to spend, is freer in his spending, and often operates in an orbit outside the goods-production system. *This* is where the mass of the American workers are in the 1970s.

They surely are not making automobiles like the Nixon Administration seemed to think they were. The money they used to buy the cars did *not* come mainly from making them. This is important to analyze, since it portends a vastly different economic America than the Status Quo sees now and is counting on for the future.

2

A Service Economy

> New environments are almost imperceptible to most people. . . . We look at the present through a rearview mirror.
>
> *Marshall McLuhan*

In the 1940s and earlier, business cycle trends, including stock market trends, largely depended upon what business did, and during and after World War II, upon what the government did. Unfortunately, we are still locked into the central idea that the American economy is a Production Economy and we commonly talk about producing "goods *and* services." This is a grave mistake. We should talk about "*services* and goods," in order to give priority and emphasis which reflect the facts of our national economic life.

Since World War II, the United States has moved from a Production Economy to a Service Economy. That is, the U.S. is the first nation in which less than half of the employed population is involved in the production of food, clothing, houses, automobiles, and other tangible goods. This, as Victor Fuchs says, has "revolutionary" implications.

The magnitude of the switch to a Service Economy is huge, but the growth, though dramatic, has been subtle and not always "seen." And even when felt, the change is often resisted. For example, Nathaniel Goldfinger, chief economist for the AFL-CIO, made this comment:

> The talk of those people who speak glibly of a service economy is the talk of those who unfortunately have not given much thought to the nature of our economy. Service jobs, most of them, are low-wage, menial jobs. It's not all surgeons and research chemists, by any means. You know, it's generally forgotten that the American consumer is an American worker, and the fact that the American market is a lucrative market is based upon the wages of the American worker.[1]

We are perhaps like Marshall McLuhan's fish, who doesn't know he lives in water. We see the material goods around us: the cars, the TV sets, the houses, the furniture, the food. We take account of them: we eat them, we use them, we buy them, we sell them, we discard them. We subconciously believe that all of this is what makes our economic world go around. We ignore a fundamental feature of our economic lives—the Service Society we swim in. It is a fact; its growth is a fact. This can be recorded in various ways:

> The Service sector's share of total employment has grown from approximately 40 per cent in 1929 to over 55 per cent in 1967. . . . In 1929 the Industry and Service sectors were approximately the same size. By 1965, the Service sector was 40 per cent larger than Industry. . . . Between 1947 and 1965 alone, there was an increase of 13 million jobs in the Service sector compared with an increase of only 4 million in Industry and a decrease of 3 million in Agriculture.[2]

From 1950 to 1970 the number of persons employed in service sector jobs jumped from 28 million to 48 million. Since 1950, 90% of net new jobs in the U.S. have been in services.

At least 55¢ of every dollar earned is spent by a consumer for services. The people who receive this income spend 55¢ of their dollars for services, and the wheel goes round and round. We thus have a growing torrent of cash flowing mainly outside the Production Society.

The following two tables summarize data on personal income and expenditures and relate these to the service sector.

It can be clearly seen that in the past forty years the amount of personal income derived from making goods has only increased

TABLE 1

SOURCES OF PERSONAL INCOME 1930-1971

Year	Source	Total (billions)	Percentage of total
1930	Manufacturing	$18.5	21%
1930	Services	$27.7	35%
1950	Manufacturing	$64.6	43%
1950	Services	$82.2	36%
1971	Manufacturing	$205.0	23%
1971	Services	$368.5	42%

SOURCE: Economic Report of the President, 1972, p. 215.

by 2%; by contrast, the income derived from performing services has increased by 7% and is still growing. The figures, it should be noted, mask the service work done in the manufacturing sector; that is, the work of secretaries, file clerks, accountants, and so forth who are employed by such firms as GM, GE, Hart Schaffner & Marx, etc. is statistically still counted in under the goods-producing umbrella. Conservative estimates peg this "buried" service activity at 20%; therefore, the actual increase in service income is larger than that reflected in the above figures—or in any standard service sector figures used today.

TABLE 2

PERSONAL CONSUMPTION EXPENDITURES 1930-1971

Year	Expenditure	Total (billions)	Percentage of total
1930	Durable Goods	$7	10%
1930	Nondurable Goods	$34	49%
1930	Services	$28	40%
1950	Durable Goods	$30	15%
1950	Nondurable Goods	$98	50%
1950	Services	$62	32%
1971	Durable Goods	$100	16%
1971	Nondurable Goods	$278	46%
1971	Services	$283	47%

SOURCE: Economic Report of the President, 1972, p. 207.

The amount consumers were spending for nondurable goods during the past forty years declined, the amount for durables increased by 6%, and the amount for services increased by 7%. The amount spent for services is going up at a very rapid rate (these figures hardly reflect the almost quantum jumps in traffic ticket costs, plumbing and TV repair costs, garbage pickup costs, etc.), and will continue to rise even more. The chart below plots the above figures since 1950 and projects to 1980 estimates derived from business community data.

CHART 2

PERSONAL CONSUMPTION EXPENDITURES *(in current dollars)*

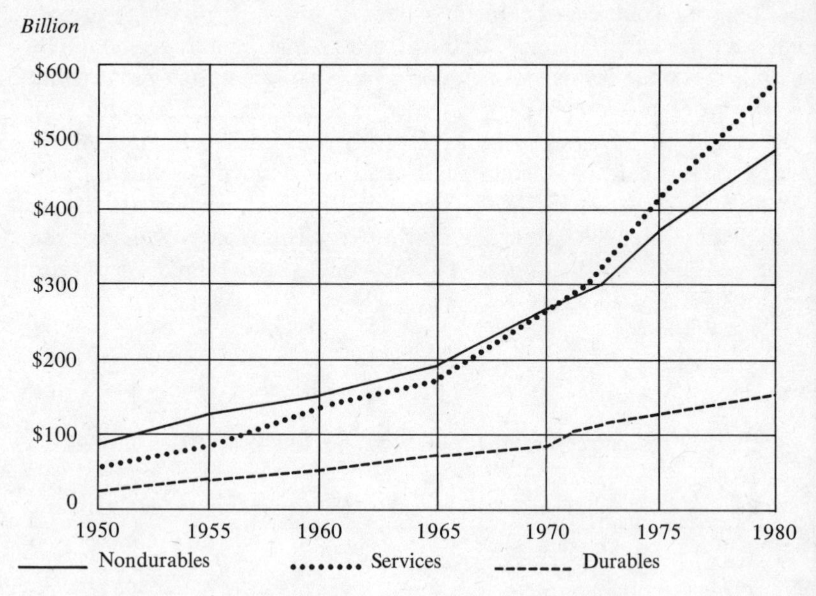

Some observers are, of course, beginning to recognize the new terrain. As Robert A. Rosenblatt said in a *Los Angeles Times* article:

> The history of California is filled with the sharp rise, and ultimate levelling off, of growth industries. Gold mining, railroading, oil drilling, movie production, munitions and aircraft manufacturing, all moved through boom periods that attracted swarms of new residents to the state.[3]

Rosenblatt concludes about California that there is, however, no "new growth industry on the horizon. Instead, . . . California is now becoming . . . a 'mature economy' in which ever-growing numbers of people will make a living in the service fields." The *amount* of "ever-growing numbers of people" is dramatized in these statistics:

TABLE 3

NONAGRICULTURAL EMPLOYMENT IN CALIFORNIA[4]

First Half 1971 and First Half 1972	
Manufacturing	increase = 27,000 jobs
Service	increase = 135,600 jobs

In other words, during one recent year, service jobs were created at five times the rate of creation of manufacturing jobs. The national statistics point clearly in a similar direction.

TABLE 4

NONAGRICULTURAL EMPLOYMENT IN U.S.A.

May 1971 and May 1972	
Production	net increase = 206,000 jobs
Service	net increase = 1,552,000 jobs

SOURCE: *Survey of Current Business,* U.S. Department of Commerce, July 1972, p. S-13.

It is curious, then, that President Nixon's New Economic Program of August 15, 1971, should have centered on the production sector, specifically, automobiles. A dynamic sector, yes, but for the long run, alas, less dynamic because of this basic transition from goods to services. It is not so curious, though, if you've read a "current" economics textbook on what to do to bail out of a recession. Status-Quo economists are trained to think "production." So ingrained is production-minded economics that even economists critical of the American economy and of Status Quo Economics ignore or minimize the facts of the new Service Society. For example, *The Review of Radical Political Economics,* in devoting an entire issue (August 1972) to a critique of Nixon's New Economic Program, failed to even mention the impact of the Service Society. Why? Presumably because they learned their economics from the Status Quo economists and rebut them on their own grounds.

With the President, the establishment economists, and the radical economists ignoring the Service Society, it is no wonder at all that Wall Street analysts are still concentrating on production figures, using the prominent business indexes which chart auto production, crude oil production, soft coal production, carloadings, and such. What we desperately need is a government compiled index reflecting the details of economic activity in the service sector which can be used like the Federal Reserve Board's Index of Industrial Production.

These critical remarks are not meant to imply that the government by spending tax money in the manufacturing sector cannot move the direction of economic activity. Nixon's Economic Program did, but the cost soon becomes prohibitive. For example:

TABLE 5

FEDERAL CREDIT PROGRAMS

1961	= $100 billions
1967	= $150 billions
1973	= $580 billions (est.)

The feedback from this enormous growth in these extensions of credit, large though they were, did not net us much bang for the buck. We cannot afford the continuance of these economic games.

And this is how the games work. According to Maurice Mann in a *Wall Street Journal* article: "In calendar 1972 nearly 60% of the total flow of funds into the mortgage market will be directly or indirectly supported by the Federal government."[5]

The editors of the *Wall Street Journal* had this to say about the system:

> What is to be borrowed must first be saved, in an economic sense, through an excess of production over consumption. When borrowing exceeds savings the borrowers are trying to get something that isn't there.[6]

Things just don't "happen." There has got to be a cause. And the gap between production and consumption had invisibly narrowed due to the immense production of more services at higher costs, thus creating less savings (even though they were at a historically high level); the savings remaining were siphoned off by higher taxes and inflation, and the consumers simply did not have the "extra" savings necessary to make even small down payments for homes (as they did after World War II when savings were abnormally large). In 1971-72 consumers were able to buy with almost no money down and pay their rents to Uncle Sam. "Buy"? Consumers still persist in talking to their neighbor about *"our* home," "we *bought* that home," etc. Astrology and astronomy come out the same to many average consumers; why shouldn't owe and own?

But the credit line tightens and there will come a day of reckoning. There always has and there always will.

What is a service job? Over the years those who have treated the subject have not reached consensus on a definition of the service industries. An essential starting point is the framework of services used in the U.S. Department of Labor's delineation of nonagricultural wage and salary employment in service establishments. Early in the Department's data gathering they included business services (e.g., accountants, advertising agencies), professional services (e.g., lawyers, hospitals), personal services (e.g., barbers, laundries), and repair services (e.g., auto mechanics). These are the activities covered by the Department's general category "Services." Their "Government" label refers, of course, to all federal, state, and local employees, including public school teachers and state university professors. The Department subsequently broadened their definition of Service-Producing Industries to include "Transportation and Public Utilities," "Finance, Insurance, and Real Estate," and "Trade." The latter refers to the wholesale and retail trade (e.g., retail store salesclerks).

Service establishments do not produce any tangible goods. For the most part they have a fairly close relationship with the ultimate consumer of their output, whereas goods-producing industries are normally remote from the consumer of the product. Unlike either a durable or nondurable good, a service is incapable of being stored and is, in effect, consumed at the time it is produced. Most service industries are staffed by white-collar workers and tend toward being labor intensive rather than capital intensive. Where this last criterion may fail to apply, as in the case of transportation and public utilities, the intangible nature of the output seems to warrant their inclusion in the service-producing industries.

TABLE 6

NONAGRICULTURAL WAGE AND SALARY EMPLOYMENT BY INDUSTRY DIVISION FOR SELECTED YEARS

	(Numbers in thousands)			Change 1947-61		Change 1961-69	
	1947	1961	1969*	Absolute	Per Cent	Absolute	Per Cent
Total	43,881	54,042	70,138	10,161	+23.2	16,096	+29.8
Goods-Producing Industries	18,482	19,814	24,158	1,332	+7.2	4,344	+21.9
Mining	955	672	628	—283	—29.6	—44	—6.5
Contract Construction	1,982	2,816	3,410	834	+42.1	594	+21.1
Manufacturing	15,545	16,326	20,120	781	+5.0	3,794	+23.2
Durable Goods	8,385	9,070	11,898	685	+8.2	2,828	+31.2
Nondurable Goods	7,159	7,256	8,255	97	+1.4	999	+13.8
Service-Producing Industries	25,399	34,229	45,979	8,830	+34.8	11,750	+34.3
Transportation and Public Utilities	4,166	3,903	4,449	—263	—6.3	546	+14.0
Trade	8,955	11,337	14,643	2,382	+26.6	3,306	+29.2
Finance, Insurance, and Real Estate	1,754	2,731	3,558	977	+55.7	827	+30.3
Services	5,050	7,664	11,102	2,614	+51.8	3,438	+44.9
Government	5,474	8,594	12,227	3,120	+57.0	3,633	+42.3
Federal	1,892	2,279	2,753	387	+20.5	474	+20.9
State and Local	3,582	6,315	9,424	2,733	+76.3	3,109	+49.2

*Preliminary.
SOURCE: U. S. Department of Labor

An examination of the postwar performance of the service sector vis-a-vis the goods-producing sector follows:

EARLY PHASE: 1947-1961

Probably the overriding feature of this period, insofar as overall economic growth and employment performance are concerned, is that the forward movement of the economy was interrupted four times by economic recessions of varying intensity. Their depressant effect on employment growth can be seen in the performance of the goods-producing sector. This was especially true for manufacturing, which accounted for approximately four-fifths of that sector's employment (Table 6). Of the absolute gain in total nonagricultural wage and salary employment during this period, little more than 10% was attributable to those industries which produce goods. Both in absolute and percentage gains, contract construction played a more prominent role than manufacturing. Clearly, the behavior of manufacturing employment—seen in the modest 5% advance for this period of nearly fifteen years—reflected the generally lackluster growth record of the economy during these years.

The performance of the service-producing industries stands in marked contrast to that of the goods-producing sector. Their contribution to total employment gains during the period was nearly seven times as great and they accounted for almost 90% of all new jobs.

Although all service-producing industries except transportation and public utilities scored advances, several industries showed exceptional advances. Trade, services, and state and local government gains were very large—about double the employment gain for all goods-producing industries. Despite a series of economic recessions, the ability of the service-producing industries to generate high levels of new employment opportunities is well established by these data. It is interesting to observe that during the economic recession of 1970, when employment in the aerospace industry in Southern California drastically declined, government employees of all sorts increased by 30,000, thus cushioning the severe shock. This, of course, sustained consumer demand, though the area was declared, among others nationally, to be a "depressed" one. Perhaps the reason the recession of 1970 did not turn into a full scale depression lay in the underlying strength of the service sectors.

MORE RECENTLY: 1961-1969

Just as the earlier period was colored by recurrent recessions, this latter phase attests to the economic expansion which began in 1961—and, more importantly, to the lessening of the impact of downturns in the economy.

Although it encompasses less than a decade, the absolute increase in total nonagricultural wage and salary employment was more than half again as great as in the earlier period, which was almost twice as long. And, as in the 1947-61 period, absolute employment gains attributable to all service-producing industries outweighed those of goods-producing industries. However, a renaissance took place in the manufacturing sector from 1961 to 1969. Paced by this pickup, the goods-producing industries increased their absolute employment gain as compared with the previous period (the bulk of this was goods-for-war, "waste" goods). They accounted for more than one out of four new jobs as compared with less than one out of ten in 1947-61. In fact, no single sector matched the job-creating performance of manufacturing in the 1961-69 period, as it remained the single most important source of all wage and salary employment. The renaissance surely masked the service growth.

During 1970 this large gain in manufacturing of war goods, in space exploration, and services was all but wiped out, and with it jobs; we experienced another recession. Without the support of the service industries, the downthrust would have been more severe. To mitigate the extent of the disaster involved in sharp reductions in war goods and space activity, the government with its powerful economic power 1) bailed the banks out of a liquidity crisis and 2) supported financially two of their largest purveyors in transport. This did not ease what the economists call "pain" of those unemployed, nor did it alleviate the problems of smaller businesses. The service industries, in sharp contrast, were supported by the spending of people buying services (e.g., auto repairs) they will not do without in good times or bad, services for which they will incur, if necessary, added debt.

The steady growth in the economy during 1965, prompted by the enlarging of the war in Vietnam, created rising levels of demand by consumers for automobiles, television sets—and *stocks,* especially in the form of mutual funds.

Even the nondurable goods sector revived significantly. Employment growth in this sector expanded more than tenfold in the years 1961-69 versus the insignificant growth of the 1947-61 period.

The percentage gain in employment of the service-producing industries during the 1961-69 period was slightly below the 1947-61 pace. However, the fact remains that employment in these industries rose by nearly 12 million in less than ten years, compared with a gain of less than nine million jobs during the longer period which preceded it. Transportation and public utilities, which had shown a net decline of more than one-quarter million jobs in the 1947-61 period, showed a gain of more than one-half million jobs in the period 1961-69. It seems quite likely that the resurgence of manufacturing activity cited above had a salutary impact on the demand for transportation and public utilities services. Except for a somewhat smaller employment rise in the finance, insurance, and real estate component, all other service-producing industries exceeded their 1947-61 performance.

There is little doubt that a strong demand for goods will redound to the advantage of the service-producing industries—because, if for no other reason, the goods are so poorly made and require service almost immediately after purchase! However, the data seem to confirm clearly that it is the overall service sector, and not the goods sector, which provides the chief source of new employment opportunities and whose dominance in this respect has been growing throughout the postwar period.

When the percentage distribution of nonagricultural wage and salary employment for the period 1947-69 is calculated, the goods-producing industries declined from 42.5% to 35%, and the service-producing industries rose from 58% to 65%. Despite the absolute growth in employment described earlier, the relative importance of the goods-producing sector in generating new jobs has been on the wane almost without interruption throughout the postwar period. These same years have witnessed a corresponding rise in the share of total employment attributable to the service-producing industries. By 1969 these industries accounted for nearly two out of every three nonagricultural wage and salary jobs. Small wonder, then, that the economy is better described now as a Service Economy.

America started out as an agglomeration of small businesses, substantially service oriented; now, late in the twentieth century, America is returning to that framework on a more grandiose scale. *Plus ça change, plus c'est la même chose.*

This would also seem to throw a wrench into John Galbraith's "New Industrial State" together with the dreams of the leaders of the "new multinational" companies, i.e., those companies that are moving abroad where profit margins are greater. History has indicated that decay is built into growth whether it be the state, the church, or business. Who in 1940 would have envisioned the demise of the Penn-Central Railroad? Who today can envision the demise of General Motors by 1990? It is interesting to observe that for years American consumers have indicated a growing preference for foreign economy cars, and only in 1970 did the large American motormakers meet the challenge. Since the profits are not as large on small cars as they are on large ones, the American motor giants are headed on a one-way track downwards as profits erode.

In 1970 domestic car sales in the U.S. were off by one million cars, and during the same period imported car sales rose about two million. Until the change of August 1971, with the New Economic Program, the imports were each year grabbing a larger share of the domestic market. Detroit, bewildered, met the change, before government aid, not with compact cars, but with cheap cars. It may not take the consumer long to "learn" there is a difference. By summer 1972 the consumer was again buying large numbers of VWs even at higher prices.

An aim of the New Economic Program was, of course, to reduce unemployment. As the plan took hold, the problem persisted. The *Wall Street Journal* on March 12, 1972 noted that total employment since 1966 presented the following picture:

> Wholesale-Retail Trade: Up 17%, or 2,269,000 jobs. Services [private, non-government]: Up 27%, or 2,634,000 jobs. Manufacturing: Down 3%, or 587,000 jobs.
>
> It doesn't take much figuring to conclude that if industry had kept up with other areas as a job supplier since 1966, employment today would be very "full" indeed.[7]

It doesn't take much figuring either to see that the *Wall Street*

Journal is plagued with the same tunnel vision that prevails among other production-oriented thinkers. The numbers are right there. Hard facts. Yet, they are not "seen." The production sector cannot supply the jobs because that is not where the action is in our economy.

3

The Service Industries

When a man changes his tools and his techniques, his ways of producing and distributing the goods of life, he also changes his gods.

Harvey Cox

The combined service-producing industries dominate the employment picture. Earlier reference was made to the differential job growth of the various service industries in two distinct periods during the postwar years. Yet, within these same industries significant differences do exist insofar as their relative importance to total employment is concerned—that is, there are laggers and leaders. Table 7 provides the data to assess the postwar performance of the various service-producing industries.

A clear lagger, for example, is the transportation and public utilities sector. Although, in absolute terms, its employment growth record in the 1961-69 period (7.2% in 1961, 6.3% in 1969) did improve relative to 1947-61 (9.5% in 1947, 7.2% in 1961), its share of total employment has trended down during the postwar years. The role of the federal government shown here in generating new jobs suggests that it, too, should be classed as a lagging sector. Despite absolute increases in overall federal government civilian employment during most of the postwar years, as a proportion of total nonagricultural wage and salary employment it reached a peak in 1952 (5%) and has been in a downtrend ever since. In fact, between 1967 and April 1972, federal government civilian employment *declined* by about 50,000 jobs.

TABLE 7

PERCENTAGE DISTRIBUTION
NONAGRICULTURAL WAGE AND SALARY EMPLOYMENT
IN SERVICE-PRODUCING INDUSTRIES 1947-69

Year	Transportation and Public Utilities	Wholesale and Retail Trade	Finance, Insurance, and Real Estate	Services	Government Total	Government Federal	Government State and Local
1947	9.5	20.4	4.0	11.5	12.5	4.3	8.2
1948	9.3	20.7	4.1	11.6	12.6	4.2	8.4
1949	9.1	21.2	4.2	12.0	13.4	4.4	9.0
1950	8.9	20.8	4.2	11.9	13.3	4.3	9.1
1951	8.8	20.4	4.2	11.7	13.4	4.8	8.5
1952	8.7	20.5	4.2	11.7	13.5	5.0	8.6
1953	8.5	20.4	4.3	11.7	13.2	4.6	8.6
1954	8.3	20.9	4.6	12.2	13.8	4.5	9.3
1955	8.2	20.8	4.6	12.4	13.6	4.3	9.3
1956	8.1	20.7	4.6	12.5	13.9	4.2	9.7
1957	8.0	20.6	4.7	12.8	14.4	4.2	10.2
1958	7.7	20.9	4.9	13.3	15.3	4.3	11.0
1959	7.5	20.9	4.9	13.4	15.2	4.2	11.0
1960	7.4	21.0	4.9	13.7	15.4	4.2	11.2
1961	7.2	21.0	5.1	14.2	15.9	4.2	11.7
1962	7.0	20.8	5.0	14.4	16.0	4.2	11.8
1963	6.9	20.8	5.1	14.7	16.3	4.2	12.1
1964	6.8	20.8	5.1	14.9	16.5	4.0	12.5
1965	6.6	20.9	5.0	14.9	16.6	3.9	12.7
1966	6.5	20.7	4.8	14.9	16.9	4.0	12.9
1967	6.5	20.7	4.9	15.3	17.3	4.1	13.2
1968	6.4	20.8	5.0	15.6	17.5	4.0	13.5
1969*	6.3	20.9	5.1	15.8	17.4	3.9	13.5

*Preliminary.
SOURCE: U. S. Department of Labor.

If the data in Table 7 confirm the lagging nature of the two service industries discussed above, they also support the view that the wholesale and retail trade sector has exhibited little trend in either direction throughout the postwar years. While the absolute gains in trade employment have been large, its relative share of total nonagricultural wage and salary jobs has remained roughly constant at around 21%, and it continues to rank second only to manufacturing as a job provider.

The finance, insurance, and real estate sector seems to have lost some of the dynamism it exhibited during the first phase of the postwar period. It should be noted here that in a separate study by H. S.

Houthakker and Lester D. Taylor, entitled *Consumer Demand in the United States: Analyses and Projections,* they found that the demand for financial services (as measured by brokerage charges) and the demands for investment counselors declined nearly sevenfold since 1929, and has remained constant, at a low level, since. "We are unable to explain this puzzling behavior," except to suggest "that the strong emergence of mutual and other investment funds in recent years was an important contributing factor in the decline of the brokerage charges," say Houthakker and Taylor.[1] Since 1929 consumers have not regarded the purchase of common stocks as a favorable place to put their excess cash. In the 1960s it looked as if a forty-fifty year trend had been broken and the small investor was returning to Wall Street by buying large numbers of shares in mutual funds. The debacle in that industry in the late 1960s ended this participation by the small investor, and as stocks recovered in late 1971 and early 1972 redemptions of mutual shares soared. At the same time, other common stocks were attracting less of the consumer's extra cash. In other words, except for a brief flirtation with mutual funds, the participation of the small investor in the stock market has been over, in reality, for many, many years. The people have given up their slight share in the popular myth of "people's capitalism." Merrill Lynch may be bullish on America, but the American consumer—if being bullish is reflected in buying stocks—doesn't share that enthusiasm.

As a source of employment from 1947 to 1961, the finance, insurance, and real estate sector grew: 4% to 5.1%. Since then, its performance has been much like that of the trade sector, although the data for 1966-1969 suggest that its employment growth potential may level at 5%.

It is within the traditional services sector and within the state and local government sector that the dominant contributions to employment growth have taken place. In 1947 their combined share of total employment was about 20%; by 1969 this had risen to nearly 30% and, thus, exceeded the share of total nonagricultural wage and salary employment attributable to manufacturing. Between 1947 and 1969 the rate of growth in state and local government employees was far ahead of employee growth in all other services. Increasingly, then, state and local governments loom as perhaps the most dynamic of the service-producing industries.

A question arises, however. The growing shift of employment toward the service-producing industries might logically indicate that a corresponding shift in the final demand for service output was occurring. This would follow from the fact that the demand for labor is a derived demand—that is, it comes from the demand for the output produced by that labor. While substantial growth in service output very clearly has taken place, a shift in the composition of total output toward service failed to occur. Table 8 uses GNP data, both in constant (1958) dollars and current dollars, as the measure of output and disaggregates this data by industry source. Whether current or constant dollar measures are used, it can be seen that the relative share of total output accounted for by services has been essentially unchanged for at least four decades. In light of the shift toward employment in service-producing industries, what are the possible explanations?

A partial explanation can be found in the behavior of the intermediate output (that sold to other firms) of services as opposed to final output of services. Given the ongoing pattern of increased specialization and division of labor, services which many goods-producing industries had performed themselves may now be purchased as an intermediate service from the various service-producing industries. Although this would serve to increase the demand for labor in the service-producing industries, since this portion of service output would not be considered a "final" output, its dollar value would not be recorded in the GNP figures which encompass only final produced goods and services.

Another explanation revolves about income and substitution effects as they relate to the purchase of services. As incomes rise, higher income levels would encourage an increase in the demand for service output. At the same time, rising service prices would tend to discourage increased purchases of services by final users. In effect, they would cause the user of this higher-priced service to substitute his own performance of that service or seek another alternative for it, or do with less of it, rather than buy it at the higher price. This would dampen the demand for service output generated by rising incomes. Although the evidence is far from conclusive, the dramatic rise in service prices during the past decade would suggest that, for

TABLE 8

GROSS NATIONAL PRODUCT BY MAJOR TYPE OF PRODUCT

Year	Total GNP	Goods Output Total	Goods Output Durable	Goods Output Non-durable	Services	Services as percent of GNP	Total GNP	Goods Output Total	Goods Output Durable	Goods Output Non-durable	Services	Services as percent of GNP
	(Billions of current dollars)						(Billions of 1958 dollars)					
1930	90.4	46.9	11.4	35.5	34.2	37.8	183.5	90.5	22.4	68.0	67.7	36.9
1940	99.7	56.0	16.6	39.3	35.4	35.5	227.2	124.0	35.6	88.4	80.0	35.2
1950	284.8	162.4	60.4	102.0	87.0	30.5	355.3	192.6	73.4	119.1	117.5	33.1
1960	503.7	259.6	99.5	160.1	187.3	37.2	487.7	256.0	97.8	158.2	176.6	36.2
1969*	932.3	459.9	192.3	267.5	377.5	40.5	727.7	392.7	172.4	220.3	267.3	36.7

*Preliminary

SOURCE: *Survey of Current Business,* U.S. Department of Commerce, Office of Business Economics.

this period at least, the depressive impact of the substitution effect on the demand for services should not be ignored.

If the substitution effect were effective in restraining the demand for service output, it might also be expected to constrain employment growth in service-producing industries. To the degree that labor productivity in services is below that of other industries, however, the depressive impact on service employment growth would tend to be muted. Evidence about productivity growth in the service-producing industries clearly suggests that the rate of growth is significantly below that of both the agriculture and industry sectors. Indeed, lagging productivity growth would appear to be the major explanatory variable for the dichotomy between the expansion of employment in the service-producing industries and the relatively constant share of total output attributable to those same industries.

The reasons for this disparity in labor productivity growth in services are complex, but the more apparent ones should be mentioned. As noted earlier, the labor-intensive character of most service industries serves to restrain growth in output per manhour; that is, services do not lend themselves nearly as much as goods production to being mechanized toward greater and greater output per manhour or machinehour. Similarly, the relatively small size of service enterprises, compared with goods-producers, would tend to limit the economies of scale which may accrue to larger productive units.

During the 1969-70 recession, the focus of the President's Economic Council and that of other status quo economic wisdom was on increasing productivity per manhour in the goods-producing industries to soften the effect of the large wage increases, thus slowing the inflation. No voices were heard to point to the service target and try and figure out how to increase an attorney's output per manhour or the garbage collector's or the nurse's aid.

A central feature of the New Economic Program of August 1971 was the resort to historic pump priming—the government incurring large deficits and spending the money primarily in the *manufacturing* sector, especially the automobile industry, since it has traditionally loomed so large in the total economic picture. In fact, it was asserted that for every 100,000 new autos sold, 25,000 jobs would be created.

By February 1972 Arthur Burns, chairman of the Federal Reserve Board and a close advisor to President Nixon for many years, in noting that the recovery was sluggish, called it a crisis of confidence. He said that the American people are too "disturbed" by unsettling events to respond normally to economic stimulus.[2] Was this the central trouble?

Perhaps this was the trouble: The American economy, a Service Economy, was experiencing a large stimulus in the service sector and not the goods sector. In the past, an economic stimulus of $50 to $60 billion had always provided an upward thrust of considerable dimensions. But as late as mid-summer 1972 unemployment remained high (5.5%-6.0%) and production was only about 75% of plant capacity (25% idle). Clearly something was amiss. Autos were being made and sold and houses and apartments were going up and being sold and rented. Consumers were going into debt at an astonishing and unsustainable rate: over $1 billion per month during March, April, and May 1972. But amid all this glitter of growing numbers the government noted:

> The absorption rate of apartments completed were showing declines. Vacancy rates are expected to rise later in the year [1972].
>
> The market for single family homes is showing signs of possible softening. The number of new one-family homes sold has been rising steadily since the spring of last year, but the number of homes for sale has been rising ever faster.

The report continued:

> The May [1972] survey findings indicate that this year's growth in outlays (for capital investment) is over, with aggregate spending expected to decline slightly in the summer and rise slightly in fall. The current expansion of capital spending, while vigorous thus far, is not shaping up as strong as the last two capital spending recoveries.
>
> The ratio of consumer credit extensions to disposable income is currently about 16½%, a high figure by historical standards and up from 15½% in the first quarter of 1971. The high level of this ratio raises a question as to how willing consumers will be to undertake further rapid expansion of installment credit; the answer will certainly have an influence on the course of durable goods buying.[3]

In addition to his auto and home purchases, expenditures by the consumer for services continued at a rapid rate and this money was flowing into channels that, with various tributaries, created a flood of cash outside the manufacturing sector.

Service expenditures by consumers have two lingering consequences: 1) higher prices and 2) low productivity. As *Fortune* magazine put it:

> The time appropriated by services is steadily increasing, and since time is money, services obviously cost more and more. . . .
>
> Because service industries account for more than half the U.S. employment and must pass on all or most cost increases as price increases, their inferior productivity performance is one of the nation's *prime* inflationary forces.[4]

And the New Economic Program was watchdogging price increases in the making of *goods*. Quite like being upstairs at the downstairs.

Perhaps much later when all the numbers are in we will discover that this was the case and what was heralded as a recovery both on and off Wall Street was, in the bitter end, nothing more than a flash in the pan, and we were right back where we started from with continued high unemployment and rising prices—rising, invisibly, at the same rate they were when the New Economic Program was announced.

In any case, whatever the reasons for the failure of service output to exhibit the same growth characteristics as service employment, this is not to say that the absolute demand for services has not grown. It has grown substantially and will undoubtedly continue to grow as levels of income rise. The clear distinction between the goods-producing sector and the service-producing sector is that the former has been able to accommodate increasing demands for its output with a declining share of total employees, while the latter has required an increasing share of total employment to satisfy the growth in demand for services.

The growing dominance of the service-producing industries in the total employment picture carries several important implications. It would suggest, for instance, that cyclical fluctuations in employment growth and in unemployment may be minimized (cf. the experience of the 1969-70 recession). This is not to imply that economic recessions will not occur or that stock prices will not fall, but rather that the lesser cyclical sensitivity of service employment will reduce the magnitude of any accompanying swings in employment or unemployment. Chart 3 reflects the cyclical nature of manufacturing employment as compared with service employment.

CHART 3

PERCENTAGE CHANGES FROM PREVIOUS YEAR NONAGRICULTURAL WAGE AND SALARY EMPLOYMENT FOR SELECTED INDUSTRIES 1946-69

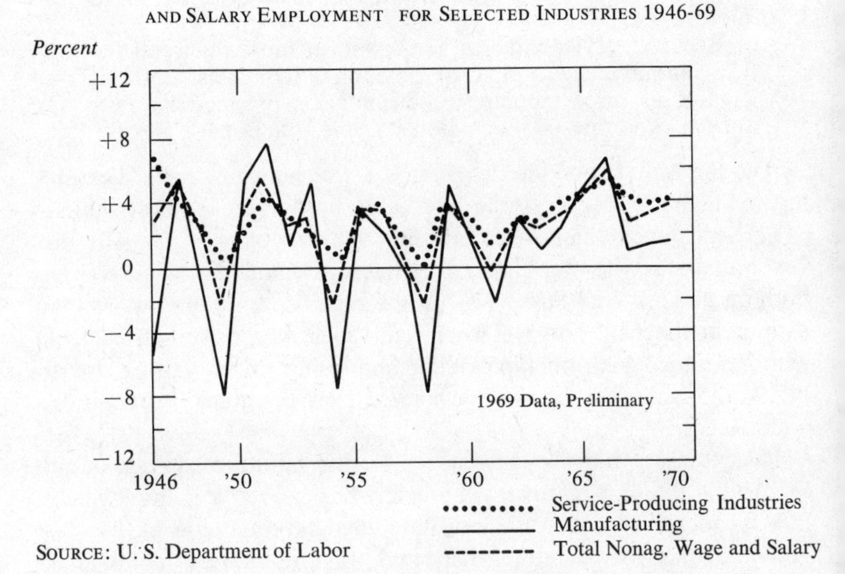

SOURCE: U.S. Department of Labor

Only in the 1958 recession did service employment fail to show an increase over the previous year. The decline in total employment which accompanied each of the postwar recessions was mirrored by the manufacturing component. Indeed, the extent of the swing in manufacturing was far greater than that in total employment. With manufacturing accounting for a declining share of total employment and with service employment increasing its share of the total, there is a growing likelihood that stability of employment over any business cycle will be enhanced.

The fact that service employment may be more stable over the business-cycle suggests that in the future the overall unemployment rate may not be as sensitive an indicator of declining business activity as it was formerly. For example, many employees of service businesses who might technically be classified as wage and salary workers are compensated more nearly on the basis of the output they produce—in effect, on a kind of piecework basis. This group would include sales personnel in wholesale and retail trade; many personal service employees, such as barbers, waitresses, and taxi drivers; employees in the insurance and real estate business; and others. Total income for these workers depends, to a considerable extent, on commissions, tips, or other supplements to a regular wage or salary. Since many services tend to be postponable, a decline in the earnings of this group may occur without a corresponding decline in their employment. Thus, this type of flexible income adjustment mechanism may cause income to fall during a general business decline, without any corresponding fall in employment or rise in the overall rate of unemployment. As the shift to service-producing employment continues, this suggests that the usual high rates of unemployment which have heretofore accompanied business recessions may be more moderate.

Although greater stability in employment over the business cycle would prove to be a desirable contribution of an increasingly service-oriented economy, the implications for price stability seem less optimistic. The price performance of the service sector is amply documented. In the past decade, the prices of all services rose by nearly 40%, compared with a rise of less than half that much for goods purchased by consumers. In the face of further demands for services, the lagging productivity growth of this sector would clearly suggest that an upward bias to price behavior is a likely concomitant of a Service Economy. See Chart 4.

A further possible implication of the trend to growing service employment is a decline in the influence of labor unions. The degree of unionization in the goods-producing sector is far greater than in services, and is traceable largely to the larger size of the firms and their greater concentration within those industries. Service enterprises are typically much smaller and more fragmented within a given service industry. Organizational efforts by unions would, therefore, be much more expensive and their control over a significant part of the labor supply within a given service industry would be more

CHART 4

CONSUMER PRICE INDEX

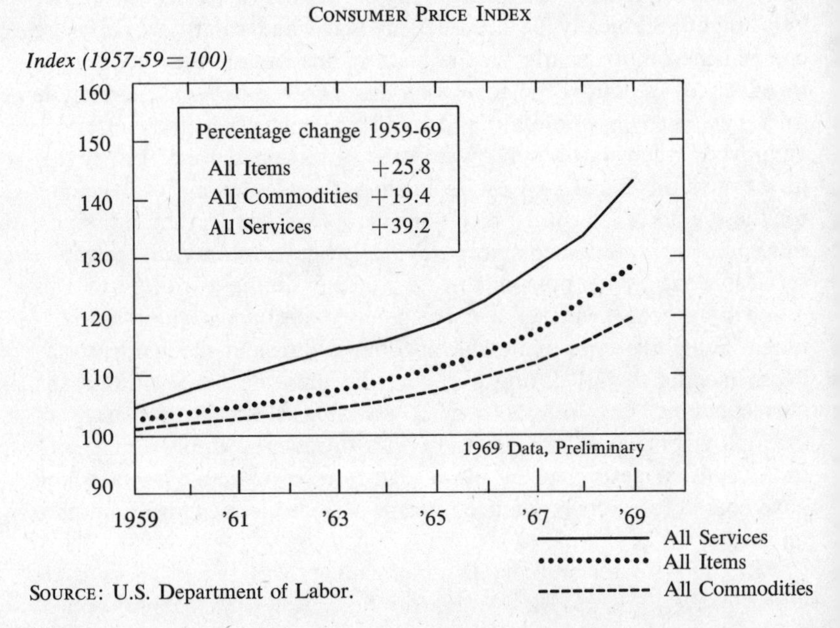

SOURCE: U.S. Department of Labor.

difficult to achieve. Thus, as goods-producing industries decline in terms of their importance as job providers, union influence may taper off.

Within the public employees sector, however, we have seen evidence that labor unions have not been unaware of growing organizational opportunities. The increasing militancy of teachers' unions, for example, is one manifestation of the success of organizational efforts in the rapidly growing state and local government sector. Strikes by public employees in the years ahead may well be more common.

Victor Fuchs notes another future implication of this profound shift to a Service Economy:

> We may see an end to the myth of the dominance of the large corporation in our society. Most people do not work and never have worked for large corporations; most production does not take place and never has taken place in large corporations. In the future, the large corporation is

> likely to be overshadowed by the hospitals, universities, research institutes, government agencies, and professional organizations that are the hallmarks of a service economy. . . . Many services are produced by nonprofit institutions . . . many occupations in the Service sector do not make special demands for physical strength. This means that women can compete on more nearly equal terms with men, perhaps for the first time in history. In the Service sector, we find women holding down almost one-half of all jobs, compared with only one-fifth in Industry. . . . We also find a disproportionate number of older workers in services . . . because it provides greater opportunities for part-time employment. . . . The transfer from a craft society to one of mass production was said to depersonalize work and alienate the worker. The advent of a service economy implies a reversal of these trends.[5]

If one is to successfully buy stocks and bonds in the years to come, then it will be necessary to pay much closer attention to the consumer: to perceive what he is spending his money for and when he shifts his attitudes and expectations. This, in turn, requires a rethinking of economic concepts. Again, from Victor Fuchs:

> One problem arises because the consumer frequently plays an important role in the production of services, but not in the production of goods. . . . In the supermarket and laundromat the consumer actually works, and in the doctor's office the quality of the medical history the patient gives may influence significantly the productivity of the doctor. . . .
>
> A second concept that may require further development is that of labor-embodied technological change. When, as in some services, formal education is important and there is job security, the rate at which advances in knowledge affect productivity will depend in part on how fast labor embodying these new advances can be added to the work force. Moreover, it is not true that physical capital is always a fixed factor and labor always variable, as is usually assumed in models based on manufacturing. In many service firms the reverse assumption is closer to reality.
>
> Another set of concepts requiring re-examination are those concerned with productivity and demand. The flow of production in many service industries is uneven, with sharp peaks at particular hours or on particular days separated by periods of slow activity. . . .

> A final implication is the likelihood that current estimates of real gross national product are becoming less useful for studies of productivity and economic growth because, at high levels of GNP per capita, a large fraction of productive effort is devoted to services (where real output is often difficult to measure) and to other activities . . . that are not measured at all.[6]

In dead center of these momentous changes lie today's Money Managers, in charge of investing the savings of millions: in bank trust departments, insurance and pension fund portfolios, and mutual funds. In declining markets especially, their record speaks for itself: abominable. They are still oriented to yesterday: quantities of money, rising and falling interest rates, numbers of cars . . . goods-focus. So, when the consumer shifts his spending for types of goods, they are unprepared. When the consumer decides to spend, they are unprepared. They simply do not know what the consumer is doing, nor do they care, for, after all, the world of buying and selling stocks and bonds has always been like *it was*—to them. In the securities market, then, the Service Economy implications for the future will also be major.

> Up to a point, it is probably true that the higher real GNP is, the more reliable it is as a measure of economic welfare. But the trend may now be in the other direction, because at high levels of GNP per capita a large fraction of productive effort is devoted to services (where real output is very difficult to measure) and to other activities that are not measured at all.[7]

Thus, any relation between rising GNP and rising stock prices is, already in 1972, unreal. Despite this, Paul Samuelson writes:

> What are the few common-sense regularities about stock prices that have stood the test of historical experience? Here are three with current relevance:
>
> Stock prices and money national income do, over long periods of time, show roughly corresponding movements.
>
> But stock prices do show more ups and downs than gross national product or *business indicators* generally.
>
> Although present and probable future corporate profits are admittedly the most important determinant of intermediate market movements, no way exists to determine what is the proper price-earnings ratio.

> Every objective study has failed to validate prediction devices that rely on anything different from *informed common sense.*[8]

It is doubtful that these comments themselves represent "informed common sense" in the light of the basic shift in America's economy.

4

Consumer Expenditures

> Our past patterns of thought are expressed in the present patterns of institutions.
>
> *Robert Theobald*

When the consumer gets ready to spend, or to save, it is important to know where the money will flow, because this is where the profits are bound to be. In 1966 personal income totaled a record $587.2 billion; by 1969 the figure had risen to $750.9 billion; by 1971, $861.4 billion. Table 9 shows where the money was spent during the 1953-1971 period. The 1971 distribution of personal consumption expenditures among the three major categories changed from the 1966 proportions. Of the expenditure dollar, 42.4 cents went for purchases of nondurable goods; another 42.5 cents was spent for services; the remaining 15.1 cents went for durable goods. Fifty percent of the total amount spent by consumers in 1971 went for the combined categories of food, clothing, housing, and household operation —generally considered essential items of living.

During this 1953-1971 period, the trends are significant. For example, although spending for nondurable goods increased more than 60%, this advance was considerably less than the rise of about 90% in total consumer expenditures. As a result, the nondurable goods portion of the total decreased from 50.8% to 42.4% over these years. During the same period, there was an increase in the percentage spent for services, from 34.8% to 42.5%.

TABLE 9

DISTRIBUTION OF PERSONAL CONSUMPTION EXPENDITURES BY MAJOR GROUPS OF SERVICES AND GOODS*

(Percent)

	1953	1955	1957	1959	1961	1963	1965	1966	1971
Total services and goods	100.0	100.0	100.0	100.0	100.0	100.0	100.0	100.0	100.0
Services	34.8	35.9	37.3	38.6	40.3	40.6	40.5	40.7	42.5
Housing	12.7	13.3	13.7	14.0	14.5	14.8	14.6	14.6	14.9
Household operation	5.2	5.5	5.8	5.9	6.2	6.2	5.9	5.8	5.8
Transportation	3.4	3.2	3.2	3.2	3.2	3.0	3.0	3.0	2.9
Other	13.4	14.0	14.7	15.4	16.4	16.7	17.0	17.3	18.9
Durable goods	14.5	15.6	14.5	14.2	13.2	14.4	15.3	14.9	15.1
Automobiles and parts	6.2	7.2	6.5	6.3	5.5	6.5	6.9	6.5	6.9
Furniture and household equipment	6.5	6.5	6.2	6.1	5.8	5.9	6.3	6.5	5.9
Other	1.8	1.8	1.8	1.9	1.9	2.0	2.1	2.0	2.2
Nondurable goods	50.8	48.5	48.2	47.1	46.5	45.0	44.2	44.3	42.4
Food and beverages	28.0	26.4	26.1	25.3	24.7	23.5	22.8	22.6	20.5
Clothing and shoes	9.6	9.1	8.6	8.5	8.3	8.2	8.3	8.6	8.6
Gasoline and oil	3.4	3.5	3.8	3.7	3.7	3.6	3.5	3.4	3.6
Tobacco	2.2	2.0	2.0	2.1	2.2	2.1	2.0	1.9	1.9
Other	7.6	7.5	7.6	7.6	7.6	7.6	7.6	7.8	7.8

*Based on current dollar expenditures.
NOTE: Payment of personal taxes is not reflected in these figures.
SOURCE: U.S. Department of Commerce

The decline in nondurable goods outlays relative to the total has been concentrated in food and clothing. Expenditures for these two groups comprised 37.6% of the total in 1953 and only 29.1% in 1971. Except for the period 1955-1958, when it showed little change, the proportion of the expenditure dollar spent on food has declined each year since 1953. (The importance of this lies in the fact that, as the famed German economist Werner Sombart emphasized, food is *the* dynamic of *all* economic change.) On the other hand, the percentage spent for clothing decreased sharply through 1957, declined at a more gradual rate through 1963, and has moved erratically since then. Outlays for nondurable goods other than food and clothing have fluctuated narrowly between 13.0% and 13.5% of total expenditures for almost two decades.

From 1961 to 1971, the ratio of automobiles and parts to total expenditures rose steadily. At 6.9% in 1971 it was almost equal to 1955, the previous boom year in auto sales. With the slowing down in auto sales in 1966, the ratio dropped somewhat. Since 1961, the percentage spent for furniture and household equipment has increased each year until 1971, while other durable goods have accounted for a fairly constant part of total expenditures.

The ratio of expenditures for housing and household operation services to total spending showed a strong upward trend during the postwar years through 1961. In contrast, the sharp increases in prices of medical services and of personal service businesses—legal fees, life insurance, and so forth—have resulted in a larger share of the consumer expenditure dollar being taken by these categories during the 1960s. Here the physical volume of these services relative to the total has shown little change over the period, and in some cases (e.g., doctors per capita) declined.

Not all groups shared in the relative rise in spending for services prior to 1961. The amount spent for personal services—such as dry cleaning, laundry, and barber and beauty shop services—increased in line with aggregate expenditures from 1953 to 1961. The percentage going for transportation decreased, as the decline in the amount spent for purchased local transportation more than offset the rise in expenditures associated with the automobile. Since 1961, outlays for transportation and personal services have not increased as fast as total expenditures.

As mentioned earlier, in the past business and government have been recognized as the sectors having power and influence to generate income, and thus to contribute to the growth of the economy. These functions have been denied the consumer sector. Fluctuations in business activity have been thought to originate in money being put in (or taken out of) the economy through business investment and government debts, or the reduction of money flow through reduced business spending and government surpluses. New trends arising through business and government activities have been thought to be transmitted *to* the consumer sector ("trickle-down economics"), but it has been assumed that changes do *not originate* there.

Two propositions are implicit in much of modern economic analysis and make it understandable why little attention has been given to consumer behavior. The first says that consumer incomes depend on the activities of business and government. The second, that consumer expenditures depend on consumer incomes.

The first proposition appears obvious on the basis that consumers do not derive their incomes from other consumers, *excepting,* of course, in *services.*

The second idea was highlighted by Lord Keynes who stated that consumer spending is a fairly stable function of income. Studies have confirmed that in the aggregate consumers spend most of what they earn (since 1945 this has been, with few exceptions, about 94%) and that the proportion of total incomes spent does not vary greatly over the long run. But *where it is spent* now becomes crucial. If the consumer continues to spend over half of his money for services, then, in time, consumers will be deriving an increasing amount of their incomes from other incomes (nurses working for doctors, etc.).

Sometime during the 1960s, Keynes' maxim, a kingpin of Status Quo Economics, seemed to be losing its validity. More and more it appeared that consumer spending was a function of "life style." No longer were consumers necessarily spending more *just because* they made more. At any income level they seemed to be spending 1) to fill one central need (e.g., a college student with a low income spending a great deal of money for a stereo set or a motorcycle or a dune buggy, then going back to his low-spending level), or 2) middle-aged people dropping out of lifetime jobs—the rat race—

and spending in entirely new directions which had nothing whatever to do with their earlier entrenched spending patterns. If this pattern persists, and indications are that it will, then a great deal of current economic wisdom must be reworked.

The following table showing the disposition of personal income shows the huge rise in disposable personal income from 1961 ($364 billions) to the 3rd Quarter, 1972 ($799 billions). Note, too, the increasing amount of personal consumption expenditures that are spent for services. The pie chart shows more recent data from a different perspective.

CHART 5

DISTRIBUTION OF THE PERSONAL INCOME DOLLAR 1972

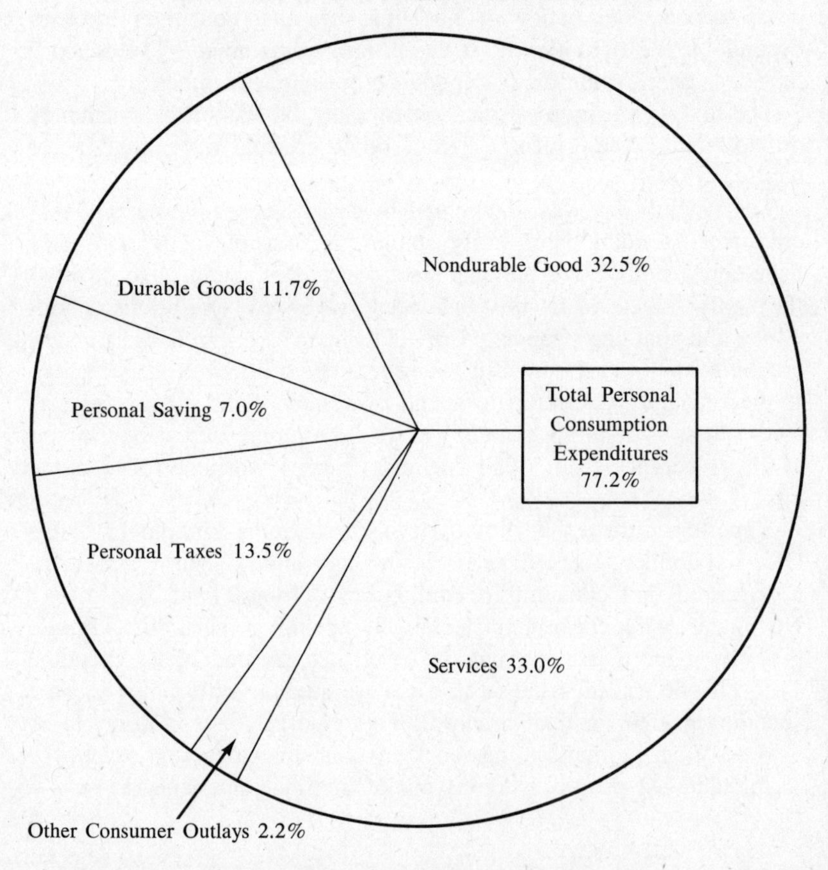

SOURCE: Department of Commerce, Office of Business Economics.

TABLE 10

DISPOSITION OF PERSONAL INCOME

Period	Personal income	Less: Personal tax and nontax payments	Equals: Disposable personal income	Less: Personal outlays				Equals: Personal saving	Per capita disposable personal income		Saving as percent of disposable personal income
				Total personal outlays*	Personal consumption expenditures						
					Durable goods	Nondurable goods	Services		Current prices	1958 prices	
	Billions of dollars								Dollars		Percent
1961	416.8	52.4	364.4	343.3	44.2	155.9	135.1	21.2	1,983	1,909	5.8
1962	442.6	57.4	385.3	363.7	49.5	162.6	143.0	21.6	2,064	1,968	5.6
1963	465.5	60.9	404.6	384.7	53.9	168.6	152.4	19.9	2,136	2,013	4.9
1964	497.5	59.4	438.1	411.9	59.2	178.7	163.3	26.2	2,283	2,126	6.0
1965	538.9	65.7	473.2	444.8	66.3	191.1	175.5	28.4	2,436	2,239	6.0
1966	587.2	75.4	511.9	479.3	70.8	206.9	188.6	32.5	2,604	2,335	6.4
1967	629.3	83.0	546.3	506.0	73.1	215.0	204.0	40.4	2,749	2,403	7.4
1968	688.9	97.9	591.0	551.2	84.0	230.8	221.3	39.8	2,945	2,486	6.7
1969	750.9	116.5	634.4	596.2	90.8	245.9	242.7	38.2	3,130	2,534	6.0
1970	806.3	116.7	689.5	634.7	90.5	264.4	261.8	54.9	3,366	2,603	8.0
1971	861.4	117.0	744.4	683.4	103.5	278.1	283.3	60.9	3,595	2,679	8.2
1972: I ..	907.0	136.5	770.5	714.9	111.0	288.3	296.7	55.7	3,700	2,716	7.2
II ..	922.1	139.5	782.6	732.5	113.9	297.2	302.4	50.1	3,751	2,739	6.4
III .	939.9	141.1	798.8	748.0	118.6	302.0	308.0	50.8	3,821	2,773	6.4

*Includes personal consumption expenditures, interest paid by consumers, and personal transfer payments to foreigners.
SOURCE: U.S. Department of Commerce; *Economic Indicators,* December 1972, p. 5.

Electronic communications and mass media can cause rapid changes in consumer spending habits, influence his decision to save, to borrow, to buy stocks or bonds or mutual funds, or simply save in a Savings and Loan, or, of all places, a Christmas Club. These changes in attitudes and expectations are known in advance, and with other consumer indicators send advance messages of what is going to happen to billions of dollars of spending power.

Time and again, businessmen in trying to assess the consumer's behavior minimize his stated intents of spending or saving. A frequent retort when these are brought to their attention: "Empirical evidence indicates consumer surveys to be unreliable." But, at the same time, they will put faith in the cost per ton per mile of hauling goods where, as some sage has noted, "No one, not even God, knows the cost per ton per mile." As production-oriented businessmen become more service-oriented and "closer" to the consumer, they will perhaps come more to rely on the research available to them. The motormakers are among the biggest offenders: They blissfully predict their sales for a model year to be high in the face of advance research indicating the consumer is saving and is not in the market for a new car, thus missing their production targets badly. But motormakers have not been famed for innovative thinking (their last significant contribution to the automobile was the air conditioner—in 1940).

SERVICE ECONOMY SUMMARY

What this book has been saying up to this point can be summarized in two different ways. First, note eight summary statements:

1. The fuel that fires what remains of the capitalistic engine *now* is the consumer. He derives the largest share of national income, spends most of what he makes, and spends a steadily growing percentage for services, not for goods.

2. What, where, and how the consumer earns and spends are critical new fundamentals to reckon with.

3. A great deal of consumer spending is for upgrading his own image by spending for services—the necessities and frivolities he feels necessary to restore his identity, an identity he has largely lost in the marketplace and factory.

4. The institutionalizing of high cost medical care has compelled

more spending for services, a disproportionate amount. Federal and state intervention will probably repair this.

5. Rising service spending accompanies a technological-knowledge society, and its effects are revolutionary: upheavals in entire industries, changing governmental spending patterns (e.g., from federal back to local) to restore neglected social needs, changing corporate structures to try to meet changes in society.

6. The "consumer revolt" undermines the fading corporate structure in many ways, including:
    a. "Excessive profits" will become a dim memory.
    b. "Let the seller be fair" will prevail. The day of "Let the buyer beware" is gone.
    c. Too many now realize they work *by* the corporation, not for it, thus are disenchanted with their work and the goods they produce, and, of course, the shoddy goods produced reflect this (requiring *more service,* sooner!).

7. Service businesses are small businesses assuring the revival of village and cottage industries that will absorb the unemployed and also provide new outlets for excess savings.

8. Different spending and savings patterns will change security buying habits, and will be powerful determinants of the waves of optimism and pessimism that will always prevail in securities markets.

Another way to summarize what this book has been saying is to compare/contrast the manner in which Status Quo Economists abstract and tabulate data (Table 11, p. 52) with an approach (Table 12, p. 53) that takes into explicit account the fact and importance of the American economy as a *Service* Economy. The same figures are used in both tables, but, simply put, Table 12 reflects the way it *is*.

TABLE 11

NATIONAL INCOME ACCOUNTS IN 1971: STATUS QUO VIEW
(billions of dollars)

Gross National Product					
GNP by Producer		GNP by Final User		Gross National Income	
Extractive Industries	$ 80.7	Consumption	$ 664.9	Wages	$ 644.1
Regulated Industries	67.0	Investment	152.0	Rents	24.5
Manufacturing	223.2	Government	232.8	Interest	38.5
Wholesale and Retail Trade	130.8	Net Exports	0.7	Profits	148.6
Services	209.3				
Government and Foreign	144.8				
Other (Depreciation, Business Tax)	199.5			Other (Depreciation, Business Tax)	199.5
Statistical Discrepancy	—4.9			Statistical Discrepancy	—4.9
GNP	$1050.4	GNP	$1050.4	GNP	$1050.4

NOTE: Total current production of services and goods in the U.S. economy is broken down three ways: by producer, by final user, and by income source. The final user account and the income account are estimated from different data. This provides a valuable check. It also gives rise to small statistical discrepancy. GNP by producer is then derived from the income data. Gategory names have been simplified.

SOURCE: *Survey of Current Business,* U.S. Department of Commerce, July 1972; *Business in Brief,* Chase Manhattan Bank of New York, Economic Research Division bimonthly report no. 106, October 1972, p. 5.

TABLE 12

NATIONAL INCOME ACCOUNTS IN 1971: NON-STATUS QUO VIEW
(billions of dollars)

Gross National Product								
GNP by Producer			GNP by Final User			Gross National Income		
Service Sector			Consumption			Wages		
Services	$209.3		Services (55%)	$365.6		Services (66%)	$421.1	
Wholesale & Retail Trade	130.8		Goods (45%)	299.3	$664.9	Goods (34%)	219.0	$644.1
Regulated Industries (Utilities, Air Travel, etc.)	67.0	$407.1				Rents		24.5
Production Sector			Investment		152.0	Interest		38.5
Manufacturing	223.2		Government		232.8	Profits		148.6
Extractive Industries	80.7	303.9	Net Exports		0.7			
Government and Foreign		144.8						
Other		199.5				Other		199.5
Statistical Discrepancy		−4.9				Statistical Discrepancy		−4.9
GNP		$1050.4	GNP		$1050.4	GNP		$1050.4

NOTE: The Service Sector figures do not take into account service activity "buried" in Manufacturing, Extractive Industries, and Government and Foreign; conservative estimates place this at 20%, thus widening the gap even further than shown.

5

Bad Numbers

News items:[1]

Second quarter, 1972, after-tax earnings of 1,368 corporations showed an average increase of 16% over a year earlier. This marks an acceleration over the first quarter when this identical group of firms reported a year-to-year improvement of 13%.

Consumer prices rose at 2.1% annual rate in the second quarter, 1972.

Estimated Gross National Product, 1972: $1,130 billion.

The prestigious National Bureau of Economic Research plans to announce later this week that the U.S. economy indeed went through a classical recession. It began in November 1969 and ended last November [1970], the private nonprofit organization estimates.

Announcements such as the above flood the mass media and Wall Street daily. "Good" or "bad" economic news, together with other exogenous events, is instantly reflected in stock prices in response to the interpretation of the "news" by the people involved. Little or no thought is given to the quality, the accuracy, of the raw data on which these stock price moves are predicted. Thus, stock market prices are often shot up or down with erroneous statistics.

Most of the data is "virtually meaningless" according to Oskar

Morgenstern, Director of the Econometric Research Program at Princeton University and consultant to the Federal Reserve Board. Morgenstern comments on five key concepts around which business statistics focus: GNP, business cycle turning points, earnings per share, Consumer Price Index, and corporate profits.

> The idea that quarterly, let alone *monthly,* figures of gross national product . . . could be obtained, even with the most modern recording devices, without appreciable error, is nothing short of grotesque.[2]

It often takes ten years of revisions to settle on a final monthly figure initially set down ten years earlier, and during this period of fluctuation of figures the GNP can have an error estimate of ±10%. It should be emphasized that deviations of 10% represent, in 1973, figures that run up to some $100 billions.

In 1971 when the Council of Economic Advisers forecast a GNP of $1.065 trillion, there was widespread skepticism. Paul A. Samuelson called it a "comic opera" forecast no more believable than the "uplifting numbers" of Fidel Castro's Cuban sugar harvest predictions. The *Wall Street Journal* reported:

> Not only did its GNP forecast exceed the private consensus by as much as $20 billion, but it conspicuously omitted the usual supporting detail. When challenged, Mr. Shultz [George P. Shultz, budget office director] explained that a "different" method was used that doesn't rely on first estimating such key components as consumer spending.
>
> This turned out to be the newly-shaped formula of his young economist, Arthur B. Laffer, which is designed to predict only the total GNP. The council tried to narrow the credibility gap by belatedly filling in the blanks, but these elements unfortunately happened to add up to a total $2 billion bigger than the $1.065 trillion. Lately, top Treasury and economic officials have been downplaying the part Mr. Schultz' protege played in the forecast, and in the process casting doubt on coordination if not on credibility.[3]

When looking at GNP figures, we must also remember the difference between constant and current dollars (i.e., the difference between noninflated and inflated dollars), a difference often glossed over. Furthermore, other effects of inflation must not be forgotten; otherwise the distortion merely magnifies.

About turning points in business cycles, Morgenstern says:

> When the time series are formed of large aggregates, such as Gross National Product or national income, it is impossible to determine any particular month as a turning point. . . .
>
> Instead of a precise *point* in time—for so complex a phenomenon as the turning about of business of a whole country—a much larger interval has to be chosen as an approximation. This poses a dilemma: current business cycle analysis demands that a time unit not larger than a month be used, yet the quality of the data will not support such fine-grained measurement. . . .
>
> We are far less certain when business turns than we are made to believe and would like to know.[4]

We tend to assume that the numbers that go into computing business activity are "fresh," as if they just happened yesterday. However, in real life many of the "fresh" figures frequently are six months old at the time they are announced, but this important qualification is never mentioned. When the activity in the business sector is observed by political figures and their economist allies, it often does not augur well to tell the whole story. In fact, during 1971 the Nixon Administration found it necessary to prohibit the experts in the Labor Department from commenting on unemployment numbers, since their candid observations ran counter to the picture being painted at the White House.

Morgenstern believes that profit calculations and reporting need a radical overhaul before we can be sure we are seeing meaningful data:

> The reader should contemplate the extent to which financial information guides action: earnings per share are a standard measure, share prices are expressed as multiples of earnings and thereby are judged as to whether they are "out of line" or not. Profit ratios, i.e., profiits in relation to invested capital, are compared for firms in the same industry or for different industries. The advisability of new ventures is judged by forming ideas about expected profits —which, however, are determined by . . . questionable features. . . . The circularity in method is striking but it will be a permanent part of our pattern of thinking until the time when economic theory develops observable meas-

> ures for profits which are free from these objections and until accountants produce substantially new ideas of constructing balance sheets composed of conceptually homogeneous figures. That time appears to be distant. But accountants could begin to use the existing tools which probability theory provides and which allow the determination of expected values. . . . The users of balance sheets, especially the investor, should be the first to insist on the introduction of a modern spirit into this sadly stagnant field.[5]

The Consumer Price Index is the best known figure in the Numbers Game. It is a rough measure, very rough, of the average price from month to month of the basic necessities of life. The wages of millions of workers are related to this index so that changes in it mean changes in their incomes. But W. J. Reichmann, an eminent British statistician, had this to say about cost-of-living indexes:

> There is no such index! The index referred to is the Index of Retail Prices. By its nature it does, of course, reflect movements in nominal cost levels but the reflection is an indirect one since it derives from an averaged expenditure list for all households. This at once gives a qualification to the word "Prices" and there are many other qualifications to the meaning of the index. . . . Perhaps the cost of living is too complex a concept to define at all.[6]

Morgenstern says simply about the Consumer Price Index:

> That it is quoted and measured in tenths of a percent is . . . simply absurd.[7]

It should be obvious that even if one were to assume the numbers were bona fide, what should enter into a cost-of-living index varies over time. Some items are no longer traded in, some have changed their function in the household, others are no longer in use, etc.

It is no small thing, then, that when the CPI is shown to be increasing at a decreasing rate, presumably an indication that the government does have a handle on inflation, the hapless housewife is bewildered when she finds, as she spends her money, that prices are creeping up each week! This was common knowledge among American consumers in the summer of 1972 while the economists were displaying statistics which showed just the opposite of real life. Upstairs at the downstairs again . . . and again.

Wall Street Money Managers spend a great deal of time *analyzing* profits—past, present, and future—but when it comes to *defining* "profits" the word itself is highly elusive. For example, see again the first news item quoted in the chapter-opening headnote; the First National City Bank newsletter went on to explain:

> Nevertheless, the recovery is more apparent than real in terms of what a dollar's worth of profits will buy. The U.S. Department of Commerce has recently begun issuing figures on after-tax profits in constant dollars, that is, adjusted for the effects of inflation. The price deflator is a composite of the average prices for consumer expenditures, reflecting the purchasing power of dividends, and the average costs of business fixed investment in structures and equipment, reflecting the purchasing power of retained earnings.
>
> If a similar deflator is applied to the Citibank profits index for manufacturing, creating a constant dollar index (1967 = 100), the second quarter 1972 level would be only 111, about the same as the peak in the second quarter of 1966 and still 2% below the record in the fourth quarter of 1968.
>
> According to the latest Commerce Department figures total after-tax corporation profits in constant dollars were still 22% below their third-quarter 1966 peak in the first quarter of this year [1972], while profits in current dollars were 2% below their high. The Commerce Department bases its profits figures on income-tax returns, unlike the Citibank's survey, which is calculated from reports to stockholders. Only last month [July 1972] the *Commerce data were revised downward again by several billion dollars,* presumably reflecting the increased impact of accelerated depreciation, the investment tax credit, and a host of other accounting differences between tax returns and published reports. Quite legitimately, these accounting procedures have led to a widening gap between the profit figures that form a part of our national income accounts and the ones that form a basis for decisions by management, stockholders and Wall Street. However, since depreciation accounts for much of the discrepancy, there is a much closer agreement in the trends of cash flow.[8]

After reading this it becomes doubtful if even God knows what the true profits were of the major corporations in America in 1972. The increasingly few that get them know, however.

Other illustrations of the elusiveness of accurate and meaningful profit figures are these observations:

> When the stock market took a depressing plunge last year [1970], investors found out that advance estimates of rapid earnings growth were often the hallmark of imaginative stock promotion and simple overoptimism. Many an earnings report turned out to be disappointing indeed. The scandals that followed such discoveries are still rocking the accounting profession and the world of corporate finance. Now the Commerce Department's Office of Business Economics has revealed that profits have been even weaker than originally announced.[9]

> In its annual revisions, the department rolled back the 1970 GNP figure to $974.1 billion from $976.5 billion. This was somewhat surprising as most administration analysts were expecting an upward restatement. The 1969 GNP figure was also revised downward by more than 2 billion, and the 1968 result reduced by about $1 billion, the department said. All of these downward revisions primarily were laid to substantial revisions in corporate profits.[10]

> Last May [1971], on the basis of public reports by companies and some tax returns, OBE estimated that corporate gross profits in 1970 were $81.3 billion. July [1971], on the basis of more up-to-date tax filings, the bureau sharply cut that estimate to $75.4 billion. The OBE also lowered its original estimate of 1969 profits from $93.7 billion to $84.2 billion. The latest revisions showed that profits were no higher in 1969 than they had been in 1966.[11]

Imaginary numbers in higher math are one thing; imaginary numbers in our economic life are another.

> In the cloudland of higher mathematics, there is a whole area of study called "imaginary numbers." What is an imaginary number? It is a multiple of the square root of minus one. What is the good of knowing that? Imaginary numbers, according to mathematicians, are useful in figuring out such problems as the flow of air or water past a curved surface like an airplane wing.
>
> In ordinary life, imaginary numbers of a somewhat different kind seem to have become even more useful. From solemn public officials and eager corporations, from newspapers, television comes a googol of seemingly definitive

> and unarguable statistics. They tell us, with an exactitude that appears magical, the number of heroin addicts in New York and population of the world. By simulating reality, they assure us that facts are facts, and that life can be understood, put in order, perhaps even mastered.
>
> Imaginary numbers sound true—that is their function, after all—and so they may serve the cause of truth. But they can serve the purpose of falsehood just as well. At the highest levels of government, imaginary numbers can delude even the shrewdest of leaders with "quantifications" of reality.
>
> The national rate of unemployment, for example is now [mid-1971] stated to be 5.6%, but that figure is based entirely on people who officially reported themselves out of work. Idle students, housewives who cannot find outside jobs, unsuccessful artisans—such people are not counted.
>
> Is nothing, then, to be believed? Yes—the evidence of the senses and the observations of the mind, but not too many of the imaginary numbers that try to provide proof. How many is "not too many"? The computer is working on that.[12]

Wall Street has its own set of imaginary numbers: the "resistance levels" and "support levels" of the Dow theorists, and the never ending array of mythical "levels" set by the "chartists"—"downside breakout," "congestion range," "high volume zone," "double top," "triangles." These concepts take on a reality that soon becomes a gospel; they are widely quoted and even more widely believed. This entire mythology is ripped to shreds time and again by the sheer facts of the activity of the market; still it clings. Old habits and ways of thinking remain the most vested of all.

The whole problem of illusory numbers can be illustrated in terms of Morgenstern's comments on national income statistics. He summarizes the problem of accuracy:

> great efforts, important contributions, eminent authors involved. . . . results: great errors, many revisions of estimates, lack of convergence of the revisions.[13]

The matter of lag and revisions is crucial. Preliminary estimates for most of the quarterly national income series (e.g., corporate profits, personal consumption expenditures, proprietors' and rental income, etc.) are made available in the *Survey of Current Business*. The following factors create problems of usefulness and accuracy of the data. In the first place, the issue of *Survey* which carries these quarterly statistics is published two months after the end of the quarter. Secondly, for the corporate profits and national income series data, the lag is an additional two months. Further, the quarterly statistics are based generally on more limited information than the annual series. However, both the quarterly data and the annual data are subject to substantial revisions after publication. First revisions are made three months after the initial publication, and in each July issue of *Survey* the statistics may be revised for the past two or three years. Finally, in some cases figures are revised after *ten* years.

> It is, of course, desirable that revisions be made when new information becomes available. But their frequency and long delays betray an uncertainty . . . permeating the whole field, which is in striking contrast with the wide-spread *immediate* use of the first given figure and the assumption that it is significant. . . .[14]

The table below summarizes for a typical period the three reliability criteria of quarter-to-quarter changes in the national income series: a measure of the extent of the average revision, the percent of times the first estimates missed the direction of movement, and the average bias (which in this series in usually insignificant). A series with large revisions (e.g., corporate profits) clearly indicates that the original estimates were poor.

In other words, during the period 1947–1958 corporate profits failed to detect the direction of movement 19% of the time; this is a poor track record. Yet, this data is widely and religiously used by security analysts trying to determine the prospects of individual stocks. Alas. As Morgenstern concludes:

> Corporate profits and gross private domestic investment . . . would be very interesting for estimating, say, future activity on the stock market, but they are definitely weak series and therefore of little use when needed.[15]

TABLE 13

SELECTED NATIONAL INCOME SERIES, 1947–1958:
SUMMARY MEASURES OF QUARTER-TO-QUARTER PERCENT MOVEMENT

National Income Series	Average revision as a % of average movement of revised estimate of change	% of time direction of movement missed	Average bias in first estimates of quarter-to-quarter movement
Compensation of employees	26%	6%	—.17%
National income	26	4	—.18
Personal income	28	6	—.15
Personal consumption expenditures	34	2	—.31
Gross national product	38	11	—.22
Corporate profits before tax	40	19	.53
Gross private domestic investment	61	19	.01
Proprietors' and rental income	96	28	.05

SOURCE: "Revisions of First Estimates of Quarter-to-Quarter Movement in Selected National Income Series, 1947–1958 (Seasonally Adjusted Data)," *Statistical Evaluation Reports, Report No. 2,* Office of Statistical Standards, Bureau of the Budget, February 1960, p. 23; Morgenstern, *On the Accuracy of Economic Observations,* p. 270.

Arthur Ross, former commissioner of labor statistics, had the following comments to make regarding the first statistical country in history:

> Public men become known by the statistics they keep.
>
> If this overblown affinity for statistics were only amusing, it would not deserve much comment in a city [Washington] replete with absurdities. But the phenomenon has a more sober aspect. Government officials are prone to take statistics too literally, to ignore their limitations, and to confuse partial truths with the whole truth about complex realities. This propensity can lead to serious, even tragic consequences.

This was demonstrated during 1971 as inflation and unemployment continued up, but at a "slower" rate; and, of course, as the Nixon Administration, in finally recognizing this fiasco, threw out its original game plan on August 15, 1971 and started a "new game." Ross continued:

> The policy-maker keeps his eye fixed on charts and tables which are sadly incomplete, increasingly obsolescent, or both. Eventually he comes to believe that poverty is really a condition of having less than $3,000 income, that war in Vietnam really is a matter of body counts, and that full employment really is a situation where the national unemployment rate is 4% or less [Secretary of the Treasury Connally made this latter assertion during the first half of 1971]. Shadow replaces substance.
>
> We need more and better statistics in order to illuminate the problems more adequately. Statistics must be interpreted with greater skill and discretion.[16]

Thus, Washington, D.C. and Wall Street, both enclaves of absurdities, rely upon elusive and erroneous numbers.

> It is astonishing that in the United States changes in stock market prices are not only reported, but also *interpreted,* in absolute terms. For example, financial papers will report that the prices of a number of stocks rose, say $1.00, neglecting the percentage significance of this change or throwing the burden of the correct interpretation upon the reader. Such restrictive reporting is as misleading as is the "conclusion" that by virtue of such price changes the aggregate "value" of all stocks has changed by the amount of the price change per stock times the number of shares outstanding.[17]

From figures with the mundane sounding label "stock market prices" to more exotic terms such as "french curve," "saucer bottom," or "head and shoulder patterns," Wall Street feasts on a diet of imaginary numbers. Distorted stock market price movements, for example, have erased the concept of investment and, in effect, substituted gambling. And risk and error compound risk and error. If we had to worry only about the Money Manager's own health, it would be tolerable. Unfortunately, bankers, politicians, consumers, the President—*all* of us—suffer. We are buying, selling, eating, warring, negotiating, dying, living in terms of bad numbers.

Is there any way out of this morass? Not easily. But as a first move, we can at least admit the problem exists. Even today most textbooks on basic economics, on analysis of financial statements, etc. make little or no mention of how shot through with lag and error our economic statistics are. Light on this subject hardly emanates from Washington. And Wall Streeters certainly show no eagerness to abandon their number fixation which they devoutly believe and promulgate. Finally, the mass media simply reflect and amplify the whole bad numbers distortion. Therefore, we *must* come to a recognition of our predicament. The sheer acknowledgement of the problem will hopefully spur us toward Ross' "more and better statistics" and "greater skill and discretion" in interpretation.

In the meantime we will just have to use the figures we have—with our skeptical eyes wide open. We cannot use no data. Money Managers, economists, securities analysts, investment advisors, financial writers—they will all continue to use numbers; numbers are their game. This present book will continue to use numbers. We simply must all be more self-conscious about the limitations of our tools. Hopefully, then, this book exhibits that greater precision and more careful analysis needed, as it attempts to zero in on usable clues about human behavior and Wall Street.

6

Psychology in Business and Consumer Decisions

> One of the few reassuring things about economics is its tendency to adopt, on occasion, the sensible ideas of the ordinary citizen.
>
> *John Kenneth Galbraith*

The emotional factor in business decisions has long been observed as a cause of the waves of optimism and pessimism that from time to time sweep industrial societies. Human folly through the ages has been well documented and still today can manifest itself as "the madness of crowds." Fads and delusions are just as prevalent in the 1970s as they were in France in 1720 when the Mississippi Scheme convulsed that country.

Over fifty years ago, Professor A. C. Pigou stated well the psychological theory of business cycles: The movement of business confidence is the dominant cause of rhythmic fluctuations that are experienced in industry; optimistic error and pessimistic error, when discovered, give birth to one another in an endless chain.

> Let us suppose the business world to be in a neutral position, not suffering from either type of error. On this situation there supervenes some real cause for increase in the demand for business activity.[1]

Then, because business men cannot forsee the results which will be produced by their own and other men's response to the stimulus (the stock market of 1968–69 being a good recent example), errors of the optimistic type will begin to be made. But why should these errors mulitply and grow so huge? Pigou's answer:

> When an error of optimism has been generated, it tends to spread and grow, as a result of reactions between different parts of the business community. This comes about through two principal influences. First, experience suggests that, apart altogether from the financial ties by which different business men are bound together, there exists among them a certain measure of psychological interdependence. A change of tone in one part of the business world diffuses itself, in a quite unreasoning manner, over other and wholly disconnected parts. . . . Secondly, an error of optimism on the part of one group of business men [e.g., Money Managers in the fall of 1968] itself creates a justification for some improved expectation on the part of other groups [e.g., the buyers of mutual funds].[2]

Thus, the optimistic error once born grows in scope and magnitude. But since the prosperity has been built largely upon error, a day of reckoning must come. This day does not dawn until after a time long enough for construction of new buildings and equipment; when marketing begins, it is discovered that they cannot be disposed of promptly at profitable prices (e.g., the franchise business in 1968–69). Then the past miscalculation becomes patent—patent to debtors as well as creditors, and the creditors apply pressure for repayment (e.g., bankruptcies in 1970). Thus, prosperity ends in a crisis. The error of optimism dies in the crisis, but in dying it

> gives birth to an error of pessimism. This new error is born, not an infant, but a giant [e.g., May 1970]; for an industrial boom has necessarily been a period of strong emotional excitement [coupled with rapidly rising security prices, and expectations that they will rise still more], and an excited man passes from one form of excitement to another more rapidly than he passes to quiescence.[3]

Under the influence of the new error, business is unduly depressed. For a time there is a relatively slow extension of facilities for production. In consequence,

> a general shortage of a number of important commodities gradually makes itself apparent, and those persons who have them to sell are seen to be earning a good real return. Thereupon, certain of the bolder spirits in industry [and in the financial institutions] see an opportunity and seize it.[4]

Business begins to pick up slowly and gradually.

> The first year or two, say, is taken up with a wholly justified expansion. But after the first year or two, further expansion represents not a correction of the past error, but the creation of a new one.[5]

And the new error grows until it has betrayed businessmen into courses which end in a fresh crisis.

There are objections by some to this line of reasoning. Professor Joseph Schumpeter believed it to be superficial, stating that the fundamental cause is "innovations." Status Quo Economics points out that the greatest single weakness of the theory is that psychological factors are not initiating forces in the economy; generally, business and individuals react to a change that has already occurred and is beginning to take shape. They say that we cannot "talk ourselves" out of a depression. They believe that favorable action, in addition to a favorable psychological climate, is necessary for recovery and prosperity.

Psychologists claim that individuals usually react according to what is in their mind. Thus, if they *believe* that business activity is going to be good in the near future, they will act accordingly (e.g., investors discounting the future in buying, when the stock market is depressed, envisioning that business in months to come will be better). Their action, fortunately, will be such that they will tend to increase the level of business activity. On the other hand, if consumers and investors generally have a pessimistic outlook, their reactions will be such that they actually *will* depress the economy. This psychological theory further points out that our roundabout method of production and the competitive element in our economy will augment business fluctuations.

This book contends that human behavior, in its psychological aspects, is, in fact, the initiator in economic activity and trends. Business decisions, good or bad, present or past, are made by people, not by computers, by the Good Lord, or whatever. People make decisions, and over time people average out with intelligent decisions; otherwise, we would be continually unglued economically. Decisions are not always right, but, as pointed out, the fact that errors compound themselves begs the fact that it is still *people* making decisions within an environment.

However, since changes in our environment are most often not discerned until too late, and since our perception as individual human beings of these changes varies enormously, it is those with the "higher perception sense" that accrue the favor of the gods; those without it become the unwitting pawns.

In analyzing human behavior and Wall Street, too often we come to it from background, experience, and education that has bogged us down with stock market myths, misconceptions, and a dogged unwillingness to perceive changes. Psychologists call this a "scotoma," a mental roadblock which prevents us from "seeing" things as they are. Contrary facts simply are not "seen"; in fact, a distorted imagery persuades people to see what they do not see—mirages.

THE CONSUMER AND MONEY

There are probably more misconceptions about "money" than almost any other single item. Since we are concerned with rising or falling stock prices, money is the main communicant, and how it is thought of by consumers and how it is thought of by economists and federal government Money Managers are not quite the same.

Money alone sends us a lot of messages daily, since most of our economic life is expressed in prices which mean we are talking about money. To understand why we choose to spend money (buy stocks) at one time and to save money (stay out of the stock market) at another is to understand how consumers view their own money.

Gunter Schmolders observed:

> We cannot possibly overlook the key role of attitudes as the long term organizers and stabilizers of human action. It is through actions and their future-oriented counterpart, expectations, that we can find a way to make the transition from individual behavior to group phenomena within a society. Attitudes towards money and its part as a symbol are the "Sesame" which opens the road to an understanding of inflation or stagnation; by virtue of their relative stability they also permit predicition, so they can be used as tools of prognosis.[6]

Restraining or inducing people to spend, save, or borrow is never an isolated affair of the money market but has repercussions throughout the entire economy. Measures of this kind quickly go beyond the cool atmosphere of monetary policy decisions into the heated climate of political and economic goals, interests, and pressures. Yet, monetary policy can ill afford to remain uncommitted in such value-laden controversies.

The ways people handle money and the extent to which they trust the monetary system are fundamental givens if monetary policy is to succeed. A cursory glance at any current economics textbook will divulge that the author is wasting a great deal of time and energy on such irrelevant considerations as the formalization of money demand, velocity of circulation, income-expenditure formulas, and the like.

At the national level, this question of "money" seems to be whether the general concept of economic processes should orient itself along the lines of stringently defined abstract models, apt to be expressed in mathematical terms but rather removed from real life, or whether it should rely on the more cumbersome and voluminous results of survey series which are, however, more immediate reflections of reality.

Changes in institutions provoke changes in behavior, and model economics cannot allow this. Different "personalities" managing money affairs, for example, and the background and environmental influences they bring to their new and influential jobs are unlikely to change, though the nature of the work may indicate they should change; they bring along their scotomas which prevent their "seeing" reality. Every slight success they effect in a downhill race against odds is seen as "victory"; every real loss is seen as corroborating their belief that future success still lies ahead. It is "just around the corner."

"It is not 'money that rules the world', but rather *people* who shape the monetary events according to their own peculiar whims," Gunter Schmolders has stated.

Age, income, education, basic personality (easy-going vs. more orderly), and other variables all influence spending and saving money; yet, curiously, notwithstanding the diversity of human characters, the differences do not cancel, *but add up*. Surveys of the Survey Research Center at the University of Michigan have found Americans, despite the individual differences cited, to be "uniform" and "conservative."

Thus, attitudes about money aggregate also. For example, lower and middle income classes perceive money quite differently than the upper income groups do. This perception is the result of environment, education, family habits, and occupation, but within the income groups it is stable. Therefore, the lower and middle income groups save quite similarly: A savings goal is set and once it is attained, most often at large personal sacrifice, people do not continue to save at the same steady rate; rather, they leave savings intact and commence spending the excess. In high income groups, once the savings goal is attained, the savings rate continues; they have more money at the outset and it is easier, therefore, to continue. As Schmolders points out: "The disposition *towards* money most often shapes the disposition *of* money." The question of whether people prefer to carry cash or have a large checking account balance or dip into savings or borrow or pay cash or use a credit card and so on is important when trying to assess how, in the aggregate, people "see" money. For example, the Michigan Surveys have indicated that most people do not "see" the purchase of an insurance policy as "savings"; instead it is viewed as "instant cash" against an untimely demise.

Psychological dispositions are influenced both by expectations about the general economic climate and the stability of the currency, as well as by attitudes toward the institutions of the currency system. Economic, institutional, and psychological factors combine to produce a fairly uniform stream of decisions about amounts to be spent and saved; each economic unit (an individual, a household, or a firm) is left with a certain amount of resources, the total sum of which constitutes his *objective* liquidity. Beyond this, though, units tend to develop a *subjective* notion about the limit to which they feel they could make additional means available, should the need for them arise (e.g., through credits or sales). So, an individual when asked, "How much cash do you have?", responds, in effect, "I have so much in my pocketbook, so much in my checking account, and so much in my saving account." He does not think, then, that he could get x dollars more if he borrowed on his car or his house. To him, *nearness* to cash *is* cash; hence, the preference by the masses for savings at banks and savings and loan institutions—or even Christmas Clubs.

The upper income groups have more sophisticated financial ideas about cash. They are aware of borrowing against their savings or using securities as collateral for cash loans; also, larger amounts of "quick cash" are more readily available to them simply because they already have ample amounts of cash. They have an entirely different outlook on "cash."

It is, therefore, the whole liquidity position that is relevant to spending decisions. In a so-called affluent community, and in a Service Society, a decision to spend is further augmented by credit cards, selling an asset, or borrowing against it.

The notion of one's own financial mobility naturally is quite open to influences of optimism or pessimism, and is by virture of this a crucial link between economic decisions of individuals and economic mass phenomena. "Subjective liquidity represents an important juncture between psychology and economics," Schmolders notes.

Attitudinal influences constitute the main influence, but demographic factors do limit conditions of behavior. For example, if certain age-income combinations correlate highly with varying rates of saving, it is pointless to assume a constant savings rate for the entire population.

The attitudes of consumers toward interest rates provides an interesting example of how rises or declines are conceived by monetary strategists (and institutional Money Managers) and how consumers "see" them. A consumer, for example, focuses on the interest he *receives, not* what he *pays.* For instance, the Truth in Lending bill was thought of as a method of affording a buyer an opportunity to shop around for lower interest rates when the true interest was made quite visible to him under the law. Instead, the consumer casually asked, "How much is the total monthly payment?" But if a Savings & Loan increases its interest payable by one-quarter of one percent, consumer savings shift quickly. That consumers do pay attention to interest rate changes affecting their income is also illustrated by their reaction to U.S. Savings Bonds. When the government raised to 5.5% the interest payable on these securities, redemptions were turned into sales; in late 1971 U.S. Savings Bonds were selling better than they had since 1945, and the total for 1971 was $5.5 billion. As a matter of fact, in 1971 savings bonds seemed to the consumer to be as sound an investment as any in the land. The stock market had lost its charm, the glitter of mutual funds was yesterday, and banks were paying only 5.0%. Insecure about the future, small investors—middle incomers of all shades—were seeking financial refuge in U.S. government bonds.

Consumers are not the only ones who appear to be indifferent to interest paid (as opposed to interest received). Businessmen, outside the securities market, often do not view rising interest rates with initial alarm, for they intend to pass the cost on anyway. Later in the process, as money dries up, they resort to many devices, as do the banks, to bypass the intent of the central bank Money Managers.

Dr. James A. Knight has observed:

> Students of human behavior see a widespread anxiety about money in almost all types of people and age groups. . . .
>
> The drive to become wealthy seems to be related [to the "will to power." Behaviorally,] the "will to power" is identical with a high "level of self-regard."
>
> Money . . . is an ego-supplement, and the possibility of getting rich—the idea of being wealthy—becomes an ideal. The attainment of wealth is fantasied and worked for as something bound up with an enormous increase of self-regard.
>
> Thus, the original and basic aim is not for riches, but to enjoy power and respect among one's fellow men or within oneself.
>
> Money has a powerful effect on our inner feelings of anxiety. In a world of turmoil and sudden change, the quest for money is motivated greatly by the desire to find something akin to a magical charm for attaining emotional security. The quest then moves the individual into competitive struggles where success becomes his form of self-validation. . . . On this competitive striving we depend for our security. Even a relative minor trauma—a stock market fluctuation—is experienced by many as a catastrophic event, a threat to values held essential to their existence as personalities. . . . Since success is their chief form of self-validation, feelings of anxiety generally lead them to redouble their efforts. It is obvious, then, that anxiety growing out of their competitive striving leads to more competitive striving and to more anxiety.[7]

Money Managers exemplify this behavioral trait: never at ease when the market is rising and filled with fear when it is falling.

R. H. Tawney observed years ago:

> When they desire to place their economic life on a better foundation, they repeat, like parrots, the word "Productivity," because that is the word that first arises in their minds.[8]

On Wall Street, the solution to today's problems can be solved with additional stock price rises tomorrow, and since productivity may provide an answer, the search for increased corporate productivity consumes a great deal of a stock analyst's time. He rarely observes the other side of the coin: the self-destruct built in to increased productivity the same as it is into rising stock prices. In late 1970, for example, the economy was observed by many to have "bottomed out" of a mild recession, though some noted that the upturn would be quite sluggish. It was not generally observed at that time that welfare payments and unemployment compensation were cushioning consumer spending. But this type of spending for nondurables had a built-in future boomerang effect: The income was not induced from producing additional goods and services; it was diverted income from others, and therefore continuing sales, even at a slower pace, were a "dollar mirage." True, goods were sold, but at an obscure economic catastrophic price; still, stock prices continued a strong rise predicated on these inherently "dollar-weak" sales.

Savings were rising at that time, too. This led the Harris Trust & Savings Bank of Chicago to observe: "High spending can be expected to boost not only home building, but also consumer spending as the year progresses"[9]—the happened-before-happen-again syndrome. Savings, it will be noted, are basically held by upper income individuals with higher salaries. Since— especially as stocks rise (which they also own in large amounts)—they have been protected from the brunt of unemployment, they spend first, but this does not insure the masses will follow this pattern.

Within the securities markets, an "easing of money" is always construed with optimism and though this may be optimism in error, it still makes for a psychological climate favorable to buying stocks. Conversely, "tight money" indicates pessimism, and sell.

One way to anticipate these government "money moves" is to study the personalities of those that wield the power—their thrust is bound to reflect their background, education, and environment.

Observing this, then, makes it fairly easy to anticipate what they will do when the "tight-easy-money decision" arises. Hard line bankers favor one approach, compassionate people favor another, and the same is true with economists. Thus, it is not difficult to find support for these moves in either direction. "In England, for example, when personal-service-background people wielded power, government spending in these areas greatly increased."[10]

Understanding how people "feel" about money helps answer such questions as why there should be rapid increases in savings deposits in a period of rather rapid price rises, as was the case in America in 1970, when savings rose from 5% in the first quarter to 7.6% by the third quarter, and when, simultaneously, the price level continued to rise at a 5+% rate. The Michigan Surveys revealed that people "resent" price rises as being unfair, and feel they are "fighting inflation" by saving and not spending. Increased savings mean fewer sales and ultimately bring on a sluggishness in general business activity, lower profits, and, finally, lower stock prices.

KEYNESIAN VIEW: INTEREST RATES AND STOCK PRICES

Since the consumer views interest rates differently from the student of Keynesian economics, it is informative to observe here the Keynes view:

> What is the nature of the speculator? He is a person engaged in the purchase and sale of securities in accordance with his own estimate of the imminent course of security prices. That speculator who believes stock prices will rise in the near future is a speculator who is impelled to buy more stock and accordingly hold less money. Very probably he will borrow on margin the better to profit from his judgment. Now, a prediction about stock prices, Keynes pointed out, is inevitably a prediction also about interest rates, since a stock yield—the relationship between stock prices disbursed—*is* an interest rate. It follows that when stock prices rise, interest rates *must fall,* for a dollar dividend of a certain amount is a smaller percentage of a higher-priced security.
>
> This is far from the end of the matter. If most speculators are convinced that stock prices are fated to rise and interest rates to fall, they will bid actively for the securities controlled by the minority of pessimists who hold the opposite

> opinion. But the very attempts of the bulls among the speculators to expand their security holdings will produce the results which caused the actions. To some extent this is another instance of the self-fulfilling prophecy. Stock prices truly rise and yields accordingly do drop. In short, interest rates shift because speculators expect them to shift and act in such a manner as to validate their own predictions.
>
> The situation is symmetrical. If speculators anticipate a decline in the market and rising yields, logic directs them to dispose of their securities and to sell short into the bargain. They attempt to increase their stock of money in order to purchase securities at a later date and lower prices. However, their effort to sell securities *before* they decline in value has the effect immediately of depressing the stock market, lowering average stock prices, and raising average stock yields. Once more today's rate of interest is the consequence of speculators' expectations and tomorrow's rate of interest. In sum, the rate of interest is indeed a premium, but a premium paid for surrendering cash, the perfectly liquid asset, for securities, imperfectly liquid assets.
>
> Upon this proposition Keynes constructed some substantial conclusions. The most provocative concerned public policy. . . . The Federal Reserve System . . . had strong weapons in their hands. Thus, if the authorities believed it inadvisable for interest rates to rise even though speculators put selling pressure on the stock market in anticipation of falling security prices and rising stock yields, then they could simply purchase on behalf of the central bank the securities which the speculators unloaded—at unchanged prices and yields. This is the most potent of monetary weapons, open market operations.[11]

Another interesting observation relative to the determination of the rate of interest is that of Joan Robinson:

> The main determinant of the level of interest rates is the state of expectations. When bondholders have a clear view of what is the normal yield which they expect to be restored soon after any temporary change, the banking system cannot move interest rates from what they are expected to be. It is the existence of uncertainty or "two views" that makes it possible for the banks to manipulate the money market. But even when the rate of interest *can* be moved in the required direction, it may not have much effect. The domi-

> nant influence on the swings of effective demand is swings in the expectation of profits.[12]

CONSUMER ATTITUDES TOWARD GOING INTO DEBT

Social commentators and others have worried for years about the effect of easy credit on financial responsibility. One of the many Michigan Surveys, however, implies their worry is unfounded. Generally, most people borrow only for important needs. Only 4% of the people questioned considered it acceptable to borrow for jewelry or fur coats. Just 9% said they would borrow to finance a vacation. On the other hand, 77% would borrow for education, 65% to buy a car, and 52% to buy furniture. This survey found that in 1970 two-thirds of gasoline credit card holders earned more than $7,500 a year and one-half more than $10,000.

Though the rich, like the poor, use credit with discretion, the affluent borrow for longer periods of time, the study found. Further, the higher the income, up to a point, the greater the likelihood of assuming debt. For instance, of those families with under $3,000 gross income per year, 17% had installment debts; of those with incomes between $7,500 and $10,000, 38%; $15,000 and over, 52%.[13]

It is interesting to observe in this regard that the consumer during the 1969–1970 recession kept the economy afloat, as noted earlier—a departure from previous patterns. In this period consumers kept their spending at a high level, though business was steadily declining, and this checked the normal downward spiral of the recession.

This is of great import when viewing future trends in securities: consumer spending means financial "good times" are ahead, sales are being made. Good times mean good business; good business means higher profits, and higher profits ultimately mean higher securities prices. This entire process takes time to unfold, nine months at least.

Since businesses are run by people, within the business framework the managers tend to shore up or spend at about the same time the consumer does. People are people.

It should be remembered that the bulk of the savings represents the efforts of the middle and upper income groups, who possess most of the money and whose habits were established in an earlier economic era.

> The bulk of the savings [in Savings and Loan institutions] belong to a relatively small number with accounts of rather substantial size.
>
> Almost half of the accounts . . . had balances of less than $1,000. These [small] accounts represented only 4% of total savings deposits, however. At the other end of the scale, accounts of $10,000 and over represented 10.6% of all accounts and 45.4% of the total balances.[14]

The younger generation, tomorrow's leaders, want to "own" less, have the attitude that money should be used now rather than at some later date, and are the biggest borrowers.

The effect of continued inflation (at any rate, so long as it continues) makes many people suspect that while banks may tell them their money will double in a specified number of years, the truth is that it may *not* grow at all or even may decrease if inflation is not contained. They perceive finally, for example, that $1,000 placed in a commercial bank in 1959 was worth, in real dollars, only $1,124 in 1969, which is hardly the road to wealth. An equivalent in U.S. Savings Bonds gained only $19.

Those who bought insurance policies years earlier have learned to their complete dismay that the cash value they had counted on for their declining years has shriveled considerably.

HOW MUCH DEBT IS TOO MUCH?

No one knows how much debt is too much. Certainly fringe borrowers—the lowest income, the least financially sophisticated black and white, the eighteen to twenty-four year age group—will be the first to learn *their* limits.

Americans pay their bills. Some abuse this, of course, but by and large people settle their debts. Despite this, people can unwittingly become debt loaded, which cuts sharply into future spending; so rising installment debts incurred by consumers, as an indicator of consumer attitudes, requires some searching into the figures themselves: What are consumer attitudes about buying (cars or beds) and how are they paying (cash, charge card, installment loan)?

The direction of consumer spending affects future securities prices since the corporation recipients of the consumer's favor will accrue profits. This is, of course, the area that financial analysts should observe more: What is the consumer buying? Analysts prefer, however, to listen to company executives tell them of their future plans, when in reality, if the plans are to eventuate in profits, it is the invisible programmer—the consumer—who calls the signals. Financial analysts, however, because of education and training, prefer to focus on production-oriented numbers, things that can be quantified. The "invisible signals" from consumers are not perceived by them.

A great deal of study has been made in the areas of where the consumer spends his money and how he finances these expenditures. Historically, a cutback in installment buying habits meant a cutback in durable goods purchased (e.g., most autos are financed). Also, in the past, consumer buying has been closely geared to the flow of consumer income: in 1958 and again in 1967–70 there was a sharp decline in durable goods buying (higher priced items financed over a long term), but durable goods and services spending remained strong because of indirect income increases in the form of tax cuts and increased Social Security payments. This tendency, as noted, is perhaps changing. Business as a whole in 1958 turned up only when the consumer received more income from increased employment, longer hours of work, increased wage rates; *that* was when he started to *buy* durable goods. In late 1970, by contrast, durable goods sales remained sluggish and future plans of consumers (surveyed in December 1970) indicated that they were not going to buy them until inflation eased and jobs became more plentiful.

In a report of the Department of Commerce in March 1959, it was calculated that during the period 1910–1929, the ratio between consumer purchases and real disposable income was 94%, and from 1947 to 1958 it was also 94%.

Total consumer purchases have had in the past a close relationship to consumer incomes, but time is critical. The Commerce study revealed that in the long run a 10% change in real income resulted in a 10% change in real purchases. In the short run, however, a 10% change in real income had just an 8% change in real purchases. This is especially significant when trying to guesstimate future company profits and security prices.

Other variables that drastically affect consumer demand are:

1. Relative prices (previously noted effect of inflation)
2. Population changes (shift in ages of population)

3. Substitute and competitive products

All of these must be observed to effectively extrapolate future consumer spending plans as indicated by various attitudinal surveys.

Consumer "attitudes" (his psychological "feeling") are, therefore, important determinants of corporate profits and security prices, and will become increasingly critical in a Service Society.

In America in the past, consumer attitudes have improved considerably *before* the incomes themselves actually grew. This was perhaps due to inherent faith in the viability of the system which has been so solid. In the 1970s, this faith seems to be eroding, and if it continues will no doubt affect this long-term relationship. In other words, incomes will have to increase first *before* attitudes change.

The disposal of earned income is not a mechanical process. It is a behavioral process conditioned by a variety of variables: life style, stage in life cycle, occupation, past income level, and so on. Yet, despite the divergence of these spreads, individual and collective, in a country as large as America, aggregative figures in the past have shown the behavior of people to be uniform and conservative. Whether this can safely be extrapolated into the 1970s and 1980s is another question. Social conflicts, wars, and such may disturb these long-term constants.

An important idea among Status Quo economists is that we can spend ourselves rich. It goes like this: If the government or the people borrow to spend (for goods), this is good, because the increase in demand will lead to more goods being made, more people going to work, more taxes being paid, debts being paid back, and Eureka!, good times ahead. But it appears that the end of this road is now in sight, especially when debts are incurred and when a disproportionate amount of the spending is going for "services"—the cost of finance, which does not accrue to the people at large, but which they *pay;* further, the gains become more concentrated in the hands of a very few. This means ultimately that the savings of the rich pile up out of all proportion to any opportunity for sound investment. The table below summarizes the relationship between personal consumption expenditures and installment credit.

Observe that steadily over the past thirty years the consumer has been diverting more and more from his current cash flow to his future cash flow (spending himself rich), a total of 212% during this

TABLE 14

PERSONAL CONSUMPTION EXPENDITURES AND INSTALLMENT CREDIT

Year	Personal consumption expenditures	Installment credit extended	Installment credit as % of consumption expenditures	Consumer interest payments (billions)
	(billions of dollars)			
1941	$ 80.6	$ 4.4	5.4%	$ .9
1947	165.0	12.7	7.7	*
1957	285.2	41.9	14.7	*
1967	492.2	84.7	17.2	13.2
1971	664.9	109.5	16.4	17.6

*Not available.

SOURCE: *Federal Reserve Bulletin,* September 1972, pp. 56, 71.

period. If he loses his job, the payments disappear and economic trouble develops (soaring personal bankruptcies in 1968, a good business year, is an example). More alarming, however, is the incredible growth in the amount being consumed by "interest" (a service cost) that in no way represents goods being sold, a rise of 1880% during this period. Instead, fewer goods are going out at much higher cost, and this situation cannot in any sense be construed as either wise or of long duration. It is also rarely observed as another cause of inflation. Equally alarming is the fact that almost half (44%) of all personal loans made in 1966, for example, were for the consolidation of existing debts. Not one economic good was purchased with this money. All that happened was that money purchased money—and that is no way to spend ourselves rich. In addition, the average size of loans has increased tremendously, from $150 per person in 1929 to $600 in 1967, most of this money being borrowed by persons who earn from $4,800 to $9,000 per year.

These facts indicate that the end is in sight for infinite debt loads for the American consumer, and that the consumer is not much aware of the interest he pays. But those who *collect it* are *very much* aware of this. It is no wonder, then, that in the aggregate personal cash flows diverge sharply, or, as some still say, in truth, "The rich are getting richer, and the poor, poorer."

The implications for Wall Street are significant. When business slows again, as it always has and always will, do not look to the consumer to bail it out by borrowing and spending himself rich, because if he does he will be borrowing not to buy goods, but merely to line some financial pocket, and *this* is no shortcut to prosperity or profit for goods-producing corporations. Stock prices will sooner or later reflect this.

WHAT THE CONSUMER BUYS

When studies are made of all services and goods the consumer bought during 1920–1958 (excepting war years), the relationship for all goods shows very little variation. But within groups there is considerably more variation:

10% change in income = 7% change in consumption of nondurable goods in same direction

10% change in income = 21% change in consumption of durable goods

10% change in income = 5% change in consumption of services (since mid-1960, this has shifted upwards)

MOST "SENSITIVE" SPENDING AREAS (1947-1958)

The 1959 Department of Commerce study explored the areas most sensitive to spending by consumers. As a future stock purchaser, a look at these is important because if the consumer becomes fearful of the future outlook and curtails spending, or, conversely, becomes optimistic and increases spending, these are industries and companies that will feel the impact first. These are ranked by "sensitivity," a measure of consumer control—i.e., these are the prices a consumer can directly control.

Services:

1. Air transportation
2. Radio and TV repair
3. Household utilities
4. Private hospital care (including sanitariums)
5. Private education
6. Auto repair

Nondurables:

1. Gasoline and oil
2. Drug preparations and sundries
3. Sport supplies

4. Stationery and writing supplies
5. Toilet articles

Durables:

1. Boats and pleasure craft
2. Housing
3. New cars, used cars
4. Books
5. Furniture

The "sensitives" have changed over the years: from 1929–1940, for example, radio and TV repair was far less sensitive, as were automobiles and housing.

THE FICKLE CONSUMER

The consumer's discretionary spending power has increased enormously since 1965—up over 20%. In the years before 1965, he had few spending choices since his income was low and was tied to making goods. Today more Americans have far more discretionary power: They can spend or save, buy a car or postpone buying one, take an expensive vacation or stay at home. The consumer's behavior is not so closely tied to his needs, as it was in the past, so he wields large "money power." But the consumer is fickle, and it pays to understand him (especially in the securities markets does it pay).

The leverage in his spending in the early 1970s came more from his increasing use of credit than from increasing amounts of cash set aside, mainly because cash savings for the masses of the people were hard to come by. The bulk of the savings were, as always, held by the middle and upper income groups ($15,000 plus).

A Department of Labor study in late 1970 revealed a sharp and sustained decline in the "real" spendable earnings of America's millions of workers. The gross weekly earnings of production and nonsupervisory workers in the U.S. were $121.56—an undeniably impressive total which dwarfs weekly pay scales around the globe. But the spendable earnings of a worker getting this gross and having a dependent wife and two children were only $106.11. This is how much $121.56 shrinks after deductions for Social Security and federal income taxes. $106.11 is the worker's basic take home pay, a rise of 3.5% over the fall of 1969. Much worse, however, the "real" spendable earnings of this worker with his three dependents was down to $77.68. This represents drastic pay shrinkage when adjusted to reflect the rise in prices since the base 1957–59 period. It took $106.11 in after-tax pay to buy what only $77.68 could buy ten years earlier. In 1970, this real spendable pay was 2% below the 1969 figure. Large state and local tax increases (70% since 1965) and "economic waste" (advertisements not seen, shoddy products, etc.) took another 30-40%, a Senate Committee reported in 1970.

So, despite increases in income, the great masses of the people in the late 1960s and early 1970s found themselves unable to stash much cash. Savings rose to 7.8% of disposable personal income—a very high postwar level, but this was for those with $15,000+ incomes. A number of families had reached this income level because of two incomes (wife and husband). Despite the constriction on the masses, there are still large numbers of people involved and large sums of money represented by them, and even for the below-$10,000-income level, consumer spending power is enormous.

Therefore, the money power of the consumer, his fickleness, and the effect on corporate profits all point to the crucial importance of the consumer for Wall Street. A truism, true. Nevertheless, the consumer is not watched by the Street as closely as he should be or in the proper way.

In the fall of 1970 the attitude of the consumer was "sluggish" and his desire to buy a new car had eroded; yet, despite this, the president of the Ford Motor Company and the president of General Motors predicted 1971 to be a big year for their cars, ranging from 9.5 to 10.0 million auto sales. This estimate was in the face of Chrysler's curtailing production on their 1971 models due to resistance to sales by a depressed and fickle consumer.

In a strong consumer-geared economy, "spend and thrive" has been the gospel of the economists. But when the consumer elects to save instead of spend, the machine tends to slow down measurably, which is reflected quite quickly in the tempo and character of business declines.

When the $15,000+ consumer (in aggregate) saves in excess, he not only reduces his expenditures, but he also of course affects the income and spending impact of those workers laid off as a result of sluggish business. Or, put another way, the first worker's failure to buy the second worker's product leads to . . . and so on. The savings process has many consequences and not all are visible.

Personal savings as a percentage of disposable personal incomes have fluctuated as follows:

1965 — 6.0%	1969 — 6.0%
1966 — 6.4%	1970 — 8.0%
1967 — 7.4%	1971 — 8.2%
1968 — 6.7%	1972 — 6.7%

The vagaries of consumer savings and spending habits are closely tied to *his perception* of the nation's economic and political cilmate. If he perceives better times, he spends; if his input is negative, he is negative. Small percentage shifts here represent in dollars huge sums —billions.

Probably because of tradition, the typical American consumer, with small savings which he prefers close to him, favors savings and loan institution or bank time deposits. The chart below shows where people preferred to save during the period 1965-1967.

To protect his insecure employment flank, the consumer will, if

CHART 6

LIQUID SAVINGS REBOUND

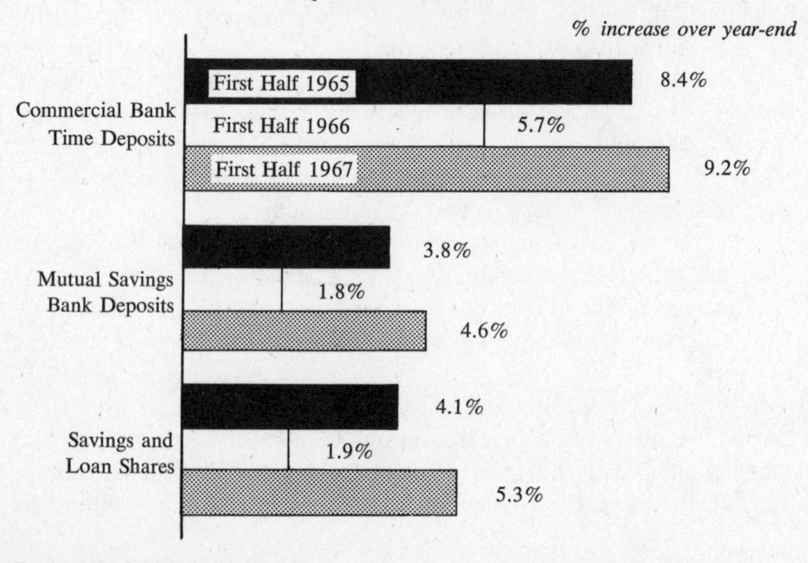

SOURCE: Federal Reserve Board

he views economic conditions ahead as potentially detrimental to him, curtail needful expenditures and build up cash savings little by painful little. When multiplied by millions of wage and salary earners, the total savings sums represent lower security prices surely to come. When spending starts (and continues), security prices will rise. The timing is not mechanical, but is influenced by the consumer's perception of the future, by his image of economic and political news.

MISERY INDEX

A rapid measure of the economic world from the level of the common man, the consumer, is the "discomfort index" invented by Arthur M. Okun, of the Brookings Institution. This index consists of two key figures which purport to measure our well-being: the rate of unemployment and the rise in the Consumer Price Index. (It has been noted earlier that these two measures themselves are subject to strict scrutiny because behind them are figures which are ignored. The unemployment index does not include, for example; part-time workers, teen-age workers, etc.) It is called here "the misery index," which is perhaps more graphic:

Year	Misery Index[15]
1971 (May)	13.4%
1970	10.4
1969	9.6
1968	8.3
1967	6.9
1966	7.1
1965	6.5
1964	6.3
1963	7.4
1962	6.7
1960	7.1
1958	8.5
1956	7.0
1954	5.1
1953	3.5
1952	3.9
1950	11.1

Perhaps the ideal year was 1953: a 2.9% jobless rate and a 0.6% price rise.

THE CONSUMER AND THE NEW ECONOMIC PROGRAM

By August 15, 1971, it had become apparent to the consumer that the economic "game plans" were not bringing *him* much relief. So, after the President's announcement on August 15, 1971, of steps being taken in different directions economically to bolster the economy, the deep pessimism that had gripped the consumer improved . . . a little. The quarterly report on consumer sentiment issued by the University of Michigan's Survey Research Center looked like this:

1st Quarter 1971 = 78.2
2nd Quarter 1971 = 81.6
3rd Quarter 1971 = 82.4
4th Quarter 1971 = 82.2
1st Quarter 1972 = 87.5
2nd Quarter 1972 = 89.3

Thus, though the sentiment index had been slowly improving *prior* to the Presidential announcement, in the quarter following the announcement it actually fell a little, but in the 2nd quarter after the announcement it rose by five points. It takes time for consumers to respond to fundamental economic changes. The analysts at Michigan stated:

> The quarter's gain (2nd) was largely due to what it called an "extraordinary" surge in the confidence of the respondents about their personal financial situations, occurring at the same time the same respondents were growing more pessimistic about the government's economic policies, and remaining gloomy about business prospects and the possibility of overcoming inflation and unemployment.[16]

Why, then, did the consumer respond as has been indicated by going heavily into debt and charging and borrowing as though there would be no tomorrow?

In this period consumers seemed to ignore facts of life which were unfavorable to him, and he was not about to forsake his standard of living level, whatever it was. Also, sheer necessity forced him to borrow: he was short of cash and *credit rich*. His auto had aged during his slow retrenchment dating back three–five years, and trying to keep it running was becoming, he thought, too burdensome; so when he got the chance (and the banks provided this with easy, long-term loans), he bought a new auto. That he may have been compounding his dilemma was not then perceived by most $10,000 and under consumers. But it would not be too many months before he would regret this decision. Anyway, spend he did for houses and cars and appliances and furniture during the spring of 1972.

What was it like, the life of this consumer? From high atop the First National City Bank in New York a chart in their August 1972 *Letter,* headed "Soaring Real Income," depicted real personal incomes in the first half of 1972 rising at the sharpest rate since the second half of 1965. They defined real income: "Real personal income is total personal income reduced by the overall rate of rise in consumer prices."

The only trouble with this is that it was simply not the case. The use of the statistics involved in putting together consumer price indexes, and their complete unreality, has been noted. No allowance was made either for increasing taxes at all levels, economic waste, and so on. The consumer by the summer of 1972 was still hurting financially, as he had been for a long, long time. Here is how a blue-collar worker reported his personal financial situation in the *Saturday Review* for July 29, 1972:

> He works as a "floor man", laying tiles and carpet and linoleum in Chicago's high-rises, making $7.65 an hour. ("No sick pay, no vacation pay, no holiday pay. You don't work, you don't get paid.") That adds up to about $300 a week. "Not take home pay," he is quick to add. "Taxes, social security, hospitalization—I figure they got $120 of it before you get home. I just can't save," he complains. "You work all week, and you come home, and it's all gone."

Still, in Washington where the numbers are gathered and with much fanfare made public, we are told that just about every family has a TV set, 95%. Four out of five American households own cars, and three families in four have washing machines, and if you earn more than $15,000 there will be two cars at home. This again moves one to examine the dichotomy between "owing" and "owning." Those who "own" homes just pay their rent to the banks, and those who "own" their cars never see the titles which are always traveling between banks and commercial lending companies. Still, the Great American Dream lingers on.

7

"Rich" & "Poor" Stock Ownership

> Equal incomes? No. People with beastly jobs—scavengers and lavatory attendants and the like—should be paid a great deal more than anyone else.
>
> *Victor Gollancz*

In our so-called "affluent society" we find, as always historically in all societies, a wide spread between personal incomes of different classes. This spread makes a substantial differences in who owns common stocks. Individuals with incomes in excess of $10,000 per year own the vast majority of common stocks. A more specific statistic concludes that "the top two-tenths of one percent of all taxpayers own 65% to 71% of all stock."[1] In addition, the great bulk of *all* common stocks are controlled by financial institutions and are managed indirectly for owners by Money Managers: those who direct the trust departments of the commercial banks, insurance companies' portfolios, pension funds, foundation investments, university endowments, and mutual funds. Actually, during the decade from 1960 to 1970, the character of the stock market changed as it came to be dominated by institutional trading; some estimates put this activity at 60% of the total in 1972. Even the large "small investors" (e.g., the Rockefeller family) formed management partnerships to deploy their monies in concert on Wall Street.

Despite the fact that the "average man" does not own much stock directly, this below-$10,000-income group nevertheless, as we have emphasized, represents the guiding force in determining basic stock market trends—i.e., in their behavior as consumers of services and goods. Only 20% of all American families have incomes in execess of $15,000 per year. With more and more women working (29% in 1950, 39% in 1970), they provide the additional income for the families. Thus, the bulk of the money spent is from the $10,000-and-under group.

The reason the vast majority of Americans do not own common stocks directly is a simple economic one: it takes all of their personal income just to live. The Bureau of Labor Statistics reported in December 1970 that due to increases in living costs and taxes during the late 1960s, it took $10,893 for a family of four to live at an "intermediate level." Of this total, $9,752 was spent for food, housing, transportation, clothing, personal care, Social Security, disability insurance, and personal income taxes. This left just $1,141 for education, recreation, savings and/or investment (common stock or mutual fund purchases). People in this income group prefer cash savings to security ownership, so very few buy common stocks. In the 1960s they put their excess cash into mutual funds which represented to them long term "savings plans," not "investments." Or they held their little excess cash in savings and loans or banks.

Other government figures showed that some 45 million rank-and-file workers—more than half of the nation's work force—averaged only $121 per week in late 1970, or $6,292 a year, well below the $10,000 group. Since it took the intermediate group ($10,000) virtually all of their income to live at a level just below the ability to participate in the "good life," the 45 million workers were even below what the Bureau estimated as a "lower level" income ($7,168). It is not surprising, therefore, that in a recent study (contrary to the myth of an all-middle-class America) 56% of American wage and salary earners said that they thought of themselves as "working class."[2]

When the New York Stock Exchange reported in 1969 that public ownership of securities rose from about 20 million to 30 million people during the period 1960–1969, evidencing "people's capitalism," there were actually very few "people" involved. The lower income individuals were involved indirectly through insurance company holdings, pension funds, investments, bank trusts, and mutual funds, but as direct purchasers they cannot be counted as a factor.

Therefore, in the following chart the "Public Individuals" category represents, in the main, individuals with incomes well in excess of $10,000 per year.

CHART 7

SOURCES OF NYSE VOLUME

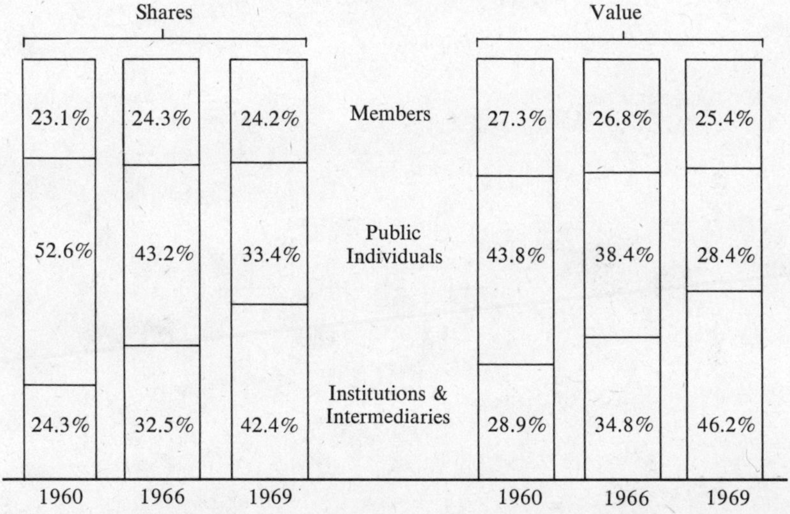

	Shares			Value		
	1960	1966	1969	1960	1966	1969
Members	23.1%	24.3%	24.2%	27.3%	26.8%	25.4%
Public Individuals	52.6%	43.2%	33.4%	43.8%	38.4%	28.4%
Institutions & Intermediaries	24.3%	32.5%	42.4%	28.9%	34.8%	46.2%

SOURCE: New York Stock Exchange, 1969.

The Stock Exchange study noted:

> The increased participation of institutions and the diminution of the role of the individual investor [over $10,000] is revealed more clearly by excluding member firms' trading for their own accounts. Institutions accounted for more than half of all such public volume on the NYSE and three-fifths of the dollar value, compared with less than one-third of share volume and two-fifths of value in 1960.[3]

In an "affluent society" only the very affluent participate directly in stock ownership, but their holdings are subject to large changes in value because the all-powerful average-man-consumer through his purchases of services and goods shifts the rise or fall in profits among the corporations that live by his wants. Security prices are, of course, sometimes referred to as "the slaves of profits."

THE ODD-LOTTER

The upper-income odd-lotter (an investor who buys or sells shares in less than round lots of 100) has declined in importance in security trading, but as Chart 8 shows he has grown wiser as a trader.

CHART 8

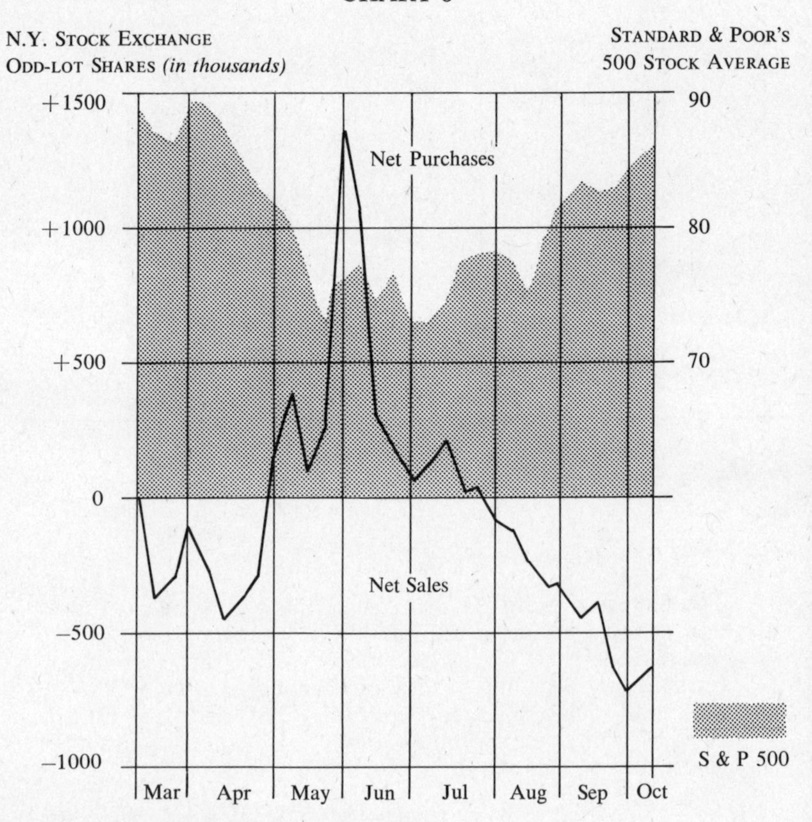

Source: Forbes Magazine, Nov. 1, 1970; SEC

Forbes magazine in 1970 had the following comments on the odd-lotter:

> He sold in October, November and December 1968 at the top of the market, and he sold through most of 1969 when the market was steadily declining. In April 1970, he began to buy heavily, and he bought still more heavily in May. Then in August and September, he began to sell heavily again.
>
> Who is he? A whizbang mutual fund money manager, a professional trader, a pension fund manager? Hardly. He is that long-despised trader, that reverse indicator, the investor who's always wrong, the odd-lotter. Today, there are fewer odd-lotters . . . than there were a few years ago, but as the chart suggests, they seem to be shrewder. By a process of natural selection, the odd-lotter has now become, if anything, a leading indicator of market direction.
>
> That belief is held by at least one long-term analyst of odd-lotter behavior, partner Sander Landfield of the odd-lot firm of Carlisle DeCoppet & Co., which handles virtually all of the odd-lot business transacted on the Big Board. Says Landfield, "The odd-lotter in recent years had made a mockery of the old contrary-opinion theory which had him dead wrong at most crucial turns in the stock market."
>
> It's a whole new investing game today, of course. Since the end of the last decade, *the proportion of odd-lot trading to total trading has declined from over one-fifth to around 7% currently*. Total trading volume, spurred by institutional buying, has soared more than threefold. The number of odd-lot traders has remained fairly constant. But the kind of person who trades in odd lots has changed.
>
> The affluence of the economy over the last ten years has turned many former odd-lotters into round-lot traders (leading one cynic to suggest that the infallibly wrong odd-lotter still exists, but he now trades a few hundred shares instead of 50). Then too, many odd-lotters have moved into mutual funds and into the lower-priced but more speculative American Stock Exchange. One market technician thinks that the mutual funds now perform the old odd-lot tricks. When fund sales are heaviest, he feels, the market is near some kind of a top, and when they are at an ebb, the market may be near a bottom.
>
> Those who remain in the odd-lot market are long-term investors with limited capital. When the market looks oversold or overbought, they judiciously buy or sell just as they

> have done in the last two years. . . .
>
> "In April and May [1970]," says Landfield, "they bought the volatile glamour stocks ranging from very substantial IBM to stocks like University Computing." This is precisely what the professionals bought, and the prices of many of these stocks have gone up by 50% or more. So, at least so far the odd-lotters have been right.
>
> On the other hand, in recent months they have resumed their long-term pattern of selling large capitalization blue chips, or former blue chips, including General Motors, Sears, Roebuck, du Pont and others. One reason: They feel the future of these companies is limited because of their huge size. Up to now the odd-lotters have again been right, but for how long remains to be seen.[4]

Despite this track record, the odd-lotter is still much maligned by Wall Street analysts and Money Managers, as the *Wall Street Journal* reported on December 12, 1970:

> The biggest bears on Wall Street these days seem to be the little guys.
>
> And that is a very bullish sign in the view of analysts and money managers who subscribe to the popular belief that small investors usually are wrong about the market—selling when they should be buying and buying when they should be selling.
>
> And right now the little guys who trade in odd-lot quantities of fewer than 100 shares at a time are selling as never before. Despite the market's spectacular rally, the odd-lot ratio of sales to purchases hit a record 2.4 early this month and still is at a lofty level of 2.2. Normally, a ratio of 1.3 shares sold for every one bought by odd-lotters is considered high by analysts who watch the odd-lot figures. Those who believe the little guy usually is wrong consider a reading of 1.5 quite bullish. . . .
>
> Right now, small investors are more bearish than they've ever been, according to Garfield Drew, who operates an advisory service that specializes in watching and interpreting trends in odd-lot trading. His odd-lot index of selling to buying has soared to a record well above 200 in recent weeks, far beyond the previous high of 160 registered at the end of 1962. That was at the beginning of the longest and strongest bull market in history. . . .
>
> Clifford Bourassa, technical market analyst for Thomson

> & McKinnon Auchincloss Inc., says it isn't particularly significant whether the odd-lotters are buying or selling, or even whether they are right or wrong. What's important, says Mr. Bourassa, is that when odd-lot figures go to one extreme or the other they often signal a major market turning point.[5]

The odd-lotter in the securities markets does *not* represent "the average consumer"—that is, the person with an income of less than $10,000 per year, whose disposable personal income in the aggregate is so large and who buys the bulk of the goods in a mass production society. It should be obvious that mass production survives with *mass* consumption and not with the consumption of the higher income classes.

Though the small investor, *as a consumer,* sets stock market trends, it is necessary to take a look at the more affluent part of our society—the Money Managers and those with incomes above $10,000—since there exists a dichotomy in behavioral patterns: The lower income group behaves quite differently from the higher income; the former are less "sophisticated" in financial matters, but financially "stronger" in the aggregate when they spend or save. Certainly in the securities markets the behavioral record speaks for itself: In the 1969–1970 stock market decline, the "sophisticated" managers took unbelievable lumps; brokerage firms folded in large numbers; the securities held by bank trust departments, the large insurance companies, the pension funds, etc. fell with the stock market averages, from 35% to 70%. None of the sophisticates saw the handwriting on the wall, since their behavior and perception is the antithesis of the consumer (the man who called the economic tune in 1970); therefore, they were blind to the events that unfolded before them. In a behavioral sense, the sophisticates literally live in another world, so they cannot really be expected to fare better when the forces which set the ultimate trend in the securities markets, the psychology of the masses, is beyond their ken, or at least not perceived by them.

LOWER-INCOME STOCK HOLDERS

Americans with incomes of less than $10,000 do not perceive the purchase of common stocks the same way those with higher incomes do. For the former, savings are preponderantly held with a view of nearness to cash. Liquidity and security are paramount considerations when employment and sources of income are uncertain, as they are for most wage earners in our mythical affluent society.

The bulk of the small security owners are not sophisticated in the Wall Street financial sense, and thus come made-to-order for the fast talking mutual fund sales people. As pointed out, these buyers regard the purchase of a mutual fund as a method of "saving," not as an investment. And because of faith, perhaps more than any other one thing, they will cling to a mutual fund purchase despite a large loss in value in a stock market debacle such as that of 1970. They give no thought to "taking a loss" and seeking other outlets for their "savings." They believe their values will come back "some day" and are prepared to wait forever apparently for that to happen. When a market move of consequence commences and their attention becomes focused on the downward trend in security prices, they will then move in a panic to redeem stocks. Alternatively, in order to secure funds for consumption purchases or a result of prolonged inflation and/or prolonged unemployment, they will redeem mutual funds as a last resort measure, along with insurance.

The direct ownership of stocks, a form of socialism for the rich, then relegates to those not so rich the purchase of shares in mutual funds, and nowhere in the financial spectrum is human folly more clearly demonstrated. The first comprehensive census of mutual fund shareholders in the United States was made during mid-1971 and it revealed that 8,450,000 owned mutual funds in 1970.

> The figures indicate that more than one in four of all shareholders in the country are mutual fund shareholders. The total of fund owners is more than double the 3.9 million individuals who own shares listed on the American Stock Exchange and almost one-half the total number of shareholders of the New York Stock Exchange. Three out of four mutual fund owners live in metropolitan areas.[6]

These *indirect* owners of a "share of American industry" are told (and they believe) that they are acquiring title to free enterprise, that they "own" chicken chains, IBM, textile mills. But the heart of the business is the unearned income creamed off the top in "fees" for management, or, more often, mismanagement. If the investment goes to zero, the manager's "fees" continue, as more money is extracted in the living rooms from other new "owners" by zealous, overbearing salesmen.

And the folly of human behavior is clearly revealed in a survey made by National Analysts, Inc., of Philadelphia during mid-1971, a survey the funds themselves commissioned to determine the public's attitude toward its product. The survey found:

> Consistent with the finding that many fund owners do not know how their fund is doing, and what its objective is, many owners believe that not having to follow the market or make decisions is a great advantage of mutual funds.
>
> Overall, keeping up with investments tends to be regarded as a chore.
>
> The average fund owner is in his mid-40's, has some college education, and earns about $13,000 per year. The average is middle income.
>
> Other characteristics of a fund owner include: less self-confident, less impulsive, less decisive, less active, more tolerant of a "quiet life."
>
> About 40% of present fund owners believe their investments are good only for the long term, more than 30% feel sales commissions are too high, and close to 20% complain that management fees are too high.[7]

Imagine! They do not know the product in which they are investing. They do not check its performance. They sit back in ignorant bliss, feeling assured that strangers will take care of them. In another era this curious quirk in human beings, this folly, was likened to putting the fox in the coop to guard the chickens; or, as Barnum is supposed to have said, "There's a sucker born every minute."

But the Money Managers never say die. For example, on August 9, 1972, the Investment Company Institute ran a full page advertisement in the *Wall Street Journal* entitled "Mutual Funds—The Record." Their figures indicated that if you had put $10,000 into mutual funds between the period 1950 and 1971, Eureka! you would now have $94,008. This was measured by the average performance of all mutual funds. What the advertisement did *not* say was that investors do not buy *all* of the mutual funds. They buy one or two or three. *They* cannot average all funds. They can only pray each night that their selections have been good ones.

Forbes magazine, in their annual mutual fund survey on August 15, 1972, came closer to the truth than the *WSJ* ad:

> Most of the mutual fund industry has redeemed itself in the

> two years since the 1970 stock market crash. Slightly over half the funds covered in Forbes' Fund Survey outperformed the Standard & Poors 500 Stock Index during the latest 12 months. And, taking the long sweep of the Forbes Survey—from 1962 through mid-1972—the *average* fund outperformed the S&P 500 average.
>
> The Forbes Mutual Fund Average appreciated by 4.9% in those ten years. Add dividends and the typical stock mutual fund earned something over 7% per year for its shareholders.
>
> *But not just in any fund.* In some cases the investor would have been better off in a savings bank.
>
> The load-charging mutual funds as a group were having to pay out more in redemptions than they took in from new sales; they were *losing* business at the rate of nearly $160 million a month in the first half of 1972.

Mutual funds do not seem to be a path to wealth for the average consumer—and recent redemptions show that he has finally learned this.

THE AFFLUENT STOCK HOLDERS

Because the "average" American needs all of his income to survive, most savings are held by those whose incomes are in excess of $10,000. Once the latter meet their living expense bills at their individual plateaus (and these vary enormously), they accrue money quickly to save or invest. Age, education, and occupation affect their living styles, financial habits, and what they "see"—ultimately, how they behave in the securities markets: when they buy and sell. Because they are so far removed behaviorally from the "average" consumer, they are, on the average, out of step with market trends when they buy and sell securities.

The $10,000+ income persons save, for example, for entirely different reasons than the average consumer: The rich save to provide for retirement or old age. The average consumer saves, if he can, for emergency purposes, which is ranked lower by the affluent, who rank savings for educational purposes still lower, since they plan to pay these expenses out of current income. The average consumer's children, by contrast, work their way through college or borrow long-term funds for schooling through various government and private aid sources.

TABLE 15

THE SIZE AND COMPOSITION OF PORTFOLIOS

(Percentages of the aggregate income received by those with 1961 adjusted gross income over $10,000)

Value of common stock[2] owned	Individuals owning fixed-yield assets[1] worth									
	Under $10,000			Between $10,000 and $100,000			More than $100,000			
	and interests in real estate and unincorporated businesses worth									Total
	Under $10,000	Between $10,000 and $100,000	More than $100,000	Under $10,000	Between $10,000 and $100,000	More than $100,000	Under $10,000	Between $10,000 and $100,000	More than $100,000	
Under $10,000	21[3]	6	2	6	7	1	0	1	1	45
Between $10,000 and $100,000	6	3	1	9	7	2	1	0	1	30
More than $100,000	2	1	1	3	2	2	4	2	5	22
Total	29	10	4	18	16	5	5	3	7	100[4]

NOTE: The information above was used to define portfolio sizes as follows:

Large portfolios (more than $100,000 in one or more asset-types) 30%
Medium-sized portfolios (where the largest asset-type had a value between $10,000 and $100,000) 40
Small portfolios (where the largest asset-type had a value below $10,000) 27

Details may not add to totals due to rounding.

[1] Savings accounts, credit union deposits, corporate bonds, preferred stock, U. S. savings bonds, U. S. bonds paying interest currently, Treasury bills and notes, state and local government bonds, mortgages and land contracts.

[2] Including mutual fund shares.

[3] Including those cases (numbering 6 percent of the entire sample) with total "savings, investments, and reserve funds" under $1,000.

[4] Including those cases (numbering 2 percent of the entire sample) where the value of any of the three asset-types was not ascertained.

TABLE 16

OWNERSHIP OF SELECTED ASSETS BY INCOME CLASS

(Percentage in each income group owning asset indicated)[1]

Asset	1963 adjusted gross income						All cases with 1961 income $10,000 or over
	$10,000–15,000	$15,000–30,000	$30,000–75,000	$75,000–150,000	$150,000–300,000	$300,000 and over	
Group I. Assets more widely owned at upper income levels							
Common stock[2]	49	77	85	96	99	99	73
Real estate[3]	35	48	53	63	60	67	47
Own corporation[4]	12	26	43	61	75	64	31
Unincorporated business interests	21	21	30	32	32	36	25
Preferred stock	19	19	32	33	39	33	24
Corporate bonds	10	17	24	31	36	35	19
Municipal bonds	10	8	23	48	52	65	19
U. S. bonds paying currently	4	10	18	21	27	35	13
Treasury bills and notes	1	6	9	14	20	29	7
Group II. Assets owned to about the same extent at all income levels							
Own home	88	91	95	92	95	99	91
Checking account	81	94	99	99	99	100	92
Cash-value life insurance	79	90	90	91	85	79	86
Private pension fund	62	61	51	51	57	54	58
Group term life insurance	49	56	58	61	70	50	55
Mutual fund shares	24	29	30	30	32	29	28
Group III. Assets less widely owned at upper income levels							
Savings accounts	67	79	84	78	74	70	76
U. S. savings bonds	46	53	50	51	46	45	50
Mortgages and land contracts	15	16	22	25	22	17	18
Credit union deposits	20	24	5	3	1	8	15
Respondents with total "savings, investments, or reserve funds" under $1,000	15	4	1	0	0	0	6

[1] Respondents with total "savings, investments, or reserve funds" under $1,000 were not asked whether they owned the specific assets listed above, except in the case of pension funds, life insurance, and housing. Therefore, with these exceptions, the percentages given above rest on the assumption that these respondents owned none of the assets in question.

[2] Including stock held in own corporation; excluding mutual fund shares.

[3] Including farms; excluding own home.

[4] Cases where the respondent held stock in a corporation of which he was an executive or director.

In investing their savings, the more affluent stress capital gains rather than current cash income; the latter is quite adequate and the former provides still more savings and more investments for the future. Three-fourths of the very affluent own common stock in round lots (more than 100 shares), and as their income rises, they accrue more stocks and less Savings Bonds and the like. Thus, when the stock market rises, they make large gains, and when it falls, take drastic losses. Table 15, from a Brookings Institution study,[8] clearly depicts this important economic fact. Table 16, also from the Brookings study,[9] shows the ownership of selected assets by income classes.

The Brookings study also discovered that before this survey (August 1966) one-half of the entire high income group had bought some common stock during the previous fifteen months. And they bought frequently: once a month or more. Their reasons for selling securities varied:

1. The stock looked like a poor risk (chief reason).
2. The time for profit taking had arrived.
3. The need to raise funds for consumption purposes arose (one in six gave this reply).

Perhaps the most interesting facet of this study, and a clue as to why this group does so poorly on the average in the securities markets, is indicated by observing where they get their investment information: A majority of the high-income group surveyed read investment advisory publications and make genuine efforts to keep themselves "well informed" in business matters with feedback from associates (an "echo effect" results, since their associates are likely to be similarly conditioned).

An observation on investment advisory services in early 1971 was summarized in the *Wall Street Journal:*

> If the leading investment advisory services are right, there's more sunshine ahead for the market.
>
> Their sentiment is predominantly bullish and characterized by rosy market letters containing an increasing number of "buy" recommendations. And this enthusiasm comes amid a more than 34% advance in the Dow Jones industrial average since last May's lows, with no major correction, or decline, to speak of during this period.
>
> However, a few analysts see some disturbing signs in the

> extent of the bullish sentiment. They argue that, historically, advisory services, for the most part, are most ebullient at market peaks, and, correspondingly, most bearish at market bottoms.
>
> Such trends are noted by Investors Intelligence, Larchmont, N.Y., a concern that keeps tabs on the view of 66 leading investment advisory services. And based on its latest reading, it thinks the market is headed for a correction.
>
> Investors Intelligence says that as of Jan. 1, 1971, bullish sentiment was the highest it has ever been since it began operations in 1963. It calculates that the services were 68.3% bullish at the turn of the year. And whenever the bulls exceed 60%, "the market appears to be at its top," a spokesman said. He added that the last time the advisory services were nearly as bullish as they were two weeks ago was in spring 1966, after which the market slumped.[10]

Psychologically, investment advisory services "sell" hope: rising prices typify hope (upness is goodness); hence, they have a sound dollar reason to tout rising stock prices. Nobody relishes falling prices; they signify disaster and darkness. After all, hell and the devil are "down there."

Interest rates have little effect on the total amount of funds the affluent maintain in savings accounts. By contrast, in the lower income groups small changes in interest received are instantly perceived and funds are moved quickly to the financial institutions paying the higher interest rate.

Also, the high-income groups who hold assets that have appreciated rarely consider selling them because no better investment opportunities appear available. Tax considerations also loom large in the buying/selling patterns of the rich, rising to 80% among those with incomes of $100,000 or more.

Since the high-income groups flock together for business, social, and other reasons, their feedback and behavior to each other on their investment portfolios are very likely to be the same. The Wall Street Money Managers, traveling in the same circles, experience this same feedback effect; thus, they share common beliefs at the same time as to trends, individual security values, profit outlooks, and so on—almost as though they were together on another planet far removed from the real life of the consumer, the "invisible programmer." Togetherness is the Money Managers' keynote: they buy together and sell together.

THE AVERAGE CONSUMER

In May 1967, *Newsweek* magazine reported the results of a survey made for them by the Louis Harris Pollsters of 3,000 representative U.S. families to find out what people think about money and the institutions that manage it:

> The survey uncovered a good deal of general ignorance about money matters, mixed with an equally surprising confidence in the people who manage the money. An astonishing 86 per cent of those covered by Social Security do not know what percentage of their salary is deducted; 72 per cent of those in noncontributing pension funds do not know how much their employer kicks in; 57 per cent of stockholders don't know what brokerage charges they pay, and 43 per cent of the sampling say they decide on a loan on the basis of the monthly payments, not on the basis of the interest rates.
>
> Faith: The clear implication is that most people are content to let the money man worry about such matters. Fully 89 per cent give favorable ratings to financial institutions, ranging from 82 per cent approval for insurance companies to 94 per cent for savings banks. In the same vein, most of those interviewed are content to trust the government to manage the economy; they show a surprising acquiescence in the tenets of the "new economics." Some 67 per cent, for instance, agree that a little inflation is the price of prosperity; majorities ranging up to 72 per cent agree that the government can stabilize the economy through its spending, and by changing interest and tax rates (one notable exception: 73 per cent say that tax increases are no way to control inflation).
>
> And even though rising prices and the publicized sluggishness of the economy have recently eroded confidence, a full 54 per cent of those surveyed predict that their standard of living ten years hence will be higher than it is today. "It's a blind faith," says a Presbyterian minister from Phoenix, Ariz. "It's just faith in the economy."[11]

In the early 1970s there was some erosion of this faith, especially among the young, ethnic groups, and intellectuals outside the universities.

Since the individual numbers of Americans owning stocks in increments of 100 shares or more is a steadily declining percentage of stock ownership, the growing effect of the influence of institutions in security trading is apparent. The number of individual 10,000 share trading on any given day has risen sharply within the past few years and will increase more in the years ahead.

Behaviorally, as noted, there exists a dichotomy: the rich and the poor do not perceive investments, money, or savings the same. It is because of this that the lower-income groups can become a drag on the economy by excess savings and more careful spending—a result of worries about inflation and unemployment, for example. At the same moment, the institution managers, believing their own propaganda, may foresee profits, say, nine to twelve months ahead, profits that will not very likely generate if the negative attitude of the masses persists and is reinforced by still more thrift—small as a savings is, individually—and unwillingness or inability to assume greater debt.

It is the perception of the total economic environment by the masses of the people that will ultimately establish stock market trends because their views are reflected in ultimate corporate profits or losses. These changes are slow to commence and slow to become apparent and slow to develop, so discernable stock market trends (gains or losses of 12%) occur infrequently, every two-three years. Untoward, genuine events may trigger more frequent action, but if there are only "pseudo-events," then the longer projection will obtain.

AN INSTITUTION'S PERCEPTION OF THE CONSUMER

Late in 1970 as the general economic picture in the United States worsened, consumers sat back with almost $50 billion in financial assets in savings, $10 billion more than "normal." Inflation and unemployment persisted and the consumer was worried.

In December 1970, the Morgan Guaranty Trust Company in New York viewed the consumer scene as follows:

> It is not unreasonable to think that the consumer's darkest hour may have passed. . . . Equity prices as measured by the Dow Jones industrial averages have staged a 30% recovery since last spring. This presumably is working to push shareholders (many of whom felt very badly pinched for a while) back in the direction of somewhat freer spending patterns,

> and it probably is having a favorable impact more broadly as well. Just getting headlines about a slumping stock market off page one of the nation's newspapers has to be counted as a fairly important positive development. The recent sharp declines in interest rates can also be included in the list of items favorable to consumer sentiment. . . . In the past, the bulge in savings often has been the prelude to buying spurts, and there is a good chance that this will be so again.[12]

Had the darkest hour passed? No. Odd-lotters were at this time selling stock, not buying stock.

Falling interest rates do *not* have the powerful focus of attention by consumers ascribed to them by economists. The consumer has a general awareness of the level of interest rates, but he is not fixated or hypnotized by them.

How people en mass perceive events is one event. How the people themselves are perceived by others is a separate event, most frequently distorted. Consumer sentiments declined sharply in the 4th quarter 1970. It was a dark hour. But this was *not* perceived on Wall Street by many.

It is critical to understand that the number of dollars saved by the consumer is only an indirect (and poor) guide as to the rate consumers *will spend*. And it is expenditure that counts—money that comes into the marketplace to be matched against the supply of services and goods.

The relationship between the quantity of money and the rate of expenditure is so tenuous and variable because of a peculiar characteristic of money—a characteristic that it need not have, but with which we have endowed it: We need not spend money the instant we receive it. In short, some production may go unsold simply because individuals and business firms sit on their money instead of spending it or making it available to others to spend.

8

People-Watching

> Seeing-is-believing is a blind spot in man's vision.
>
> *R. Buckminster Fuller*

People control the stock market since they buy and sell the shares; as long as the people behave "properly," so will the market. But the behavior patterns vary among high-income and low-income people, professionals and amateurs in the stock market, speculators and investors. However, the masses of the people—the principal determinant of stock market trends—over time appear to respond in a uniform and consistent way, albeit slowly. The three major forces that set the level of business generally are business spending, government spending, and consumer spending. The last is by far the mightiest machine in propelling the economy. It is, therefore, critical to "people watch," to observe the behavioral patterns that condition the spending of the masses. To reiterate, mass production cannot exist without mass consumption, and the spending by the masses for services and goods will inevitably mean profits or losses for the businesses that cater to their wants and needs, and, in a longer analysis, establish stock market trends (a mirror of profits and losses).

People watching is not a hopeless task, since they telegraph their intents through three major confidence surveys compiled and made public by private and government institutions: the Survey Research

Center at the University of Michigan, the National Industrial Conference Board in New York, and the U.S. Department of Commerce. Generally, each of these organizations surveys selective samples of people to find out if they are in a "buying" or "selling" mood, confident or not.

The public is ambivalent in its feelings about the validity of polls. Americans, after all, are polled to death, so why attribute weight to more pollsters who try to plumb the attitudes of the consumer toward his future spending/savings plans? "How Good Are Consumer Pollsters?", *Business Week* magazine asked in an article by that title. Among its examples of users of confidence surveys was GE:

> General Electric Co. makes a variety of uses of the Katona [Michigan Survey Research Center] and Census [U.S. Dept. of Commerce] surveys. The Katona index has had a "rather good track record in the past," says Robert W. Pratt, Jr., manager of consumer behavior research. Corporate headquarters uses Survey Research Center as one of the many inputs in its total economy forecast. The various consumer divisions use it individually, in the way that works best for them. Even some of the nonconsumer divisions keep tabs on it.
>
> "Primarily, we use the index as a flag," says Pratt. "Marketers criticize the index because it doesn't always do a marketing job. But Katona is not a marketer. Our own research confirms the impact of sentiment on buying. People don't behave like economists. Katona sends out the flag that warns us: maybe we had better be a little more perceptive just now. He offers us a tool. It is up to us marketers to figure the applications."[1]

The thrust of this book is that these surveys do a great deal more than merely send out "flags." Behavior is really all there is and if the indexes provide a clue about this changing economic behavior, they perform a major service.

The buying or selling moods of the masses are conditioned, of course, by their general economic environment, and this can be basically set by the financial actions of the federal government: for example, the surge in business caused by the step-up of the Vietnam war or the decline in business concomitant with the Nixon Administration. Within an economic environment the masses act and react, spend and save, and it is the tremendous buying power (or, conversely, savings power) of the masses that make the wheels of the American economy go around (or slow down).

Some critics of consumer sentiment indexes challenge their reliability as predictors of what consumers will do, since people can and do change their minds. But so can/do businessmen change when they plan expenditures for plant and equipment; they can go ahead or they can stop. Yet, more credence is given by many people watchers to a businessman's sentiment on future spending than to a consumer's. This is curious, because they are both "people," both behaving as "people," both spending as "people."

Put another way, some charge that these indexes only reflect the present rather than predict the future, because consumers simply are not future-oriented in any orderly way. Of course, impulse buying does go on all the time and some sudden-need purchases (e.g., a refrigerator to replace a defunct one) cannot be neatly discretionary. But we all *do* plan our personal finances ahead in a general way. Consumers *do* prefer to keep some semblance of order in their own personal finances. Man is goal-oriented generally. If we did not have goals, there would be no sense in planning money-spending ahead, nor would there be any savings.

During World War II, Americans earned a lot of money doing war-related work. Strict rationing of essentials and unavailability of other goods did not allow them to spend as they ordinarily would, so they saved; at the end of the war, savings amounted to 25% of disposable personal income. Many government and business economists had predicted that when the war ended the country would face a depression: production of war goods would begin to approach zero, jobs would vanish, and the economy would collapse. Instead, the American consumer, with a lot of money to spend, went on a spending spree; as factories shifted from war goods to making autos and refrigerators and washing machines, the consumer began buying, buying, buying. Don't discount the consumer and his dollar power—and his attitudes toward the next several months. He is "thinking ahead."

To gain a better understanding of how the consumer reacts to his environment, let us use the last half of the 1960s as a case study. Here is a recapitulation of the behavior of the consumer masses during the period 1965–1969 (Caution: No two economic environments, no two business cycles, no two economic yesterdays are exactly the same. Each must be reckoned separately with the variables then predominating. Therefore, the summary below is only to give the reader a sense of what to look for, a "feel" for what he should be observing.):

It has been noted that the consumer believes he can fight inflation by saving, not, as classic economic logic dictates, by stocking up on goods before prices go higher (thus intensifying inflationary pressure).

In 1965 the feeling of the people was that rising prices would reduce their future buying power and more money would be needed for necessities; so they *saved,* and reduced discretionary spending for frills at the same time. The result was not the flight from money to goods predicted by Status Quo Economics, but a move from less essential goods to money reserves. Consumer sentiment declined, sales of durable goods slowed, installment debt declined, savings rose. Incomes continued to rise during the period, so net asset accumulation jumped.

In early 1967, consumers had adjusted to the Vietnam war talk and the possibility of a surtax being imposed. Tight credit eased, interest rates fell, and the consumer became more optimistic. He perceived "good times," for a while at least. Meantime, inflation was accelerating to the point that consumers had to incur installment debt or dip into their savings in order to maintain their customary standard of living. As they became more buoyant psychologically, they threw caution to the wind and began incurring installment debt at a very rapid rate, at an annual rate of over $12 billion. Savings started down at the same time. So, when the surtax took effect in mid-1968, its advent had been discounted and "boom" psychology was predominant. Prices began to rise sharply.

During the early months of 1969, consumers began to feel the squeeze of the monetary and fiscal restraint applied by the government to bring inflation under control. It was not likely that they could cushion the impact on their spending by reducing their savings rate very much further. As inflation persisted and the value of the consumer's dollar fell, down came the consumer's optimism: car sales fell; household appliance sales, TV sales, and household furnishing sales lagged. The graphs on the following page chart the 1965–1969 period.

CHART 9

RISING PERSONAL INCOME WAS PARTLY ABSORBED BY HIGHER PRICES AND TAXES.

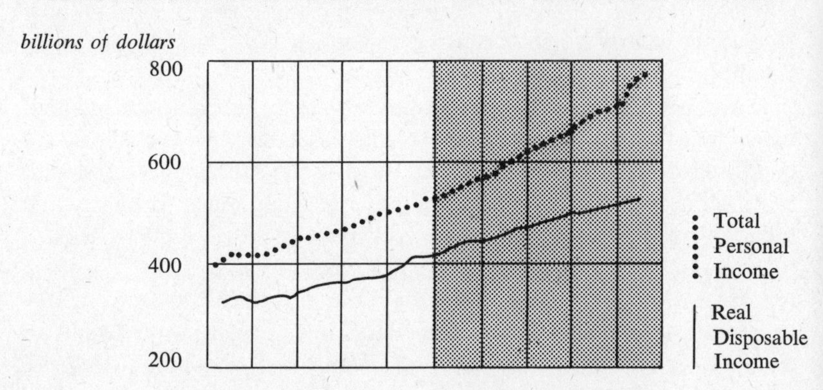

CONSUMERS FIRST INCREASED SAVING, HELD BACK DEBT, THEN BECAME LESS CAUTIOUS.

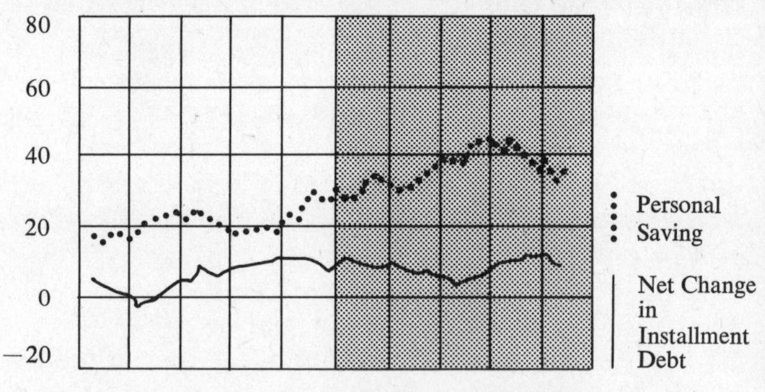

DISCRETIONARY SPENDING LEVELED FROM 1965 TO 1967, THEN ROSE IN 1968.

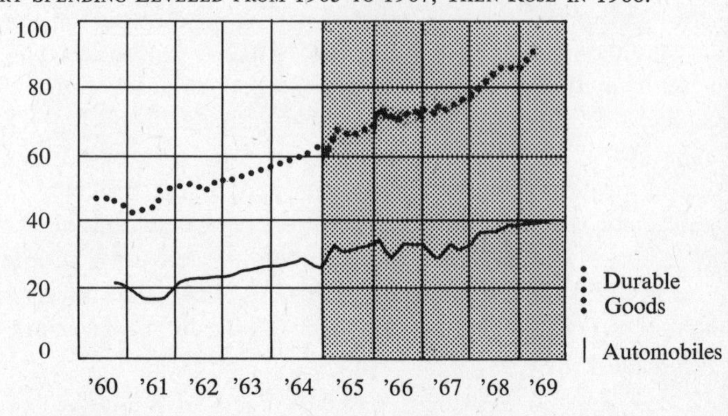

SOURCE: U.S. Department of Commerce, Federal Reserve Board

The $10,000-and-under consumer manages his personal finances with adroitness. Being human, he errs at times: overspends or saves too much; but in the main and on balance he keeps afloat financially. In discerning his future moves, we must remember our assumption: He is basically conservative and uniform in his economic behavior.

The "modern American consumer" is over 200 million people, some 77 million wage and salary workers, most of them living in family structures physically separated from one another. But in McLuhan's real-life electronic sense, we are, though physically apart, a "village"—witness to or involved in decision-making processes. We are electronically and psychologically a "crowd." For example, the TV national newscasts include recaps of Wall Street's action for that day as reflected in stock market averages (mass media influence), so when two neighbors meet while hauling their garbage cans to the street for emptying by the garbage men, they can knowledgeably talk about the stock market's action. When the President makes an economic address on network radio and TV, everyone knows about it at the same time. In an economic-decision-making sense we are profoundly influenced by this new instant transmission of financial and economic news; we are a "crowd." We all know what the Dow Jones averages are. Separate decision makers meld into aggregative economic totals; a total often becomes much greater than the sum of the parts in a true national economic sense.

Gustave Le Bon noted the most striking characteristic of a crowd:

> Whoever be the individuals that compose it, however like or unlike be their mode of life, their occupations, their character, or their intelligence, the fact that they have been transformed into a crowd puts them in possession of a sort of collective mind which makes them feel, think, and act in a manner quite different from that in which each individual of them would feel, think, and act were he in a state of isolation.[2]

Over seventy-five years have come and gone since LeBon wrote. Technology has redefined a crowd; we don't have to rub elbows anymore to be a crowd. But people are still the same.

There has always been among stock traders a recognition of "psychology;" it has been variously described as "investor confidence," "the mood of the investor," etc. Such appellations, however, represent at best hurried value judgments by analysts with no fundamental understanding of either psychology or behavioral economics. To them, when people buy, they are "confident;" when they sell, they are "not confident." In the aggregate, in fact, the sum total of the decisions of the crowd may be, and frequently is, completely contrary to what it is perceived to be by Money Managers.

Let us look at a sample three-month period: the first quarter of 1970. The general mood of the masses was reflected in consumer sentiment as reported by the Michigan SRC: The index for all families fell from 86.4 (August-September 1969) to 79.7 (October-November), representing "primarily consumer expectations concerning the future course of business conditions which have become more pessimistic . . . under the impact of unfavorable news about rising unemployment, sluggish sales, and tight credit conditions."[3]

What was the actual economic behavior of the masses during the first three months of 1970? The chart below capsules the answer.

CHART 10

PERCENT CHANGE FIRST QUARTER 1969 TO 1970

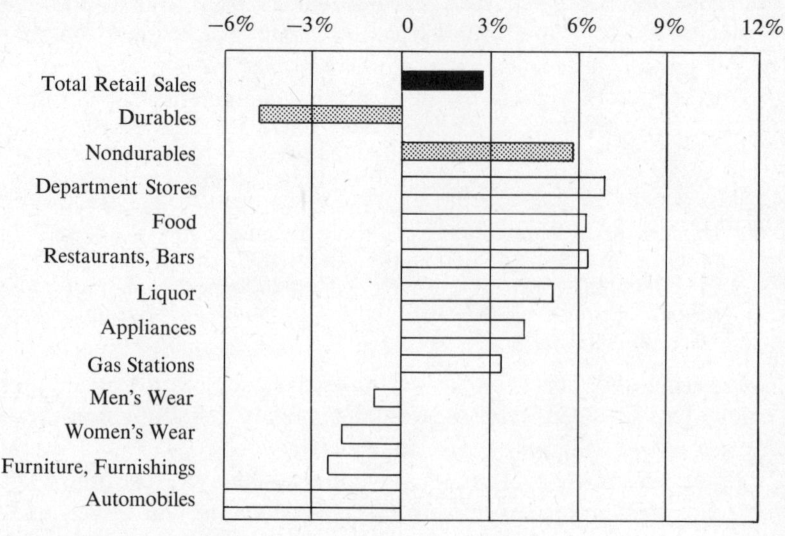

SOURCE: U.S. Department of Commerce

During this period consumers did more than just tighten their purse strings; they knotted them. In many areas the actual number of dollars spent had dropped. But even where the spending was up, it merely reflected higher prices caused by inflation, not an increased volume of goods being sold. Either way, this meant bad news for Wall Street and business generally. The stock market finally took note of this erosion in April and May of 1970 when the averages slid sharply, some 36% or more.

Spending by consumers for the first quarter of 1970 ran about 2.5% ahead of the same period in 1969. But prices were 5% higher, so in fact, when the inflation was taken into account, consumers were buying less in 1970.

Demand for nondurable goods was up about 6%, about the same as the inflation for that part of the economy, so the net result was no real change in buying.

In durable goods, however—items with a lifespan of more than three years—spending fell more than 4%, despite a 2.5% price inflation, adding up to a total loss in real volume of 6.5% or more.

About the only place the consumer was putting his money was in the bank. By March 1970 consumers were saving about 6.5% of their disposable income versus 5.5% the year earlier, and disposable income had increased, so they were, in fact, putting away a lot more dollars.

Retail food sales in the first quarter of 1970 were running some 6.5% ahead of 1969, but food prices were up slightly more than this figure, resulting in no real increase in volume.

Restaurants and bars reported sales about 6% ahead of the first quarter of 1969, but prices had gone up close to 8% because of increased wage costs, meaning real volume dropped.

Home furnishing sales were sluggish during the first half of 1970, only 1.5% ahead of 1969 and significantly behind the rate of inflation. Furniture stores reported an actual decline in dollar sales in the early months of the year, and dollar volume had remained off despite a 5% increase in prices.

Appliances, on the other hand, had fared relatively well. Dollar sales volume was up 4% over 1969, while prices went up a modest 1.5%.

In apparel, dollar sales barely matched 1969 levels despite a 4.5% price hike. Sales by women's speciality shops were down 2% in the face of a 4% price increase, while men's wear was up about 5%.

Department stores were doing a little better than clothing and furniture stores for the first half of 1970, up 5.5% in the face of a 4% to 5% price increase, depending on the product line.

Automobile dealers reported a 7% drop in sales dollars, but with a 2% price rise the real decline was nearly 9%. Gasoline station sales bucked the trend. Sales were up about 3%, while gas prices were actually about 1.5% lower than 1969, creating an actual increase in volume.

To effectively use mass psychology in economic analysis, it is imperative, as a beginning, to subject inputs, such as just described, to close scrutiny, together with employment of other variables: how the purchases are being made, cash or charge, etc. The sentiment index *alone* is not an Aladdin's lamp, so that a cursory brush with rising or falling figures will *not* indicate what the market will do in "x months." Retail sales *alone* will not suffice or reveal trends either. Regrettably, it is not that simple. As a matter of fact, "retail sales" is a good example of a "bad number" still watched closely by Status Quo Economists. Not only is the data gathered by arcane methods, but in a Service Economy the figures reveal a great deal less important information than in a Production Economy.

HOW DOES THE CONSUMER PAY?

Another important aspect of consumer behavior is how he chooses to pay his bills, how much debt he incurs, the kind of debt, and when he incurs it. Debt overloading imposes constraints on future spending, so his liquidity, or lack of it, is an important determinant in his reference frame as to whether or not he will spend and when. His spending habits are closely observed, but the consumer often is unyielding, saving/retrenching in excess of normal, or incurring too much of the wrong kind of debt at the wrong time, which prevents his spending in any case. Despite the fact that the average American is supposed to have a high school education or less, he nevertheless manages his own personal finances with the astuteness of a financial expert. He is not (as is so frequently reckoned among sophisticated investors) stupid. When he won't spend he is called "reluctant," "worried," "penny pincher," and other words far too strong to pass on here.

The late 1960s saw the forward thrust of the bank credit cards, and since the consumer pays little attention to the interest he pays (focusing instead on what he receives), the 18% interest charge on these cards eludes him. *Business Week* magazine reported in an article entitled "The Santa Claus That Makes You Pay":

> As recently as 1965 there were fewer than 5 million bank credit cards in circulation. . . . Bank credit cards in 1969 accounted for less than 2% of the $120 billion worth of consumer debt outstanding—but a year ago [1968] the figure was under 1%. Within a decade, if the bankers are correct, the figure will soar to 25% or more.[4]

This will be a force to reckon with in the years ahead in evaluating consumer liquidity. Until the consumer learns to exercise his financial astuteness in this area, it will be a trap—short-term debt that will cause him "pain," to use the language of the classical economist.

Other short-term debt includes bank or loan company installments, department store accounts, and an accumulation of other "personal debt." The chart below shows the rapid growth of average family debt from World War II to 1969:

CHART 11

THE MOUNTING BURDEN OF FAMILY DEBT

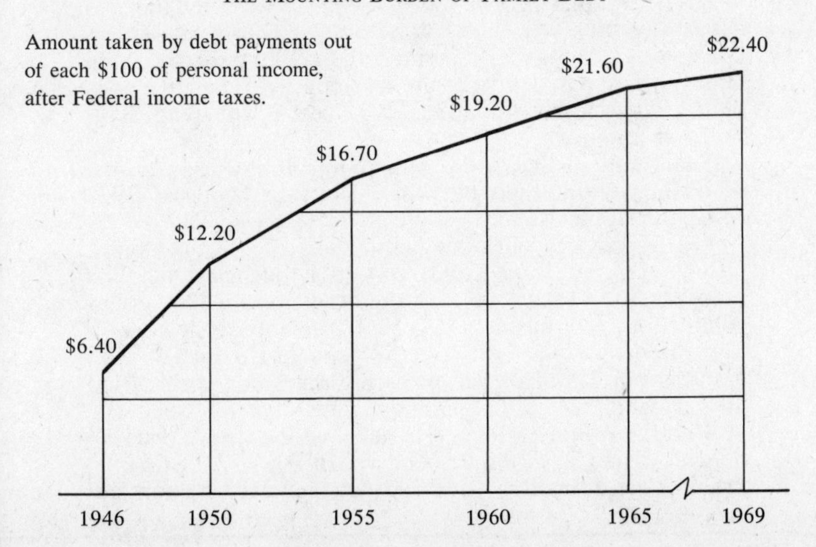

SOURCE: U.S. Department of Commerce U.S. News & World Report, June 22, 1970.

If general business conditions and prices remain fairly stable, the average consumer manages to repay his debt on time. But sharp recessions and excessive inflation compound his troubles. As *U.S. News & World Report* described it:

> Personal debts, mounting for a quarter century, are threatening a financial crackup in more and more families.
>
> Debt delinquencies are in a sharp rise. So, in many cities, are personal bankruptcies. Creditors appear to be taking a tougher line.
>
> Pressure tactics applied to debtors are the subject of hearings set June 22 and 23 [1970] by a new National Commission on Consumer Finance.
>
> The pattern of bill paying is far from uniform around the country. In New York City and State, lenders, bill collectors and credit bureaus report no great change in recent months.
>
> In most other communities across the country, a careful check by "U.S. News & World Report" reveals a picture of growing troubles. . . .
>
> A long rise in interest rates has exaggerated the problem. As recently as 1951, less than 16 cents out of each $1 in payments on personal debt was absorbed by interest charges. Now, nearly 25 cents in each $1 of payments goes for interest charges.
>
> A sharp increase in living costs, often outstripping family incomes, also is straining family budgets.
>
> Easy consumer credit, too, is being blamed for the rise in past-due bills.
>
> For years, the experts assured the country that growing family debts posed no threat—as long as prosperity continued. Now, in recession, excessive debt is engulfing thousands of families. . . .
>
> One result is that more and more businesses, doctors, others are putting their overdue bills in the hands of debt-collection agencies.
>
> The American Collectors Association, Inc., Minneapolis, receives reports from 2,600 collection agencies handling accounts for about 800,000 credit grantors. The dollar volume of new business received by those collectors in May [1970] was up more than 58 per cent from a 1967–68 base period. The increase in the last year alone was about 40 per cent.
>
> Both the volume of new accounts and the size of overdue bills are rising, says the association. In April, for example, the average amount of overdue debt involved in new ac-

counts assigned to collection agencies was $85.01, up from $68.01 in April, 1969.

Says Joe Galdiano, spokesman for the association:

"People are going out and using credit without really knowing what it's all about. The average person doesn't know the responsibility he assumes when he opens an account. It's a shock to him at the end of the month to find he has been spending more money than he's making."[5]

Since some consumer debt creation also has the other side of the coin, asset creation, a better perspective of the consumers' total financial position between 1960 and 1970 is shown below:

TABLE 17

FINANCIAL ASSETS OWNED BY INDIVIDUALS

	1960	1970
	(billions of dollars)	
Savings deposits	$168	$ 370
Corporate stocks and bonds	401	615
Life insurance & pension reserves	152	275
Other assets	254	360
Total assets of individuals	975	1,620
Total debts owed by individuals	185	405
Net assets of individuals	$790	$1,215

SOURCE: U.S. Department of Commerce.

This is not as bright as it first appears, because the relative freedom from debt and ease of securing liquidity is largely reserved for those whose incomes exceeded $10,000 per year. In late 1970, the average consumer was under severe future financial constraints, and could not be cajoled by anyone to spend, "to get the economy going." By straining to pay his past debt load and straining to increase his pitiful savings cash balance (estimated to be less than $1,000 for the vast majority of Americans), his failure to spend was dragging the economy (and, later, the stock market) down with him, and he was, alas, hoist by his own petard.

We accept readily the misconception about consumers being too much in debt because we have a convention in America which holds that when goods are delivered to consumers they are consumed immediately and therefore have no market value from then on, that the goods do not produce monetary income regardless of their use, and that there is no well organized secondhand market (except for autos).

As we entered the 1970s, consumers were more and more involved in *financing money, not goods*. This is even worse than borrowing just to consume, as some have done before, because when you borrow to consolidate debt there is no consumption period.

Here is one example of nonsense borrowing. A consumer can "buy" a $45,000 poorly constructed home for 5% down ($2,250). This home was in the first place not in fact built to last and to live in; rather it is (literally and figuratively) a paper house, with parasites chewing at it in a long line leading to Washington where a mortgage of doubtful value is stored. In this arrangement the house part is relatively small and the finance part (service) relatively large. The Service Economy *is* different in many, many ways; here the operation is *seen* as good (i.e., a house was built), but the service element (in this case the financial waste) is invisible. This is patently a dimwitted way to revitalize an obsolete construction industry or to benefit legitimate consumer needs.

Despite these views, though, the record over a long time indicates that in general the low-income families cannot and do not incur substantial amounts of installment debt. It is vital, however, that government-created economic environment not be designed to produce unemployment. Otherwise, as with illiquid corporations or illiquid financial institutions, the consumer-masses will quickly find their backs to the wall. It is only when the consumer's discretionary income melts before rapidly rising taxes, rapidly rising prices, shorter work weeks, that we head for mass disaster for the consuming masses and, later, lower corporate profits with a fall in securities prices.

WHEN WILL THE CONSUMER SPEND?

Classical thought has indicated that it is axiomatic that as consumer income rises, so will consumer spending. (The new phenomenon of "life style spending" is still invisible.) Like most of our preconceived myths, though, the experience of 1969–1970 dispelled this idea. Consumer income rose (since August 1969, such income had risen from an annual rate of $785 billion to $811 billion), being pumped up by the federal government, but the consumer instead of spending, saved. By late 1970 his savings amounted to 7.6% of his disposable personal income, some $10 billion above normal, a total of $52 billion—a huge pent-up green power. Obviously, a small percentage shift in savings represents, in the aggregate, very large demand *when* spent.

However, it appears that buyers do go on "strike." They will spend only when *they* perceive an economic environment that is favorable to *them, not* one favorable to the government. If a government has budget problems, tries to stop runaway inflation with classical techniques, and thereby imposes "economic pain" on the consumer, the consumer invisibly rebels. That was our experience as the 1960s came to a close.

At a time like that, the banks became more liquid with the aid of the central bank, but were having difficulty putting these funds to work, much less the savings of the masses, so the savings became a double drag: not working directly or indirectly.

The consumer masses have struck before: 1948–49, 1957–58, 1960–61, 1966–67, in addition to 1969–70, each time marked by exogenous circumstances creating an economic situation perceived to be unfavorable for *them* by the masses of the American people.

Consumer behavior has traditionally baffled economists and bureaucrats alike. Back in the early 1950s, the Truman Administration, in anticipation of an inflationary upsurge in spending and investing, slapped on price and wage controls six months after the Korean war broke out. Instead of going on a buying spree, however, the public tightened its belt; as a result, prices dropped sharply, and, for the duration, never approached official ceilings. The trouble was purely and simply psychological. The consumer skewed his behavior to the "images" he perceived.

Psychological or behavioral deterrents to spending in the late 1960s had been slowly building. The rise to prominence of Ralph Nader, Champion of the Consumer, was no accident. He brought the age of "consumerism" to flower, which centered the masses' attention on the fact that much of what they were offered in the marketplace was either unsafe, too expensive, or not worth buying. One product after another was attacked and the reputation of large institutions shattered in the process: Savings and loans companies in

California were subjected to large class action law suits for failure to rebate to consumers interest they had earned on putting consumers' prepayments of taxes to work; color TVs that allegedly exposed consumers to radiation were highlighted as health risks; cereals and soaps came under fire. One national news magazine headlined "No One Seems To Give a Damn" in a lengthy article depicting the faults in the marketplace. These inputs were perceived by the public; they weighed heavily on the consumer. He had tried the appliances, he had been exposed to the merchandise; as a worker, the consumer didn't care much about the product he helped manufacture, whether it was an auto or a toaster, since he did not intend to buy it himself, knowing it was not well made.

During the period 1969–1971 we developed an Economic Lo! and Behold! With a steady rise in unemployment there occurred a steady rise in savings. Status Quo wisdom and all of the conventional economic textbooks have told us that this should not happen; instead, when people are out of work, they will draw on their savings in order to have some income with which to pay their overhead which continues. And now something new under the sun! Where were the answers? Who could explain this? We turned to the Status Quo and were solemnly advised that this shouldn't occur. As they looked through their rearview mirrors, sure enough, it had not happened before, so they were unprepared for the economic exigencies of the here and now.

Perhaps the main reason that this happened is that America is now a pluralistic economy: the private sector, the government sector, the not-for-profit sector (all including a vast array of service workers). Thus, manufacturing unemployment could and did rise, city and state payrolls were cut, but large sectors of the economy, outside these sectors, came through unscathed. Large numbers of people worked and saved like mad; they were economically scared. Coupled with the savings kick was a reducing of the monies spent for day-to-day living, and so the Lo! and Behold!

In a mass consumption society, loss of employment is a powerful psychological and spending deterrant from the ken of the consumer. Despite the affluence that is visible, the average American consumer in general, hovering at a financial break-even level, fears deeply loss of his income source through layoff. As his unemployment stretches out, he tries more desperately to shore up his precarious financial position by all sorts of devices, the principal one being curtailing consumption. Thus, prolonged unemployment turns off the spending valve.

In a behavioral sense this is further reinforced in the community when the "opinion leader" is thrown out of work. Since the opinion leader is the dominant authority in any small neighborhood (he is the one most highly regarded by his neighbors for his expertise in all economic matters), he feeds back negativism to his neighbors which becomes locked into their subconscious mind and lurks there to further reinforce their non-spending attitude.

The added pressure of debts comes into the picture, dampens spirits more, and makes matters generally even worse.

Studies at the Michigan Survey Research Center have indicated that the consumer does *not* move swiftly when he decides to stop saving and start spending. It is, instead, a slow, long, drawn-out process, and for it to become meaningful in a country as large and diverse as America, it takes at least nine months to spread throughout the economy. So, from the moment the sentiment indexes bottom or indicate an upturn, months lie ahead before the economy in general feels the effects. This means, naturally, long-delayed profits for corporations, and this will be reflected in the securities markets. It is one thing to guesstimate future profits; it is an entirely different thing for the profits to materialize. Thus, Money Managers are frequently off target for two reasons: They do not perceive the consuming masses properly and their own psychological predilection indicates profits coming sooner than it is possible for them actually to come. Conversely, when the consumer stops spending (e.g., in 1970–1971, reflected in using credit less), this too takes time to become "visible" and felt economically.

Since we tend to see what we want to see and not what is in fact "out there," it is doubtful that Money Managers or high-income groups will ever perceive accurately the psychology of the masses. Historically, they never have (while decrying the "madness of crowds") and it is doubtful that they will change. Change itself is an "ordeal," as Eric Hoffer has emphasized.

The amount of cash which consumers keep in savings accounts, bank accounts, etc. is only an indirect, and frequently very poor, guide to the rate at which they will spend that cash. *Spending* counts, and only spending, and the consumer will oblige when economically the environment is favorable to *him*. Rising inflation, rising unemployment, unexpected large "bad" news—and his pockets are closed and locked. This is how women reacted in 1970:

> In two surveys of how women economized on their food and non-food budgets, Foote, Cone & Belding, the nation's eighth largest ad agency, found that not only have most women tightened up on their budgets, but that the richer and better educated women are stingier than average.
>
> In interviews with more than 1,500 women the agency found that more than three out of every four have cut back on food expenditures this year compared to last, and that two out of three extended the cutback to non-food items on supermarket shelves as well.
>
> Income makes a difference in how women economize, or try to. Those in families with incomes below $5,000 per year said they have initiated new economies this year, presumably because their budget is already stretched to the limit.
>
> Women with incomes above $5,000 say they are doing much more comparison shopping and buying of sale items than in the past, while those above $7,000 add that they are buying in quantity and eliminating snack foods more often than women with lower incomes while sharing tactics with the others.
>
> Women from higher-income families, with $15,000 or more, are above average in terms of the proportion who do comparison shopping and buy at discount stores, say the surveys.
>
> The proportion of non-white women who economize was above average. Generally, says these reports, they are more likely to use meat substitutes such as casseroles to stretch the food budget and are less likely to buy in quantity. Non-whites are also above average in the proportion who shop for sales and use coupons for non-food items.
>
> Is all this a temporary phenomenon? "As long as the cost of living continues its inflationary trends, consumers are going to remain extremely cost-conscious," says Foote, Cone & Belding. That could keep the ladies on alert for quite some time.[6]

9

The Pulse of the People

> Without due recognition of crowd thinking, our theories of economics leave much to be desired.
> *Bernard M. Baruch*

As noted in the previous chapter, modern technology has redefined a crowd, though crowds still act in ways known to tradition. Persons no longer need to be in physical contact (e.g., ghetto riot, religious revival meeting) to get the "crowd feel" or to react with a sense of "oneness" in decision making (e.g., Wall Street).

If most people "feel" things are good they aggregate these feelings and buy stocks. Any good economic news that promises an individual more for his buck is bound to register favorably; news that bodes less for the buck is bad news. Economic news is pocketbook close. For example, the cost of living index and percentages of unemployed are numbers which touch consumers directly or indirectly. Yet, the news that these numbers are rising at *slower rates* is less important to the average man than his pragmatic, pocketbook experience that they are *still rising;* his wife reminds him of this every time she returns from the supermarket and he knows it when he pays for movie tickets. Even their children become very cost conscious and shop like rag merchants (try raising the price on a popular fad-type child's toy; the feed-back is astounding); those first seeing an increase in price rapidly tell their friends—and so on.

To play games with the vast American consuming public today at the national level by juggling numbers leaves the real decision makers insulted and unreceptive to the wishes of the power people when attempts are made to get them to spend or to save.

Selective perception is another aspect of our economic life this book has emphasized. As William James said:

> Consciousness is always interested more in one part of its object than in another, and welcomes and rejects, or chooses, all the while it thinks. . . .
>
> But we do far more than emphasize things, and unite some, and keep others apart. We actually ignore most of the things before us. We notice only those sensations which are signs to us of things which happen practically or aesthetically to interest us. . . .
>
> In a world of objects thus individualized by our mind's selective industry, what is called our "experience" is almost entirely determined by our habits of attention. A thing may be present to a man a hundred times, but if he persistently fails to notice it, it cannot be said to enter into his experience [e.g., consumer sentiment indexes and behavioral economics].[1]

Objects which violate our established habits of perception are simply not taken into account at all. Thus, Institutional Managers are by training conditioned to a world of numbers: earnings per share, dollar sales, tons of coal, tubes of toothpaste, etc.—and the "invisible programmer," the average mass consumer who buys these things, is not "seen."

What we think about the future is an important factor in what kind of a future there will be as far as the stock market and the economy are concerned. How the consumer sees tomorrow today will ultimately affect production plans, plant expansion, and other capital outlays. The results of a single consumer's thinking, multiplied by millions, can have a dramatic effect. If most people *think* the economy is going to get better, it probably *will* get better, and if they *think* it will get worse, it probably *will*. This we call self-fulfilling prophecy.

The state of the consumer's thinking determines whether he will spend his money or save, whether he will assume a debt to buy something or put off the purchase (increasing disposable income permits this). The state of mind of the consumer affects what economists call discretionary income, that is, what is left over after basic costs (food, housing, clothing) and taxes.

Wall Street's view, however, often runs differently. When the public was in the market and got very jittery, many big investors felt most secure about stepping in. They reasoned that under such conditions, stock was moving out of weak hands and into the portfolios of strong, informed holders. In other words, "consumer psychology" was applied inversely. The institutional track record of the 1966–1967 and 1969–1970 stock market would indicate this view to be in error; but to err is human, we are reminded.

Expectations play an important role in the demand for money (and securities); certainly a root cause of future failure is built into erroneous "expectations." For instance, in July 1968, in a discussion of this subject, the New York First National City Bank's *Monthly Economic Letter* commented on the outlook for capital spending:

> In recent quarters manufacturers have persistently and considerably overestimated what they would spend for capital formation. Past plant and equipment spending continues to show up in enlarged capacity, and the overall plant utilization rate has not changed significantly since late last year. As long as that rate hovers at around 85% compared with more than 90% two years ago, it requires fairly robust sales expectations to induce a much larger volume of plant and equipment formation. Thus far manufacturers have not been convinced that such expectations are warranted.

On July 1, 1970, the *Wall Street Journal* reported in a front-page story entitled "Cautious Consumers":

> Most American families are managing their financial affairs better than many of the nation's largest corporations.
>
> So claim many economists who study consumer debt, savings and spending. The comparison may be unflattering for some chieftains of U.S. industry. But analysts say [here expectations come into play] the relatively sound financial position of most consumers could help bolster the sagging economy in coming months. Indeed, many economists predict consumer spending will help revive general business activity later this year.

Why were they so very wrong, as reflected by late 1970, when the economy continued to sag as the consumer continued to save (1.3% more than in 1969, about $7 billions)? Especially why in the light of a previously published National Industrial Conference Board survey which noted early 1970 attitudes?

> Out of 10,000 families surveyed in March and April, 19% of the sample think that business conditions are "bad," up from 16% in a comparable survey in January and February.[2]

A reasonable answer would seem to indicate that most analysts and economists are not "tuned in" to the "average consumer." Life styles, occupations, and such strongly influence their individual or group "expectations."

As an instance of this, a Conference Board analyst stated:

> "The thing that counts is the consumer's actual financial position, not what the surveys tell about his morale." [The *WSJ* article continued:] Accordingly, . . . consumer spending in coming months should constitute a strong "plus" for the economy.
>
> Among those who attach considerable importance to the consumer's role in coming months are economists at U.S. Economics Corp., a New York based consulting service. "The time has come to stop thinking and talking recession and to begin taking account of the developing signs of increased business strength," the service stated in a recent report to clients. The most encouraging sign of business improvement, the report went on, is that the average consumer should soon begin "to buy more closely in line with his rising income."

The Spanish say, "The last thing we give up is hope."

These examples bring to the fore the wide discrepancy that always exists in "expectations." Time and again expectations are in error; especially is this true on Wall Street where error in expectations cause catastrophy.

Wall Street's view of expectations is seen in this *Wall Street Journal* story of January 11, 1971:

> The opinion that there's a "correction" in the stock market's future is gaining currency on Wall Street. Expectations of such a temporary pull-back stem from the market's sharp

> climb during the final weeks of 1970. After spurting nearly 88 points since mid-November, the Dow Jones industrial average reached a recovery high of 842 on Dec. 29, 1970.
>
> Stock prices, said one analyst, go up for two reasons, both of which are present: One, he explains, is an expansive monetary policy, "and when money is flooding in and business isn't using all that is available, then some leaks into the stock market." The other is the creating of expectations by everyone of increases in earnings. "Everyone is accepting the expansionist philosophy as the Government's new policy. And every analyst is in the process of projecting earnings of his favorite company into the anticipated expanded economy of 1972 and is concluding the stock is a bargain. As the stock market goes up, people will feel richer and will tend to spend on non-necessities. Consumer's psychology will be better. . . . The current market isn't characterized by speculation because the public is still 'mostly bearish'."

The Continental Illinois National Bank (Chicago), in their *Continental Comment* economic news letter for September 29, 1967, viewed expectations then as follows:

> Generally expectations have concerned: the size and timing of a tax increase, the method of financing the deficit, the renewed vigor in the economy, the influence of the auto strike, loan demand this fall, the question of inflation, and speculation as to changes in monetary posture—just to name a few.

Conspicuously absent from this Big Bank's expectation list is the *consumer*. Apparently at Continental they still believe H. L. Mencken's apothegm: "No one ever went broke underestimating the average American's intelligence." The Bank continued:

> Now a paradox . . . is developing. The Federal Reserve has pursued a vigorous easy money policy since late last fall, and since January bank reserves have increased at a 9% compound annual rate almost twice the rate of 1965 and mid-1966 and four times the rate of 1964. In spite of the abundant availability of funds and the large increase in bank credit, primarily from investments, long rates have continued to move steadily upward to record levels, and recently rates in the short markets, especially the 90 day Treasury bill, have also climbed sharply. These unorthodox

> movements in interest rates show how important the expectational factor, fired by various rumors, can be at times in determining the level and structure of interest rates.

This provides an interesting example, too, of how expectations are frequently distorted in real life.

Behavioral excesses of Money Managers are repeated time and again. Money Managers' expectations of ever increasing profits are reflected in the securities markets; prices of stocks become higher than they would normally be in order to reflect the level of current dividend income they produce, and become tied to the entire "growth" idea with the huge multiples in earnings per share (100 times earnings and such). With the focus on the latter, sight is lost of the central issue: inadequate consumer demand in conjunction with top-heavy capital structure now loaded with interest charges. When these payments are missed, due to decreasing cash flows, then the roof caves in. Expectations of future growth are destroyed. At this time the high multiples per share vanish into thin air as panic selling takes place, and, to quote a cliche, "financial houses are put in order."

Someday there will come a realization among Money Men that the minimum rate of profit that businesses must have to continue investing and operating is not the 20+% return on investment capital that GM earns, but a more "normal" return of 8-12%. Greater than this is a ripoff. Money Men must also come to recognize the level at which plant and machinery investment are greatly in excess of the consumer's ability to purchase the goods that can be ground out. An interesting example of this discrepancy occurred late in 1972: Factories were operating at approximately 84% of capacity, but business was planning an expenditure of some $130 billions for 1973 in order to increase production with more and better machines. Plant expansion at a time of idle plant capacity! Waste and nonsense.

Expectations become disproportionately large, but in a behavioral sense this is normal among Money Men—because to them the whole machine must always go *up*. In observing human behavior in Wall Street, this disproportionate rise in expectations seems always to come first, but despite this it is not "seen" by Money Managers, because they are living in a different world. The moment their behavioral excesses commence, unseen countervailing forces are at work to destroy them. These forces (the consumer and his behavior) are what we must understand.

Easy money is seen on Wall Street as a source of future corporate profits. This perception in the marketplace leads to rampant speculation (and peculation) which is then seen as "the market is showing great strength" (especially is this true after the stock market has been greatly depressed). Speculation and strength are seen to be the same, though obviously they are not.

How do the masses of the people, by contrast, "see" easy money? Until it is manifested in lower prices for the things they buy, it is not seen by them at all; and until prices finally fall, they resist buying. The masses of the people, except in the purchase of a house or an automobile, are seemingly oblivious of the economic impact of the price of money—interest. What they pay in interest, with the exceptions noted, is ignored; what they receive grabs their attention.[3]

We do learn by experience, but yet every new experience must be absorbed under the same old head. We have our mental filters which often screen out deleterious news, and we frequently repeat an action which we have previously suffered and swore we would not repeat. William James again:

> Most of us grow more and more enslaved to the stock conceptions with which we have once become familiar, and less and less capable of assimilating impression in any but the old ways. . . . Old foggism is the inevitable terminus to which life sweeps us on.[4]

As Harold Leavitt says:

> Most of us recognize that the world-as-we-see-it is not necessarily the same as the world-as-it-"really"-is. Our answer depends on what we heard, not on what was really said. The housewife buys what she likes best, not what is best. Whether we feel hot or cold depends on us, not on the thermometer. The same job may look like a good job to one of us and a sloppy job to another.[5]

Or in Joseph Pearce's words: "Our world view is bound by our world-to-view."

Kenneth Boulding has used the notion of "image" to characterize how we view the world.

> Behavior depends on the image. . . . Knowledge has an

> implication of validity, of truth. What I am talking about is what I believe to be true: my subjective knowledge. It is this image that largely governs my behavior. . . .
>
> What, however, determines the image? . . . The image is built up as a result of all past experience of the possessor of the image. Part of the image is the history of the image itself.[6]

Even James' "quality of voluminousness" envelops us. Though he emphasized this in a physical sense (that of sensations—"the entrance into a warm bath gives our skin a more massive feeling than the prick of a pin."[7]), this phenomenon becomes a center of attention in Wall Street as expressed in stock market volume. Some abstruse individuals who manipulate numbers on the Street and who prefer to be called "market technicians" or, more recently, "computer selectionists," attribute a kind of reverence to volume.

Another trap we often fall into is forgetting that all words are abstractions. They are not the object or the event itself; words only refer to something else. As words get farther from the object or the event, their meanings become more difficult to maintain and to transmit, and their value as instruments for communication decreases.

That Wall Streeters believe their own propaganda seems apparent, but perhaps worse is that what Wall Streeters believe tends to lead hapless others to believe the same thing. Thus, errors in judgment gather unreal dimensions as they move the market up or down. Wall Street deals frequently in pseudo-events.

Daniel J. Boorstin characterizes a pseudo-event as follows:

> 1) It is not spontaneous, but comes about because someone has planned, planted or incited it. Typically, it is not a train wreck or an earthquake, but an interview.
>
> 2) It is planted primarily (not always exclusively) for the immediate purpose of being reported or reproduced. Therefore, its occurrence is arranged for the convenience of the reporting or reproducing media. Its success is measured by how widely it is reported. The question "Is it real?" is less important than "Is it newsworthy?"
>
> 3) Its relation to the underlying reality of the situation is ambiguous. Its interest arises largely from this very ambiguity. Concerning a pseudo-event the question "What does it mean?" has a new dimension.

> 4) Usually it is intended to be a self-fulfilling prophecy. The hotel's thirtieth-anniversary celebration, by saying that the hotel is a distinguished institution, actually makes it one.
>
> In the last half century a larger and larger proportion of our experience, of what we read and see and hear, has come to consist of pseudo-events. We expect more of them and are given more of them. They flood our consciousness. . . .
>
> By this new Gresham's law of American public life, counterfeit happenings tend to drive spontaneous happenings out of circulation.[8]

The stock market, supercharged as it is with emotions, is especially subject to the extra emotional impact of pseudo-events. News that it is thought will affect security prices, such as a raising or lowering of interest rates, is frequently timed for release after the market closes, to minimize its impact that day; or before the market opens, to maximize its impact the next day. For example, in the spring of 1968, when President Lyndon B. Johnson announced a halt to bombing in Vietnam and his intention not to run for reelection, he chose a Sunday. August 15, 1971, the date of President Nixon's economic message on price and wage controls, was a Sunday.

The pseudo-event: On August 25, 1970 the *Los Angeles Times* headlined a front-page story: "Nixon Aides See Economic Upturn." The report continued:

> President gets encouraging report for balance of the year.
>
> Paul W. McCracken, chairman of the Council of Economic Advisers told newsmen what he had told the President:
>
> "Generally, we felt that the evidence we are looking at now is encouraging. . . . It has been possible to cool off a highly overheated domestic economy without throwing the economy into a very sharp recession or depression.

The event: By year-end 1970 unemployment had risen to 6% and inflation continued at the rate it had been two years earlier. The GNP actually fell for the first time in twelve years and the Industrial Production Index continued downward.

For better or worse, the level of the stock market serves as a broad gauge to the average man as to the economic health of the economy. When he perceives it rising, it is "good"; when it falls, it is "bad." But with an innate sense of financial balance reflected, for instance, in his personal finances and their management, he is *not* inclined to spend or save until *his own* little world measures up to *his* expectations. If unemployment and inflation continue in the face of a rising stock market, the consumer (with growing disposable personal income) will not spend (he can save), since Wall Street is far removed from his pocketbook and unemployment and inflation are as close as his corner supermarket.

But the average man does not have an easy time of it keeping track of real events and pseudo-events. In an electronic age both kinds of events are instantly and voluminously transmitted and received—and often perceived with significant impact. Vivid images themselves too frequently overshadow pale reality. Boorstin speaks to this situation:

> The new power to report and portray what had happened was a new temptation leading newsmen to make probable images or to prepare reports in advance of what was expected to happen. As so often, men came to mistake their power for their necessities.
>
> Then came round-the-clock media. The news gap became so narrow that in order to have additional "news" for each new edition or each new broadcast it was necessary to plan in advance the stages by which any available news would be unveiled. . . . It was increasingly necessary that the news constantly change or at least seem to change.
>
> News gathering turned into news making.
>
> The American citizen thus lives in a world where fantasy is more real than reality, where the image has more dignity than its original. . . . We have become eager accessories to the great hoaxes of the age. These are the hoaxes we play on ourselves.[9]

News flashes across the desks and the minds of people on Wall Street in a torrent, and in the emotional background of the market itself the news is rarely weighed, evaluated, or reasoned; it is simply transformed, without thought, into "buy" or "sell." It is only later that the pseudo-event is realized to be just that; too late the event transcends. Then as surely as the clock turns, pseudo-event will become a new "event."

Wall Street abhors "dead time." The nature of the business is speed. Prices of stocks and bonds oscillate with astonishing rapidity. To prevent being trapped, participants must be able to separate pseudo-events from real events, to dig through the morass of numbers in search of reality. The underlying truths will ultimately prevail. The market does indeed respond to pseudo-events, but in the long run the basic substance of the economy governs the outcome, and the consumer—his attitudes and his behavior—is at the root of this.

Sometime late in 1970 the Money Manager's in-house economists "found" the consumer. He was discovered because he was not spending like he was supposed to. Without looking for the reasons behind the consumer's lack of spending confidence, the experts decreed that spending by the consumer was just around the corner: he always had spent and he always would. Perhaps because they had just really discovered the consumer for the first time and were therefore inexperienced in understanding him, their forecasts proved in error. Here is the way the *Wall Street Journal* reported the matter on January 25, 1971:

> Many money managers are counting on the consumer to play a leading role in the comeback of the economy and the stock market.
>
> "We are looking for the consumer to be the driving force that will move the economy ahead and give us a fairly good recovery," asserts Edward N. Button, executive vice president and chief of the investment management division of Anchor Corp., which runs Fundamental Investors and five other mutual funds with assets of $1.8 billion. He explains: "We think the economy has bottomed out and started up. And we hope the improvement in retail sales that began in the second half of December and is continuing this month is what we were looking for."
>
> This pickup in consumer spending has helped make Anchor "quietly optimistic about the economy." It expects the recovery to be "a reasonable one, but not as dynamic" as in some previous recoveries, Mr. Button says. And, he adds, it anticipates "some slowing of inflation, but no significant decline in the rate of unemployment before the second half of 1971." However, he suggests that "we could be setting the stage for the continuation of the economic recovery into 1972 at a sustainable rate."
>
> What this means for stock prices, he states, is that "the general trend of the market could be upward for quite a

long period of time, provided you don't get too much speculation or enthusiasm in either the economy or the market." But he quickly adds: "Obviously there are going to be periods of correction and weakness. And it wouldn't surprise us to see a relatively mild correction at any time."

An improving business picture with an upturn in consumer spending the "key" factor also is foreseen by Landon T. Clay, vice president of the $40 million Vance, Sanders Special Fund. "We think consumer psychology will be improving through the year and we see some indication of it right now in the retail figures," he asserts. Argus Research Corp. notes that in the four weeks ended Jan. 9 retail sales showed a year-to-year gain of 5.9% compared with a rise of only 1.9% in the four weeks ended Dec. 12; and, excluding food stores and auto dealers, retail sales in the Dec. 13-Jan. 9 period were up 8.7% against a 5.5% gain in the prior four weeks.

Although the recovery may be slow, says Mr. Clay, "the direction is unmistakable and it's clear that the Administration very much wants business to improve." Helping to spur the turnabout, he explains, are the increase in liquidity of banks and the lower interest rates that "make corporations more willing to rebuild inventories." He expects "better corporate earnings" to appear in the latter part of the year.

"The combination of better profits and lower interest rates should lead to higher stock market prices," he suggests. "As yields of interest-sensitive securities [such as bonds] go down, the price earnings multiples of stocks should improve."

One factor that represents potential support for the stock market is "the pessimism and skepticism that still holds many investors in their grip," contends Robert S. Waill, vice president of Inverness Counsel Inc. These investors' eventual return to the market will greatly bolster a recovery, he indicates.

One place where this skepticism remains entrenched is in the ranks of small investors. This is apparent in the pattern of odd-lot tranactions. During the final weeks of 1970 the odd-lotter sold about twice as many shares as he bought. He has continued selling on balance this month, although at a reduced rate of somewhat more than 1½ shares sold for each one being bought.

To watch "retail sales" totals is very often deceptive. For one thing, within "retail sales" the all important service sector is not weighed (statistically) significantly enough; furthermore, in our Service Economy "retail sales" account for only $.45 of every dollar spent. For another, some components are far more "sensitive" to consumer spending than others. Finally, the "year-to-year gain of 5.6% reported above was a net *loss,* since it represented price inflation and not goods.

Landon T. Clay "expects 'better corporate earnings' to appear" later in the year. The market did rise strongly during this period partly because of expectations (misplaced expectations, but expectations nonetheless). However, the profits expected later could not in fact appear until *much* later; presumably this was not perceived.

Finally, odd-lotters' transactions, though closer to mass reactions, are not mass reactions, since the masses own almost no stock directly.

In actual fact, the consumer began to spend again a year later, in January 1972. It was in the main spending on the cuff: huge extensions of credit allowed the consumer to purchase automobiles, homes, and durable goods. The $10,000-income consumer did not have cash at this time, but those who control his financial destiny were eager to extend credit.

Back to 1971: the *Wall Street Journal* carried another article that same day, January 25, 1971:

> Businessmen in coming weeks will be watching eagerly for signs to bear out the many forecasts that consumers will provide the main propellant to economic recovery in 1971. Also getting close attention will be trends in wage settlements and other costs of doing business. A look at some aspects of consumer behavior and corporate costs shows there's room for optimism and pessimism on both sides.
>
> "Almost without exception, forecasts of the U.S. economy for 1971 have looked to the consumer to lead a recovery movement," says Raymond J. Saulnier, a professor of economics at Columbia University and former chairman of the President's Council of Economic Advisers. A Reynolds & Co. survey headline terms 1971 "The Year of the Consumer." Robert B. Johnson, economist at Paine, Webber, Jackson & Curtis, figures a rise in consumer spending of about 7.5% this year will provide the "major stimulus" to recovery.

The consumer, of course, is the giant spender in the economy, accounting for over 60% of gross national product. And he is being cast as a hero of the economy at a time when some other sectors of spending—notably those of business and the Federal Government—aren't expected to post sizeable increases.

Consumers, who have shown restraint in spending since mid-1969, have the capacity to spend more. Although personal income rose only 7% in 1970, the rate of increase in income after taxes in the first half, before the auto strike, was the highest since 1948. Personal savings of over $50 billion in 1970 were up a whopping 35%.

Savings have been running at the rate of 7.3% of after-tax [disposable] income, up from the average 6% rate of the 1960s. With disposable income reaching an annual rate of nearly $700 billion, a decline of one percentage point in the savings rate would mean an additional $7 billion in consumer spending.

Moreover, spendable income this year will be augmented by as much as $10 billion resulting from reductions in income taxes and increases in Federal workers' pay and in Social Security benefits.

But what about consumers' willingness to spend? Here, economic analysis moves into an area of sentiment and attitudes. "The economy is more than a mechanism," notes the Council of Economic Advisers. "Consumer behavior has been especially difficult to predict in recent years, and may be more complex than had been thought previously."

Surveys on consumer confidence and buying intentions are far from scientific and are sometimes contradictory. A recent Conference Board survey found six-month buying plans down considerably from a year ago. But, based on a Census Bureau survey, the Commercial Credit Co. forecasts first-half spending up 17% for new cars and 21% for single-family houses.

The unpredictability of consumers was demonstrated in 1968. The 10% surtax imposed in mid-year was expected to cut spending and ease the inflationary pressures of high demand. Instead, consumers went on a buying binge, drawing heavily on savings.

There's a widely held notion that consumers who expect prices to rise will try to beat inflation by buying in advance. Actually, rapid price increases, as in the past year, often seem to stimulate savings. For many, rainy days seem to spur incentive to maintain the purchasing power of savings

> in event of even rainer days.
>
> Over the long run, it can be argued, it's plausible that consumers would save more of their incomes. The number of affluent families is rising steadily and studies indicate the affluent tend to save larger shares of their incomes than do poorer families.
>
> But, for now, postwar history is persuasive. The high savings rate is unlikely to persist, and that's a big plus for the outlook.

The article fails to note evidence available but not "seen": In 1968 the consumer prepared for the surcharge and reserved money to pay it—then continued to spend, thus dealing a mortal blow to its intent. "Surveys . . . are far from scientific" seems to too easily minimize consumer sentiment indexes; the evidence simply urges that those that work should be used—and there are such consumer confidence surveys which can be integrated into a consistently and fruitfully workable system.

On August 4, 1972, the *Wall Street Journal* carried this front-page view of the consumer:

> CONTRARY CONSUMERS
>
> They Step Up Outlays Though
> Their Worries About Economy Persist
>
> Polls Show Public Is still Pessimistic
> on Inflation, General Trend of Business
>
> "But, I'm Doing All Right"
>
> When you're worried about inflation, unemployment and whom George McGovern will pick for his running mate, you're not likely to rush out to buy a new car, a lawn mower or a double-knit suit, the theory has it.
>
> But the theory is wrong.
>
> Most recent consumer polls indicate that the public is still totally unconvinced that inflation is disappearing. Consumers also worry about politics and joblessness and, on balance, see almost as much bad as good in the general business situation.

Consumers do ignore storm signals, though. But years of steady erosion of their standard of living caused by inflation and taxes caused even the sturdiest to grow reckless and say, quite literally, "To hell with the consequences. I know I won't live forever." So he went further in debt—with high cost credit insurance, naturally, to protect his heirs (and the Money Men).

During 1969 and late into 1970, the consumer saved and paid off his debts. His disposable income rose 14% in 1970 to $700 billion; yet, installment debt had fallen more than it had since 1942; savings accounts were rising late in 1970, at a rate two times that of the previous five years.

Consumers can spend; *and* consumers can *save*. The power of "easy money" is transferred, then, from the reservoirs, the banks, to the *people*. People Money Power waxes even larger in a Service Society, since services are where the action is.

It was never planned to give the masses this power (though Status Quo Wisdom said so); it was, in fact, reserved for the Power Elite.

10

The Consumer of Stocks

> It's a good thing to turn your mind upside down now and then, like an hourglass, to let the particles run the other way.
>
> *Christopher Morley*

Buying or selling stocks is often thought to be something apart from buying or selling services and goods. This attitude seems illogical, since it would appear that the findings of marketing and motivational wisdom apply with equal vigor in buying and selling securities.

This brings back again the concept of "perception": we very often perceive what we *want* to see. With security prices we *want* to see them rise, but we may not see that the basic causes for making them rise do not exist. Economists fighting inflation see a temporary slowdown as a final result, given a time lag. The "slowness" exists in the eye of the expert, but not in the eye of the inexpert (he "sees" inflation ended when the price he pays for something today is no higher than it was last week).

Our perception is based on:

1. Stimulus factors: e.g., power words.
2. Individual factors: the character of the person "perceiving" plus his past experience. (Can a person who has never experienced panic, except in reading about it, perceive it?)

Before our perception can be aroused, attention must be aroused—in the securities markets attention given to a stock. The stock may even be a gift from someone, or a potential buyer may be given "insider" information. In any case, his focus is centered on that stock. Attention also comes into play in stock market trends—moves of ± 12%. Most day-to-day stock market moves are too small, not "eye-catching"; and with no attention, no perception.

Motion produces attention—sharp, fast rises of stock prices; abrupt drops.

An announcement by a prominent person, especially with the use of radio and TV, usually gets attention. The message (with appropriate power words) attracts attention: interest is centered, perception may be altered. We also "perceive by exception"—e.g., the death of a President, the invasion of Cambodia; then the perception causes havoc with stock prices.

But even with attention aroused we do not always *see* the situation. There is the phenomenon of negative adaptation: After a period of unchanging application, a stimulus may cease to produce its characteristic sensation. We develop a new adaptation level; we become satiated. Vietnam war news is a classic example.

Our lack of true perception may also encourage a vicious circle. During the late 1960s and into the 1970s, we saw rises and falls of security prices which became traumatic for those owning the stocks. This may well reflect our unwillingness to recognize basic changes which have occurred in our society and our economy—the wiping out of scarcity and its replacement with abundance, Buckminster Fuller's "more with less," etc. Our myopia, our fixation on Status Quo Economics, has led us, Robert Theobald concludes, on a path toward "increasingly wild fluctuations" on the stock market. He argues:

> The stock market is sheltered from any serious examination by a collection of long-established screens, among them slogans put out by the stock exchange appealing to the public's desire to promote growth ("Become an owner of American industry"), and the advertising of those concerned with persuading individuals to buy and sell stocks. . . . In effect, the operations of the stock market are presented to the public as essential to the financial health and economic growth of the nation. . . .
>
> In effect, then, the stock market is little more than a method of moving the right to an income on capital from one person to another and predominantly from one rich

person to another. For although it has been estimated that at least 15,000,000 Americans own stocks and shares, the vast majority of holdings are very small and almost all wealth is concentrated in a few hands: in 1953 just over 1 per cent of the population—about 1,800,000 people—held 80 per cent of all corporate stocks and virtually all state and local bonds.

Given that the transfer of the right to income is the major role remaining to the stock market, can we expect it to continue to fulfill this function in an orderly manner? In order to answer this question, we must understand the process by which the value of shares is set. It rests on a foundation little more substantial than the belief of stockholders as to what the value should be. Indeed, in most cases the connection will be even more tenuous than this, for the stockholder's valuation of a stock will be based not on what he thinks it is worth but on his best estimate of the level that interested parties would assume to be appropriate, since it is at this level that the stock will actually be bought and sold. The process of autointoxication seems almost limitless. The price of the stocks of any specific company can rise to dizzy heights for a period without producing any increase in offers to sell, because everybody will hold on to the stocks, feeling sure that all the other interested parties are *convinced* that the situation is viable. . . .

The fact [is] that the stock market, like all nineteenth- and early twentieth-century institutions, is conceptualized as functioning in conditions of scarcity.

The coming of abundance destroys its viability, for its primary function was to allocate *scarce* capital. In today's conditions, when capital is no longer scarce, its functioning is inappropriate. An immense volume of savings is generated every year by private individuals, pension funds, payments for insurance, payments to mutual funds; all this money seeks profitable investment. Depending on the views about profitable investments held by those with control over funds, money can be invested through the stock market in marketive shares, which are risky because they are liable to sharp increases and decreases in price, but which have the prospect of providing the greatest gains in value. . . .

Abundance reduces the value of money as well as of all ecofacts [services and goods]. If the stock market is to carry out its traditional role it should recognize this fact. This would mean that the yields from shares would decline sharply. Such a result appears unlikely because the over-

> whelming message conveyed by the financial community is still the shortage of capital, a message which is reinforced by the government's determination to use a high level of interest rates to protect the balance of payments position of the United States. In reality, the equilibrium rate of interest, and therefore the value of capital, in the United States is only a fraction of the present level maintained by the government.
>
> If the stockholder fails to understand this implication of abundance, his actions will necessarily become increasingly unrelated to the realities of the situation. . . . Waves of optimism and pessimism, unrelated to the facts, would sweep through the market and increasingly wild fluctations in the stock averages would occur.[1]

The use of words frequently transforms the word into the event. Mass media will not allow the stock market to just rise or fall—it must "surge" ahead (up 5 points) or "plunge" (off 5 points). All of the cliches and power words are reintroduced again and again: bold headlines, radio blasts, TV newsmen with charts (drawn to distort the minimal). Wall Streeters daily invent word explanations of stock market behavior; the fluctuations in securities values must somehow be explained and justified. These verbal inventions are then dispatched to newspapers and other media to cover the nation. With the power of words, the event then takes on the character of the words; for example, when the quantity of money is increased, this becomes a signal for "easy money" and "good times" and stocks rocket up. The rise then becomes "reality" in the minds of those exposed to the inventions, and the spectacle, which by now it is, assumes unwarranted dimensions; these in turn all too often influence the behavior of investors (including the inventors who receive their own words, now distorted, in feedback) and the result is ultimate financial chaos.

We become word distorted. False images add up to an apocalyptic crisis. We are overwhelmed, inundated by words, words, words. Power words no longer have power. Art Buchwald capsuled the problem in one of his inimitable columns:

Overkill In Superlatives
Is Most Popular Trend Ever

The President, whether he likes it or not, is the trendsetter in this country, and when he speaks in superlatives, it is no surprise that everyone starts picking up the habit.

I imagine the first time we knew we had a President who pulls out all stops was after our astronauts landed on the moon. The President was quoted as saying:

"This is the greatest week in the history of the world since the creation."

Then, last week [January 1971], before he gave his State of the Union speech, the President called it "the most far-reaching, the most bold program in the domestic field ever presented to an American Congress."

This kind of talk cannot but affect all American families.

For example, the other night, just as our family sat down to dinner , my wife announced, "I hope everyone has washed his hands, because I have cooked the greatest meal ever served in the Western Hemisphere."

"That's good," I said, "because I've had the hardest day anyone has has ever had since Gutenberg invented the printing press."

My 15-year-old daughter said, "We had the worst test in school today since the Spanish Inquisition." . . .

My wife said, "After the most delicious apple pie anyone has ever tasted, I want every one to help me with the largest pile of dirty dishes I've ever seen."

There were the loudest screams of protests ever uttered by an American family, but no one could escape.

Then we all went into the living room to watch President Nixon give his "State of the Union" speech which Atty. Gen. John N. Mitchell described as "the most important document since they wrote the Constitution."[2]

Sometimes it seems as if Wall Street is dealing in pseudo-event securities. Institutional advertising or executives addressing groups of financial analysts develop for the audiences images that may have no relation to the content of the message or, worse, to the strengths and weaknesses of the business institution. Americans are faddists, and security traders, hooked on images, become obsessed at times with "chicken stocks" or with free champagne and red carpets on airlines as the "stocks of tomorrow." In marketing behavior, for example, women in our culture have been more receptive than men to pictures of babies; in buying securities, stock buyers have been, for instance, often more receptive to IBM than a competitor, due to IBM's "cleaner image": spare logotype, antiseptic machines and buildings, conservative dress of personnel. In other words, the consumption of stocks often revolves around the attention-getting value of various securities. Every person has an attention threshold for each of his senses. The greater the intensity and clamor for attention among many stimuli in a given area, the more dramatic must be a stimulus just to be noticed. In a rapidly rising stock market, securities may have to double in price—small rises are not perceived; hence, the temptation to manipulate prices by insiders to achieve this, a practice as old as the stock market itself. It is because of this that we view stock prices on an absolute basis rather than a percentage basis. Common practice and tradition dictate that we talk in so many points or dollars, not percentages: the market, when quoted, moves so many points, not fractions of a percent; the latter would quite obviously be perceived as too small.

To repeat this chapter's opening thesis, securities should be thought of as commodities. We should understand that, behaviorally, persons relate to buying and selling stocks the way they relate to buying and selling other commodities. Some customers, for example, are very worried when making the final decision to buy stocks (or high-priced goods); brokers try to overcome anxiety or resistance with honey-like reassurances. When persons sell, taking a loss, they dread it. The dread often prompts postponement of the decision (to lose money) until the bitter end, so mass selling on a sharp fall in prices is not uncommon. A principal motivation for buying stock is, of course, a tangible return, a monetary gain—buy low, sell high. But, as with the purchase of other services and goods, stocks are bought for a mixture of reasons: social status (associates or neighbors are "in the market"), future security (especially among upper income individuals), personal interest or self-realization (amusement, gamesmanship, hobby, curiosity). Purchases of securities are quickly rationalized. Think of the reasons a husband uses to overcome family resistance to his buying a sports car. Often stock purchases are kept from the family until a gain is made. We also rationalize by stating that many people are buying "our" stock. But many people also suffer from hemorrhoids.

In the final purchase decision, rational economic objectives often dim and social and psychological satisfactions loom large. The same orientations toward shopping in a store appear to exist in the securities market as well; we find at least five types of buyers:

1. economic—the tough customers
2. personalized—"I buy what my broker tells me."
3. ethical—"My banker thought it a good buy."
4. apathetic—"I don't care what it is; buy something."
5. impatient—"Get it over with quick."

Studies indicate that in purchases other than stocks "rational" behavior is found only about 20% of the time. When we remember that stock buying is, behaviorally, like other buying, we recognize that about 80% of securities purchases are probably made "irrationally." This sort of puzzling behavior has been ascribed generally to emotions, impulse, habit (cf. boardroom sitters), newness to the marketplace (cf. first time at a race track and at a broker's office: almost the same).

In other words, there is a tendency to buy "images" and "package design," ignoring the basic economics involved. As in the supermarket, purchases are very often based on rhyme, not reason.

Why do some people like risky stocks? For the same reason that some people work harder on tasks where the probabilities of success are fewer: if success does come, it represents a great achievement to them.

An important factor in stock buying, of course, concerns the rate of saving of the customers. A prospect irrevocably committed to saving his money obviously is not a prospect. Psychologically, people have conditioned themselves quite differently than economists tell us. As noted, economists, all vintages, state that people can always be counted on to spend, that they never go on strike, that time has indicated more or less regular savings rates, that if savings should jump up it is "unusual" and people will revert to a "normal spending pattern," and that finally after any prolonged savings period there will be a sharp spending spree. But people don't behave like they are supposed to behave: Most times when affluent people form a habit for savings to meet an objective, they continue, after the objective is reached, to save at the same rate. Because of this, good times and rising corporate profits are not self-perpetuating. This curious behavioral pattern can, unless closely observed, create havoc with securities prices.

The masses of the people, though not owning stock, yet do directly have an effect on the course of large trends in the securities markets. It has been noted that moneyed people, or those dealing with people with money, are very different from the great majority of consumers in psychological-sociological motives. The majority of Americans seem to be inherently conservative in their spending and saving patterns. Since this is true, their optimism or pessimism can more easily be measured. Attitudinal market research is no longer in the diaper stage, although it is often so perceived by financial writers and security analysts; errors in market research are brought forward as proof. However, marketing research successes are swept under the rug by the same groups. Yet, this information—the psychological inputs—is, in the end, more powerful than the numbers orientation that exists. (Numbers are very helpful, however, in separating the wheat from the chaff in individual stock selection.) As a sample of the attitudinal research on consumers, note the Survey Research Center report, "Consumer Buying Habits: Analysis of a Ten-year Study":

> During the past fifteen years or so we have had a substantial price inflation. Has the will to save been impaired by inflation? We find that the American people are aware of the increase in the cost of living. They are even greatly concerned with it and resent it. During several brief periods in the past ten years, inflationary tendencies led to restraint in spending and therefore to higher rates of saving. This happened because the American people never lost their confidence in the essential soundness and stability of the dollar. Even in 1951, following the substantial advances during the Korean war, the majority of people predicted that, in the long run, prices would stabilize or decline somewhat.
>
> A very large majority of people express a preference for government bonds and savings accounts over such investments as common stock and real estate.
>
> Even among people with higher incomes, investments with fixed money value continue to be preferred over other investments with fluctuating money value, although by a much smaller margin than in the lower income groups.

> There is good reason to conclude that the will to save is not likely to be diminished by inflationary tendencies, unless the price advances are larger and more rapid than those which we have experienced.[3]

As inflation hung on in the late 1960s, however, the attitude of Americans changed. A Michigan survey made late in 1970 reported:

> Most Americans believe inflation is relatively painless and are reluctant to make any sacrifices to control it.
>
> Anti-inflationary measures which threaten to bring about unemployment are strongly opposed by most Americans.
>
> Most of the families questioned said they protected themselves against price increase by economizing or postponing certain purchases.
>
> Even though inflation reduces the buying power of fixed savings, consumers found some compensation in the safety of their deposits—no possibility of capital losses—as well as the interest received.[4]

This is, of course, completely contrary to Status Quo Wisdom.

The behavior of large masses of people saving will inevitably, in time, affect corporate profits in a mass consumption society—and consequently security prices. Too much saving is an extraordinary profit and security price depressant.

A psychological dichotomy seems to always arise in an inflationary period: The Money Managers, spurred by easy money and the early rapid rise in corporate profits that accompany this (in the years prior to 1970), begin to move into the market in great strength (as in late 1970 and early 1971). This happened in late 1970 even while the masses were gloomier and gloomier toward future purchases. As the Continental Illinois National Bank and Trust Co. noted in January 1971:

> Consumers aren't yet ready to unleash their much-discussed spending power. . . .
>
> The survey . . . indicates that people think business conditions currently are worse than they were a year ago, that prices will continue to increase, and that the battle against inflation is being lost.
>
> Asked about areas in which they planned to economize or cut down on purchases during 1971, 58% of those polled mentioned entertainment; 52%, clothing; 47%,

> recreation and hobbies; 46%, travel and vacations; and 36%, food.
>
> Some 65% of the families polled said they didn't plan to make any major expeditures this year for a new car, furniture, appliances, color television sets, a new home, or other expensive items. Of those who did plan major purchases, some 60% planned to make payments from current income or cash. Another 20% planned to use bank loans.[5]

Expectations, it has been emphasized, play a large role in economics and stock prices.

Which group, then, will prevail? Answer: The masses who make the profits possible. Profits develop *only* if the scared consumer spends. To "expect" him to spend when surveys of his attitudes indicate he does not intend to, is to invite financial disaster.

What makes a consumer a pinchpenny?

1. Fear of the unknown future.
2. Habit.
3. Future personal planning (regardless of prices).
4. Unemployment (job insecurity that is inherent for most workers).
5. Exogenous events: war, poverty, "public squalor," etc.

People tell their plans, but we persist in theorizing differently:

> Keynes expressed his belief in a "psychological law" that as an individual's income rises, that individual will spend part, but not the whole, of the increase in income on added consumption. Another way of putting this is to say that individuals or society will divide any increase in income into (a) added consumption and (b) added saving. (Since saving is defined as that part of income that is not consumed, a and b will necessarily equal the given increase in income.)[6]

This applied before World War II and in a Production Society. Up until 1969, the ratios obtained. But in 1969 something happened: with *more* income at their disposal consumers decided *not* to spend, and the beautiful theory became bankrupt. Were the old ratios "normal" or simply wedded to an age now gone? "New ideas must go into old heads," William James said.

Credit has been around a long, long time, but in recent years it has acquired a new dress to the point where, with the use of credit cards, for example, money has acquired an even more intangible value: it is now "electronic money." Data machines and computers move money around from here to there. As the Money Managers and the consumer move still further away from the real thing, value, and into electronic money, the "worth" of the latter diminishes and overextensions become much easier with dire consequences almost in direct relation to distance of the transaction from the value of the thing being valued.

Marshall McLuhan has observed:

> Nose-counting, a cherished part of the eighteenth century [is an] ineffectual form of social assessment. . . . The public, in the sense of a great consensus of separate and distinct viewpoints, is finished. Today, the mass audience (the successor to the "public") can be used as a creative, participating force.[7]

This observation can be carried a few steps further. Participation (all-at-onceness) by the masses *has* changed everything, including Wall Street, especially how Wall Street is seen from the "inside" and by the masses "outside." The "insiders" play their own game, as they always have—apart from and oblivious of the "outsiders." The outsiders, possessing the real dollar power, control the Wall Street profit game from just over Wall Street's horizon. While Wall Street is estimating profits, Main Street is estimating survival. The extension of our sense perceptions has altered the way both sides perceive the world, neither "seeing" the other.

The "expert" inside Wall Street is the man who stays put. The amateur "outside" has broken the ground rules, has written new ones, and is player and umpire at the same time.

An American is uniform in his perception of the economic world around him. This attitude, curiously, is a negative attitude toward conformity, not positive:

> He was reared in a tradition which taught that the ideal man chose his life without his knee to convention, and the fact that his ancestors did not necessarily measure up to this ideal is beside the point. His concern is with the fact that *he* does well.
>
> But perhaps the major source of his discontent is the scanty reward he receives through conforming. If the pattern of his life fulfilled him, he would be inclined to

> cherish it. But a growing number of Americans express a sense of emptiness and discontent that sits oddly with the affluent complacency ascribed to them.[8]

It is in large measure because of this that the "controlling" mass spenders are so frequently misread by the mass media, by politicans, and by upper-income Money Managers.

The great majority of Americans are uniform simply "because they conform unwittingly to the prevailing set of beliefs . . . normal neurosis." Louis Wirth observed that "the most important thing . . . we can know about a man is what he takes for granted, and the most elemental and important facts about a society are those that are seldom debated and generally regarded as settled." Such implicit assumptions are the premises from which thought begins, the starting point for any course of action.[9]

The changes in savings rates in recent years can perhaps be attributed to rebellion against "normal neurosis"—an *unwillingness* to accept unemployment as a cost of fighting inflation, coupled with no land to return to. The individual no longer is taking for granted these assumptions, and since these thoughts and actions are now broken, he *changes his* perception and takes on a new dress. Thus disguised, he is not perceived in his new role until too late. Those environmentally removed from the masses "become conscious of the belief they had taken for granted only in the moment they perceive that it is false."[10]

Until the beliefs are challenged, they remain unremarked and unassailable—invisible strait jackets on thought and thus ultimately on action.

Normal human behavior, then, is not natural, but rather habitual behavior that over a period of time has become typical in a particular society. Thus, savings rates in the consumption function have been closely defined and counted on to repeat ad infinitum, i.e., "normally." But late in the 1960s the pattern shifted, the habit was broken. Why? The previously noted tendency to spend more as a function of life style is one reason. Also:

> When normal behaviors leave him deprived [a result of inflation, for example], the adjusted individual is relatively helpless. In the first place, he does not have a clear idea of what he is seeking (e.g., define "a better life"): he has learned a set of customs, not an understanding of hu-

> man needs. In the second place, he has learned to take for granted certain deprivations in certain areas in his life.
>
> The normal neuroses are generally endured, precisely because of their prevalence.[11]

The rising prices of the late 1960s alone almost guaranteed that the consumer would be unwilling to accept additional unknown unbearables, so he saved. Unless recognized and acted on by Money Managers, the result of this behavioral switch will continue to cause financial chaos in securities markets.

If a better informed individual now has enough self-understanding to make a valid choice, he will choose to act in ways which lead to his satisfaction. He can make "valid choices of his behavior in the light of his needs."[12] This is the "awareness of self" observed by David Riesman in *The Lonely Crowd.*

Needs are the mainspring of human behavior. And here the needs of self-image loom large:

1. The need for an acceptable self-image.
2. The need to verify this self-image.
3. The need to expand self through action.

(A distinction: Self: that which the individual is; self-image: his conception of what he is.)[13]

To act effectively, "conceptions of reality must be approximately accurate reflections of reality." Unemployment and its consequences are viewed far more clearly by those closest to it than by those who make it possible.

Corporate profits are viewed in quite the same manner. Therefore, projections of profits (discounting of stock prices) must be "approximately accurate reflections of reality"—not predicated on the theory that "one X" will give a "Y." "One X" may make "many Ys," none of which was expected nor foreseen. More tangibly stated: An easing of money will insure better business in the future when its effect is realized. It may. But it may not. Pseudo-solutions or, at best, quasi-solutions too often result; later they feed back distortions (not solutions), and the distortions set off entirely unexpected chains of events. Wave mechanics (many "Ys") rules now, not Newtonian cause-effect. This significant change is invisible and perhaps is the root source of security forecasting that becomes wrong. The behavior of people is neither "seen" nor weighed.

11

The Black Box Model

> The consumer has more power for good or ill than the voter.
>
> *The Last Whole Earth Catalog*

In the previous chapter we mentioned the rate of savings and noted critically, in passing, that many economists still assume that the amount of money consumers save moves in a constant but narrow range, that for consumers to save more than "normal" is an aberration. There is good reason for this assumption; for many years it was *true*. However, beginning with the 1970s the old pattern broke up. The figures in Table 10 (p. 50) point to this fact. In 1971 savings rose to a record 8.2%. The significance of this pattern change can be seen most quickly by zeroing in on one calculation: A 1% shift in consumer savings rates means from $7 to $8 billions spent or saved; this is a powerful and determining force in the swing of business and the business cycle.

What about this consumer behavior of the early 1970s that created the savings "aberration"? Why did it happen? A speculative answer worth noting is that consumers per se seemed to be employing what corporations have long exercised as their sole prerogative. The consumer was taking advantage of "depreciation" and "retained earnings" from his cash flow.

Depreciation: With more income and a sustained cash flow, the consumer was able to make depreciation work *for* him instead of against him. For example, in the purchase of a new automobile he was able to trade his auto at a time when he could maximize its depreciation rather than be (as most consumers always have been) locked into the arcane depreciation techniques developed to sell new autos.

Retained earnings: As the corporation had long done, the consumer now was able to move an increasing percentage of his income out of the spending cash tributary into a tributary that led to an institution where the money earned money for him. It also provided the cash to retire old debt, thus increasing liquidity. Since the consumer does not yet enjoy the access to the banking system as a last resort place for credit, as the giant corporations do, he made his own place.

This illustration about consumer savings makes again the point which this book has continually emphasized as a major thesis: Status Quo Economics and production-oriented economists are inadequate to analyze and predict economic and business trends in the country. We have examined some of the contexts of this: U.S.A. as Service Economy, consumer sovereignty, etc. Now it is time, in good American cliche slang, to put the money where the mouth is.

Some years ago I concluded that almost all projections of Wall Street stock market prices have, in general and over time, been largely in error. Yet an enormous amount of time and thought have gone into stock market price forecasting by concentrating upon Wall Street, its figures, and so forth. It appeared to me that perhaps the key but neglected area was that of the consuming masses and their behavior—i.e., the human element. It seemed logical, then, to scrutinize "man," not "matter." Most economic and financial analysis, as we have noted, is embedded in quantitative matters which have been counted for so long that it is assumed historical patterns will prevail and repeat. Faith in production numbers and "imaginary numbers" has been given formal credentials in the leading-lagging-coincident-indicators syndrome.

But what if historical relationships decayed? What if "matter" were not central? What if . . .? It was at this point that I began my focus on consumer sovereignty. The problem became how to convert consumer intangibles (his expectations, his attitudes, the images he used, the influence of power words and the mass media upon him, etc.)

into tangibles—i.e., how to put the behavior and the psychological aspects of the consuming masses into a form usable for establishing a quantitative relationship between the consumers and the stock market. I had to keep in mind the truth I knew about "bad numbers," but yet use numbers. I assembled a model—a system combining mathematical calculations and subjective judgments; I called this my Black Box. Let me explain.

Price provides the basic tool. The consumer is the ultimate price determiner and decision maker. He will either spend at the price asked or reject that price and save. Price is a reasonable, easy, and consistent measuring rod. How much is the consumer spending? What is he buying or not buying? How is he paying, cash or credit? Is he building up a large inventory of durable goods that require more maintenance? Is he moving "down on the hog," giving up steaks for hamburger or hairdressers for home permanents? I developed a list of what I considered the most sensitive areas of consumer spending—"sensitive" in the sense that they respond most quickly to changes in a consumer's income and reflect almost immediately his feelings not only about present but also about future spending. For example, here are nine sample variables I use (there are thirty in my complete list):[1]

1. air transportation
2. utilities
3. food (not in terms of using it or not using it, as in air transportation, but of upgrading/downgrading shifts in expenditures)
4. telephone (e.g., downgrading in terms of minimizing toll calls, eliminating extension outlets)
5. automobile gas and oil
6. postponable automobile repairs (e.g., body work, painting)
7. hairdresser
8. entertainment
9. Savings and Loan Association balances

It will be observed that these measures are not the same as measures pondered by Status Quo Economists. Their attention is riveted on production (tons of steel hauled, number of automobilies sold, barrels of oil produced, tons of freight moved), but in a Service Economy this now represents secondary actions. More traditional categories are not by any means to be ignored; however, they should be considered *after,* not before, the consumables and more sensitive indicators noted above. For example, I look at such variables as:

10. durable goods sales (e.g., automobiles, TVs, furniture)
11. level and direction of state and local government expenditures
12. consumer intentions to buy (as reflected in regular studies, especially those of the Survey Research Center at the University of Michigan)
13. liquidity of the consumer

Once a list of variables has been drawn up, a simple weighted index number can be arrived at, or more elaborate mathematical formulas can be put together with calculus and computer.[2] Any interested reader can prepare his own index and put into it what he thinks to be significant. For those unfamiliar with making a weighted index number, the following brief summary will suffice for now.

An index number is a special kind of average. It gives in a single figure an indication of the variation over time of a group of related variables; a variable is a quantity with different values under different conditions. Measurements of the same variable are recorded from time to time; these reveal the trend in values of the variable. The Consumer Price Index is probably the best known index in this country. It is a government-computed figure released monthly by the Bureau of Labor Statistics. Figures look typically like this (for the first six months of 1971): January: 119.2, February: 119.4, March: 119.8, April: 120.2, May: 120.8, June: 121.5. The base 100 of the index is 1967. The CPI is a rough measure of the average price from month to month of what has been determined as basic necessities of life in the United States. This calculation is no idle exercise, because the pay scale of millions of wage earners is tied to this index and changes in it mean changes in their incomes. In brief, the CPI points to the rising or falling cost of maintaining the same standard of living.

The index of consumer prices is computed by averaging, in a special manner worked out by the government, the prices of many basic necessities in order to provide a single number that will represent all the variables which make up this group of necessities. As an illustration, let us make our own price index on a small scale, by going to the dairy aisle in the supermarket and buying four items: milk, eggs, oleomargarine, and cheese. As an average family, we might consume each month:

40 half-gallons of milk
10 dozen eggs
8 pounds of oleo
2 pounds of cheese

In shopping on the same day of the week (e.g., Friday) and noting prices from the same week (e.g., first) each month, we might find the following:

	Feb	March	April	May
milk (per h-g)	$ .60	.59	.59	.58
eggs (per doz)	.65	.60	.61	.59
oleo (per lb)	.39	.39	.35	.30
cheese (per lb)	1.10	1.00	1.00	.95

Multiplied by the quantity we (as average family) use each month, the totals result:

	Feb	March	April	May
milk	$24.00	23.60	23.60	23.20
eggs	6.50	6.00	6.10	5.90
oleo	3.12	3.12	2.80	2.40
cheese	2.20	2.00	2.00	1.90
Total	$35.82	34.72	34.50	33.40

The monthly totals show us a general downward trend in dairy prices (This illustration indulges our wishful thinking!), but it would be simpler if we chose one particular month (e.g., April) as our base, 100, and related other months to it, giving us, then, a dairy price index. This we calculate by dividing the total for each month by our base (April) total. Thus we have four weighted aggregative price index figures:

	Feb	March	April	May
Index	103.8	100.6	100	96.8

Index figures need not be constructed, of course, from such obviously quantifiable variables as prices of groceries. The Survey Research Center in Michigan employs, as noted earlier in Chapter 1, an Index of Consumer Sentiment, calculated to "measure" consumers' confidence in the economy, their willingness or reluctance to buy, projected months into the future. SRC's experience indicates that its index leads expenditures on consumer durables by six to nine months. The following chart graphs seven years of SRC findings:

CHART 12

INDEX OF CONSUMER SENTIMENT

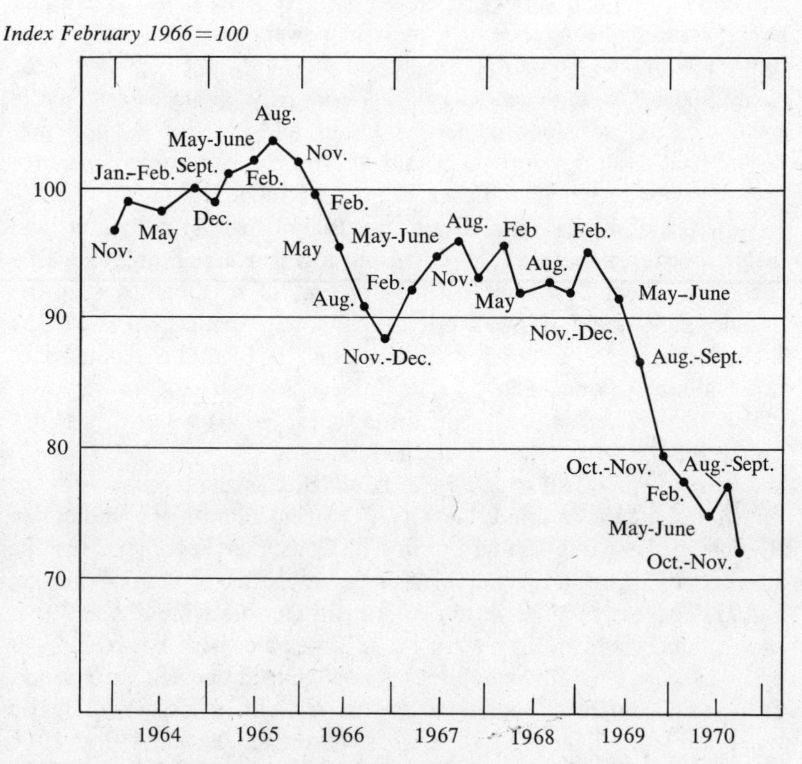

SOURCE: Survey Research Center, University of Michigan

More recent figures indicate a slightly less pessimistic attitude about the economy on the part of consumers. For instance, the figure for the last quarter of 1971 was 82.2; for the first quarter of 1972, 87.5.

In my own case I have worked out a set of variables and given them certain values, based both on actual experience and on hypothetical historical cases. After obtaining my weighted numbers and my base, I related these to the Standard and Poor's Composite 500 Stock Index. My first Black Box model was constructed in 1965. It initially had twenty-five variables, later refined to thirty. In addition to the variables listed above, I have incorporated more exogenous and less easily defined ones, such as war prospects, conservative and liberal frames of reference of leaders in power, etc.[3] This, of course, introduces greater human appraisal and escalates the chance for error in my Black Box, but such variables are nevertheless necessary factors to consider. Observation, experimentation, and practice in constructing a Black Box develops skill and ability to make reasonable predictions with higher and higher degrees of reliability.

Now a look at the reliability of my Black Box. As a hypothetical historical exercise, after I felt I had put together a workable model, I carried my Black Box back to 1956 and ran "forecasting" tests for the decade 1956–1965. It was not possible to compile a Black Box Weighted Index Number for earlier than 1956, because data were not available prior to that time. In forecasting four stock market *declines,* the Black Box was right three times. Now I was ready to try my technique in a real before-the-fact situation.

During the first half of 1965, the Black Box gave out "plus" signals, but in August they turned "negative," coincident with the findings of the Survey Research Center's Index of Consumer Sentiment. On the strength of this I projected in August 1965 that the stock market would decline sometime within the next three to six months and that the decline would be in excess of 12%—somewhere between 20% and 25%. Five months later stock prices obliged and fell. In my personal management of money, I had moved out of large holdings in one blue chip, selling at $187 per share before the decline; in late 1966 the stock bottomed at $125. Actually, in managing one trust fund, I made $125,000 in ten months during this 1965-1966 period, and was in the market only twice.

In forecasting three subsequent market declines after the 1965-1966 success, the Black Box was right three times. Not a bad batting average—100%! The record of these eight cases is summarized in the following table. Since 1956 there have been eight declines in the

DJI index ranging from —12% to —37%. In every instance but one, Black Box estimates of the depth and breadth of the decline were correct.

TABLE 18
DJI DECLINES OF 12% OR MORE

Black Box projections		Actual results		
Lead time (months)	Index signal date	Dates	Duration (months)	DJI decline (percent)
none	May 1956	Apr 56-Feb 57	10	—13%
1	June 1957	July-Oct 57	3	—19%
3	Oct 1959	Jan-Oct 60	10	—17%
—	no signal	Dec 61-June 62	6	—27%
5	Aug 1965	Feb-Oct 66	8	—27%
none	Nov 1967	Sept 67-Mar 68	6	—13%
1	Apr 1969*	Dec 68-May 70	17	—37%
1	Mar 1971	Apr. 71-Nov 71	7	—17%

*Although the 1969-1970 decline actually commenced in December 1968, the Black Box did not pick up the signal until April 1969. However, the market did not begin its precipitous drop until May 1969; therefore, if an investor had not sold in December, but waited until May, the loss would have been negligible.

In forecasting a turnaround, that is, "finding the bottom," the Black Box is not as useful. In my first before-the-fact use of the Black Box, after its forecast of the decline in 1966, the reading leveled in September 1966 and one month later the stock market turned up. More recently, in June 1971 the Black Box signalled up and in November of that year the DJI hit 790 and turned up—a lead of five months. Since then, in March 1972, the Black Box indicated a sharp upward turn; eight months later the market broke through the DJI 1000 barrier for the first time. However, these have been my only successes in forecasting turnarounds; the Black Box caught the other turns only after they had been going on for a while. The explanation for this seems to be that psychological feelings of pessimism among the masses of consumers linger on and on. Consumers seem to be "from Missouri." Being *told* that things are "getting better" is not enough; it must be *proved* to them. It will be recalled that the consumer is stubborn and selfish; only when *his* personal economic situation improves does he respond positively. When business and government activity take off under traditional "trickle-down" economics, it takes time to "trickle down," and sometimes the "trickle down" itself, at the consumer level, adds up to less than one, so the consumer remains pessimistic. However, his behavior near the top, when Wall Street is most euphoric, is sensitive. Since the consumer has no one to assist him in bailing out financially, he intuitively seems to know when to pull in his financial excesses; he cuts his spending and charging activity with almost no notice. He is "turned off," and is not tuned in to manipulators who tell him that things are better, or that there will be two cars in every garage or chickens in every pot.

My experience with the Black Box during the period 1970-71 will help give detail to the ideas and themes I have been expressing, though my success here was not 100%.

In February 1970 over two thousand economic and financial experts met in New York at the Third Annual Institutional Investor Conference. This group made the following estimates on the future of stocks:[4]

Predicted DJI average for first half of 1970—

Most Money Managers	800-824
Large Portfolio Managers	850-874
Most Brokers	800-824

Predicted DJI average for February 1971—

Most Money Managers	900-924
Large Portfolio Managers	1000+
Most Brokers	850-924

A rosy future indeed seemed assured to these financial experts—though one could have wondered at their confidence in their own accuracy if their recent track record had been noted. At their previous annual meeting in February 1969, a similar poll of consensus about DJI predictions had been taken. The majority of the experts had then estimated that one year later—February 1970—the DJI would be somewhere between 1000 and 1100. Well, one year later in February 1970, while they were sitting there making predictions about February 1971, the DJI was only 750. That they had missed their projection 300 points or more did not dim their optimism.

But my Black Box was not optimistic. On March 30, 1970, it forecast a DJI of 675-700 for mid-July of that year. At the time of prediction the DJI was 784.65. By May 4 it was moving toward my forecast: it was then 714.56. By the third week in May it had dropped to 631.16. This, however, proved to be its bottoming out. In mid-July the DJI was at 711.66. The next day, July 16, it rose to 723.44, the highest since May 1.

It was in July 1970 that I was interviewed by James Flanagan of *Forbes* magazine. At that time I broadly outlined my research into the economic psychology of the masses as a significant indicator of stock market forecasting.[5] When the interview took place, the stock market was in a run-up, thus missing my prediction. Despite this, I forecast a turnaround, with the market reaching a level of 600 "soon," because my indicators still read negative. "Soon" passed into fall, into winter, and into spring, and the stock market surged ahead. My own readings became increasingly negative: the consumers, the masses of the people, were "economically turned off"; they were saving, not spending, getting out of debt—in short, gloomy. Still, stock prices rose, some 300 points!

It was admitted on Wall Street late in 1970 and early 1971 that consumer spending held the key to economic recovery, and most Wall Street Money Managers, looking in their rearview mirrors to past consumer behavior, confidently predicted the consumer would spend.

In early February 1971:

> Many economists government and private believe consumers will spend more and save less this year.
>
> Americans in 1970 saved more than 7% of their disposable personal income, exceptionally high by historical standards, as inflation, unemployment and sluggishness plagued the economy.
>
> "I think the savings rate is going to come down," said Dr. Harold C. Passer, assistant secretary for economic affairs in the Commerce Department. "I think it will be heading in the direction of 6% by the end of the year."
>
> With the economy expanding and business getting better, many economists say consumers should be using up their huge supply of savings at a faster clip.[6]

The *Wall Street Journal* in a front page story on March 8, 1971 observed:

> To an unusually large extent this year the government is counting on something other than its fiscal and monetary policies to make its forecast come true. This is what the authorities are calling "the confidence factor," and confidence is all the harder to establish when professional private

> economists are filling the press with talk of the government's economic policy "credibility" problem.
>
> Chairman Arthur F. Burns of the Federal Reserve Board has been hitting hardest and longest on the confidence theme, in arguing that the central bank has already provided ample liquidity, so all that's needed is for people to have the gumption to borrow and spend it: "The strength of the economic expansion during and beyond 1971 will depend principally upon our success in restoring the confidence of consumers and businesses in their own and the nation's economic future."

Arthur F. Burns had indeed been hitting this notion hard. A few weeks earlier in testifying before the Joint Economic Committee of Congress, he summed up the crucial role of the consumer:

> Ultimately the shape of business conditions during 1971 will depend on what happens to spending in the largest sector of our economy—the consumer sector. For many months, the mood of the average consumer has been cautious, if not pessimistic. The personal savings rate has remained high. Consumer liquid assets have been built up at an unusually high rate. No one can foretell how soon this mood will change.

In February 1971 the Institutional Investors again held their annual convention in New York and again exuded their usual confidence and estimates. They forecast that by the end of the year the DJI would be somewhere between 950 and 1200.

Such optimism continued into the spring. A headline in my local newspaper[7] read:

EXPERTS PREDICT DJ AVERAGES REACHING 1000

One thousand on the Dow Jones Industrial Average—a magic figure stock market observers had talked about often, but a figure never reached, though the averages sniffed it in the December 1968 high of 994.7. Now the impossible seemed possible, seemed inevitable even. Analysts everywhere saw the industrial average marching over 1000 by 1972. (The DJI finally closed at 1003.16 on November 14, 1972.)

On June 19, 1971 the DJI fell 17.09 points and the *Los Angeles Times* reported that "analysts blame a combination of glum reports."

But the mood on Wall Street was far from glum the first week in July:

> Howard Stein, chairman of Dreyfus Corp., a mutual fund management company with assets of $2.8 billion, is in general accord with the view that the stock market will work its way higher. But he thinks the gain over the next few months will be modest—not dramatic.[8]

On July 6, 1971 the DJI closed at 890.19. (Five weeks later to the day it closed at 839.59)

On July 9 the *Wall Street Journal* carried this front page story:

> **Bull or Bear**
> **Most analysts believe share prices will rise after recent weakness.**
> **Next quarter forecast 1005**
>
> How robust is the stock market?
>
> The Dow Jones Industrial Average closed yesterday at 900.99 up from a recent low of 873.10 on June 28 but far below the 1971 high of 950 set on April 28.
>
> A considerably larger body of opinion still adheres to the view, nearly unanimous in the early months of this year, that the market is exceedingly healthy. The optimists contend that the basic climb in share prices from a Dow Jones low of 631.16 on May 26, 1971 is still in progress. They view the recent decline from the April high as merely the sort of temporary drop that often occurs during the early stages of a general recovery in economic activity.
>
> Robert H. Parks, a Vice-President of duPont Glore, Forgan, Inc., states "The outlook suggests that we are still in the middle of a major bull market for stocks, despite temporary but inevitable corrections."

Even aberrations were normal, and optimism was sustained:

> The 8% drop in the DJI from the high of 958 reached in April constitutes a "normal correction in a bull market," according to the Alexander Hamilton Institute.[9]

The Black Box still read 600 for the DJI. Since the model is constructed around the economic behavior of the consuming masses, it simply could not point up, because consumer confidence was low.

Consumer confidence continued to shrink, but the shrinkage was presumably invisible in key high government councils—or else it was felt that the shrinkage would disappear if washed sufficiently in a sea of *talk* about confidence. In mid-July President Nixon's then chief economic spokesman, Secretary of the Treasury John Connally, said:

> One of the things that I hope to do is to try to make it abundantly clear that the President has confidence in the progress that is being made. He has confidence that this is going to be a very good year. He thinks the American people express that confidence in the retail sales that are going on. They are the ones. The concern is largely among the academicians around the country and those who, for political reasons, want to continue questioning this and questioning that.
>
> I don't think there is a lack of confidence throughout the country or you wouldn't see people spending at the rate they are in terms of retail sales.[10]

(Retail sales, an arcane and incomplete measure, were up 2.5% in real dollars from the preceding year;[11] but this small increase was probably due to normal population increases moving into the marketplace.)

Two weeks after Secretary Connally's statement, the *Los Angeles Times* in a front page article entitled "Consumer Holds Cure for Economy in His Pocket," stated:

> What has $50 billion in savings and holds the key to economic recovery? Answer: the American consumer.
>
> For months economists, businessmen and government officials have been watching and waiting for individuals to resume their traditional habits of savings and spending. Most agree that if they do the gradual economy recovery taking place would be greatly accelerated.
>
> Sales of automobiles, after leaping forward in the first months of 1971 after the long strike against General Motors Corporation, slacked off in the second quarter. Purchases of other "big ticket" items such as major appliances increased only moderately in both quarters.
>
> While historically individuals have saved roughly 6% of their disposable income, the rate went to 7.9% in 1970, and in the second quarter of 1971 hit an unprecedented rate of 8.4%.

> Earlier figures estimated the savings rate in 1970 as 7.3% and the rate in 1971 as 7.0%.
>
> The percentage differences are small but in terms of dollars that were saved by individuals rather than spent the disparity was $9 billion the first three months of this year.[12]

The Black Box continued to read 600. But, curiously, one of the variables, the consumer attitude studies from the Survey Research Center in Michigan, registered slight upturns at the end of the 1st Quarter 1971, and the end of the 2nd Quarter 1971. However, the Conference Board survey which early in 1971 had been pointing up, turned down in May-June 1971:

> Consumer Buying Plans, which rose sharply during the early months of the year, have fallen back during the last two months.
>
> After making steady improvement through the first four months of the year, buying plans sagged during May and June, the latest survey period. Plans to buy automobiles and major appliances over the next six months are down significantly.
>
> Consumers have become more optimistic about general economic conditions. Only 27% label current business as "bad," down from 36% in the previous survey. And looking ahead, 27% expect their incomes to improve over the next six months, up from 24% in the March-April survey.[13]

The gloom pervading the country was revealed (in other than economic behavior) in a Roper Survey of July 1971, which noted that "64% of the American people believe the country to be on the wrong track."[14]

Early 1971 had seen predictions of a DJI of 1000 and forecasts of lavish consumer spending. Seven months into 1971 the consumer was being characterized as "tight-fisted":

> **TIGHT FISTED CONSUMERS HURT ECONOMY PROGRAM**
>
> Weary of inflation and high unemployment, the nation's consumers have cut back sharply on their plans to make major new purchases this year, the government said. . . .
>
> The administration has been counting on stepped up consumer spending to accelerate the pace of the economy.

> But the new report suggested even further slackening of business activity.
>
> The report, based on a survey taken earlier this month by the Census Bureau, shows consumers are more reluctant to buy new cars, major appliances, furniture and carpets than they were when a similar study was taken in April (1971).
>
> The Census Bureau said an index measuring expected new car purchases declined by 10% from the last survey.
>
> The number of major appliances reported likely to be purchased within the next year declined from 26.1 per 100 households in April to 24.1 in July.
>
> The percentage of households expecting to make major expenditures on furniture and carpets declined from 28.4% to 24.4%.[15]

And businesses were being called "tightwads." As the consumer tightened his belt further, so did the corporation. On August 2, 1971 the *Wall Street Journal* front-paged this item.

> **The Tightwads**
> **MANY COMPANIES PLAN LITTLE CAPITAL SPENDING DESPITE THE RECOVERY**
> **They cite overcapacity now, uncertainty over imports, taxes, and pollution rules**

In a *Newsweek* column entitled "How Odd of the Public," Clem Morgello wondered:

> In all the years that anyone can remember, the individual investor has never behaved as he is behaving now. The bull market is more than a year old, and prices as measured by the Dow Jones industrial average are up 41 per cent. Yet the public is staying resolutely out of the market.
>
> The phenomenon shows clearly in the odd-lot figures, which are a pretty accurate guide to the behavior of the public in general. Odd-lotters started to buy more stock than they sold as the market was in the process of bottoming out in May 1970, and they remained buyers for three months (chart). This is typical behavior [?], for odd-lotters are inveterate bargain hunters.
>
> As price continued to rise, the odd-lotter turned into a

seller—and that is also the normal pattern [?]. What isn't normal is for him to stay out so long in the face of persistently rising prices. Some brokers have the feeling that the period of heaviest public selling may be past, but there is no real evidence that the public is about to step up its buying.[16]

CHART 13

A SURPRISINGLY RELUCTANT INVESTOR

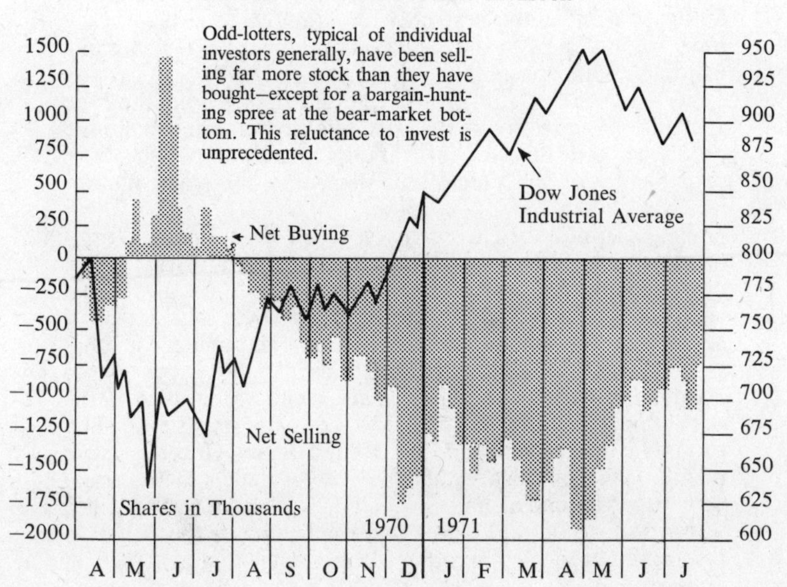

Once again the reluctant consumer was felt in Wall Street. By August 9, 1971 stock prices had fallen to 842 on the DJI from their 1971 high of 958. In stark contrast to the joy of fall-winter 1970-71, the investment community began to show signs of loss of confidence—again belatedly. (It should be noted here that this is not unusual, because Money Men *theorize* about the consumer as they have been taught in basic economics books to do, rather than *observe* human behavior.)

> **INVESTMENT CIRCLES EXHIBITING DIMINISHING CONFIDENCE LEVEL**
>
> While optimism on the state of the economy continues to be the watchword in Washington, the mood elsewhere has been quite different. As the year rolls along, a diminishing level of confidence is obviously developing in business, economic and investment circles [note: no mention of eroding consumer confidence].
>
> In recent weeks, particularly, a wave of pessimism has engulfed Wall Street—and it may be encompassing Main Street as well [note: it *started* on Main Street]. It is being reflected in a sagging stock market and the cautious commitments of both consumers and business.
>
> Security analysts and other commentators said that the growing malaise over the nation's mammoth economic problems and the administration's domestic policies was responsible for the precipitous decline in the stock market last week.
>
> The leading stock averages suffered their greatest drop in more than a year with the Dow Jones Industrial Index down almost 30 points.
>
> The financial markets were beat last week by a series of adverse developments, including: The continuance of great tension in various labor negotiations; the 50% cut in the dividend of the United States Steel Corporation; unfavorable economic statistics, particularly the data on the leading economic indicators and the United States' foreign trade position; the disclosure that the federal deficit in the fiscal year that just ended had reached $23.24 billion; the sharp upward move of gold prices and weakening of the dollar as this nation reported another drop in its gold reserves in June.[17]

Conspicuously absent from this list of "causes" was emphasis on the consuming masses. This is tragic and stupid. They are out there. They have all the money. They spend. They save. They send messages. They keep the machine running. Or they stop it. But the Status Quo focuses on production and dividends and arcane "leading economic indicators." Thus they continue to misread the consumer—or not read him at all.

How could so many knowledgeable persons misread the inputs in 1971? Probably for at least two reasons. In the first place, they had (and still have) a fixation on historical relationships, on the Status

Quo Syndrome. On August 9, 1971 *Newsweek* carried a stock market story entitled "The Bull's Waning Signs":

> In recent weeks this column [by Clem Morgello] has frequently dwelt on economic developments to help explain market behavior. . . .
>
> Plainly, the technical condition of the market is growing worse, although the majority of the indicators still point upward and do not yet indicate that the bull market is coming to an end.[18]

Although the stock market is getting worse, by 120 points, it is "technically" getting "better"! At best technicians can only report past history. To look through this rearview mirror with imaginary numbers and extrapolate the future is sheer nonsense since each stock market cycle lives its own life, by its very nature separate and distinct from any other cycle that ever occurred in the past. Despite this, a great deal of the extra money on Wall Street flows down research channels dedicated to this myopic view of yesterday or yesteryear. And a large section of the investing public bets their money on this output! With friends like this. . . .

In the second place, many experts would not have recognized a genuine consumer if they had stumbled over one. Unnoticed was the fact that the consumer has acted (and will again act) autonomously of the production-money-machine. After World War II a depression was calculated by Wall Street and their in-house economists, because war spending was over and the machine would grind to a halt. But the consumer held record savings, some 25%, and went on a spending spree; he was optimistic with the end of the war and needed to replenish and refurbish his consumer package. The economy boomed. Again in the Korean War the consumer confounded the Status Quo. Still again in 1955: radically restyled cars brought the big spending public out. By contrast, during 1970 and into August 1971, the consumer saved (rising to 8.2%) and paid off his debts. He got liquid. Why? The common man has no federal government to run to his financial aid when he is burdened with debt; he digs himself out. Major corporations and banks can count on the central bank "as the bank of last resort," as Arthur Burns has said. By contrast, small businesses and small consumers can go broke.

Also, consumer storm clouds got blacker: unemployment continued up and prices continued to rise, despite promises to the contrary. The basic consumer is economically insecure, and this dictates his behavior. Contrary to the much believed American myth, he will not "risk it." Practical living experience furnishes all the documentation the consumer needs about the beneficence of business, large or small. He has learned, as Tawney observed, that "competition is used to obscure dishonesty."

Wall Street was not faring well from any quarter in August 1971. Also that month there appeared this *Wall Street Journal* item:

> **BIG BOARD "MISINFORMED" PUBLIC, CONGRESS ABOUT "CRISIS," SEC COUNSEL SAYS IN BOOK**
>
> A Securities and Exchange Commission staff official has charged that the New York Stock Exchange "misinformed" the investing public, its own membership and Congress about the financial problems during the "crisis" years of 1969-70.
>
> In a soon-to-be-published book attacking Wall Street, SEC special counsel Hurd Baruch attributes this partly to exchange reliance on "inaccurate" reports from the firms themselves, partly to faulty analysis by the exchange of such reports and partly to the "traditional cloak of secrecy" that the exchange throws about its members.[19]

When the stock market closed on Friday, August 13, 1971, the DJI was 856.02, reflecting the stagnant consumer confidence we have been pointing to and the expected DJI drop to 600 the Black Box had been forecasting. Then came President Nixon's surprise blockbuster which broke the trend. On August 15 he delivered his now-famous major economic address. The scope of the new game plan underscored the great waste and futility of the previous game plan. Money Managers and the consumers hastily perceived the message as "good news" and on Monday August 16 the DJI rose 32.93 points, the largest one-day gain in history, on a volume of 31,730,000 shares, also the largest one-day trading in history.

(The opposite of this good news was the receipt of the same news in Japan as "bad news"; its stock market took the sharpest fall in its history: over 300 points in two days. Up or down, exogenous events cut a wide swath; large fortunes are made and lost.)

The sharp rise on Wall Street also brought out the consumer: there were on August 16, 1971, 60,000 individual transactions, one-third more than normal. But the Money Men were on the choice seats: 196 trades of 10,000 shares or more.

One week after the President's speech, the *Wall Street Journal* reported:

> A resurgence in the confidence of businessmen and consumers is viewed by many on Wall Street as the chief boon of the administration's new economic policy.
>
> "It's a bold plan and it may well succeed in raising the confidence level, prompting people to begin spending again," asserts William A. Tenson, executive vice president of the Bank of New York, which manages several billions of dollars of investment funds. "A lack of confidence is really all that had been holding the economy back."[20]

Additional cautious hopes found expression:

> Most economists seem to agree . . . that the plan's biggest benefit is its shock value. They hope that Mr. Nixon's bold moves will convince consumers that inflation can be bludgeoned into line and the economy restored to sustainable growth.
>
> That would encourage people to save less and start buying new cars, dishwashers and new clothes—a process that would create more demand, more jobs and more growth.
>
> A single percentage point drop in the current 8.4% rate of consumer savings would add 8 billion to the national output of goods and services, according to estimates of Robert Oster, senior economist in Los Angeles for the Bank of America. "The theory is that, while incomes are frozen, prices are frozen too. So people might be willing to go out and buy things while the prices are stable." Analysts figure the cut in car purchase taxes might help the process along.
>
> Professor R. M. Roseman of California State College at Los Angeles doesn't quite agree with the notion. He argues that unemployment, not so-called "consumer psychology," may be the chief problem that has to be dealt with. Therefore he predicts that the Nixon program of tax cuts won't get the results that an increase in federal spending could. "Whatever people's state of mind is," he says, "if they don't have the income they can't spend it on purchases.

And if companies don't have the sales they can't spend the money on investment."[21]

Consumers discount their own future, much like Wall Street purports to do with stocks, and the view from the ken of the common man, the consumer, was about like this: prices frozen at the highest levels ever, wages locked in lower, and a tax refund to come in several months that for a family of four in the 16% bracket would amount to $32. The consumer could hardly wax euphoric over this package, and some experts were noting this:

EVEN BANKERS FEEL CONSUMER LEFT OUT
Paycheck Must Come In Before He Can Spend It

America's labor leaders aren't alone in their misgivings over President Nixon's new economic package. Officials at several of the nation's greatest bastions of capitalism—though they welcome the latest plan's promise to restore orderly growth—are starting to question whether too many of its benefits will end up in businessmen's pockets and not enough in the hands of the workers.[22]

By September 16, 1971 one month had passed since the economic message of the President, and the *Chicago Daily News* reported:

Freeze fails to spur consumer optimism

The government's new economic policies have not generated an immediate upsurge in consumer optimism, according to a survey by the [National Industrial] Conference Board, a business research organization.

The Board said it had surveyed 10,000 families across the country during the three weeks since President Nixon's mid-August announcement and found buying plans up slightly, but consumers "no more confident than they were earlier this summer."

The survey showed 8.5% planned to buy an auto in the next six months, up from 7.8% in the May-June check, and 3.5% planned to buy homes, up from 3.1% in May-June.

In the latest survey, 34% planned to buy a major appliance in the next six months, down from 36% in May-June. The Board said plans to buy washing machines, television sets, and clothes dryers all declined.

CHART 14

OUTPUT LAGGED BEHIND SALES

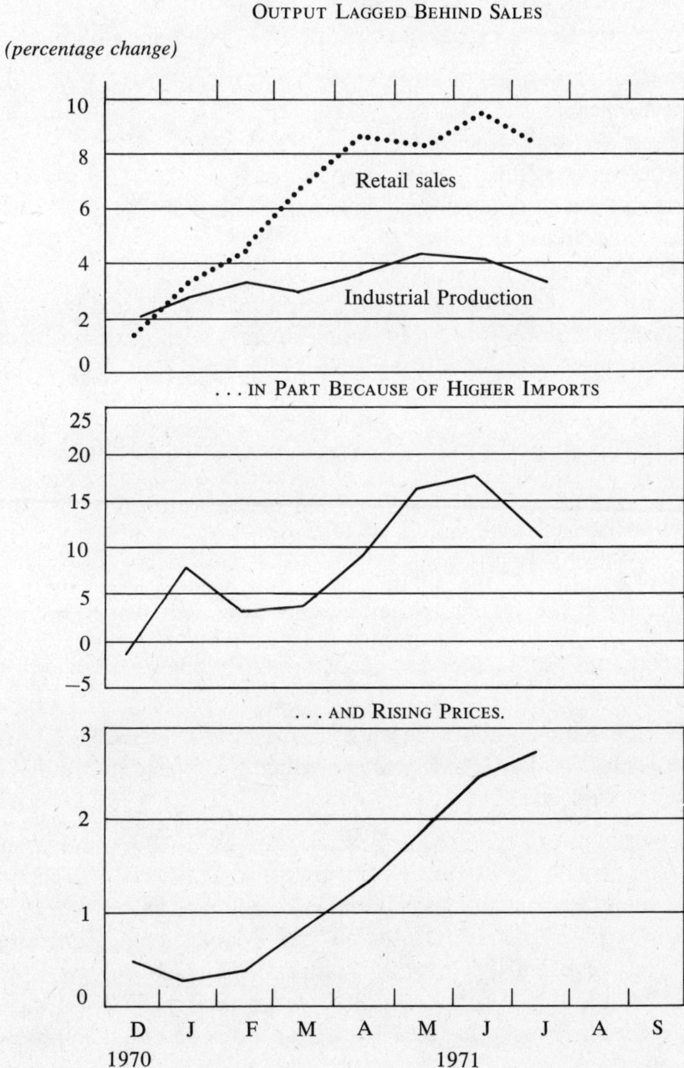

The charts show monthly data expressed as percentage changes from the level attained in November 1970, the month tentatively identified as the trough of the 1969-70 recession. The series are, respectively, monthly retail sales, industrial production, merchandise imports, and the consumer price index for commodities.

SOURCES: Department of Commerce, Federal Reserve Board, and Bureau of Labor Statistics.

Additional evidence of the importance of the economic behavior of the masses of the people is apparent in Chart 14 (from the September 1971 *Economic Letter* of the New York First National City Bank).

What the Bank is pointing out is this:

1. Retail sales sagged, so
2. Industrial production sagged;
3. Part of this was due to more imports and
4. Part was due to rising prices (continuing inflation).

What the Bank did not say was:

1. The people call the economic shots.
2. The people were, as noted earlier, economically "turned off."

Where, then, will corporate profits come from? Sales must be made for wheels to turn and profits to be made. The Bank *Letter* made this additional comment:

> Beyond the period of the wage-price freeze, the anti-inflationary thrust of the program also centers on *influencing public opinion*. The *hope* is that the demonstration of the Administration's willingness to take direct action will lead to a downward revision in *expectations* regarding the future rate of inflation. If the public comes to expect a lower rate of inflation, the theory is that interest rates and wage demands will be scaled down with the result that the revised expectations will tend to become self-fulfilling. [italics added]

The National Industrial Conference Board survey referred to above would indicate that this Bank was whistling past the graveyard. So common on Wall Street.

What was the Black Box projection for 1971-1972 and what actually happened? In August 1971 the Box registered "decline." This was manifest almost a year later. For example, in August 1972 a survey report by Capital Research and Management Company, Los Angeles, revealed that of 1,801 stocks listed on the New York Stock Exchange, 1,113 were down 30% from their 1967-1968 highs —i.e., 62% of the stocks down 30%! Of the 1,801 stocks, 426 (24%) were down 66%!

All the while that this erosion was taking place, it was *masked* by the stock market averages: the DJI during this period was down just 6% from its 1968 high. This confirms again that there can never be a broad recovery in stocks on Wall Street until the lowly consumer somewhere along the line also shares in the "prosperity," instead of merely being sent the bill for it.

The heralding on August 15, 1971 of the New Economic Program—or as one economist called it, "the new era of economics"—had apparently little positive impact in depth, despite the wild gyrations on Wall Street. There were big individual winners, but then there always are, up or down. And there were also big losers, as always.

The disenchantment of the consumer noted in mutual fund redemptions seemed to extend to *all* stocks, as is evidenced here:

TABLE 19
HOUSEHOLDS, PERSONAL TRUSTS, & NONPROFIT ORGANIZATIONS

Percentages of other corporate shares (excluding mutual funds) as a percentage of total financial assets.
1945-1954 = 30.44%
1955-1964 = 40.19%
1965-1971 = 43.66%

SOURCE: Federal Reserve Board, *Flow of Funds,* 1972.

Since stock holdings of personal trusts and nonprofit organizations are large and quite stable, the differences represent, in the main, the household sector, i.e., the consumer. Between 1945 and 1964 his holdings increased by 25%, while the DJI increased 96%. From 1964 through 1971 the consumer's increase was only 7%, while the DJI declined 2%. Thus, the consumer did not enjoy much of the large appreciation in stocks during the last twenty-seven years. Someone did, however: the few large holders of all stocks represented by trusts, pension funds, insurance companies, banks, etc. It is no small wonder, then, that the consumer remains wary of Wall Street and the Money Managers. In its August 7, 1972 issue, *Newsweek* characterized this behavior as "The Public Hangs Back."

The Money Managers will miss the consumer in the years to come, but it is difficult to see how the consumer will miss the Money Managers, since there are many other places where he can put his money, get a tiny bit of action, and behold! get it back. Those who talk of return *on* one's investment rarely mention the return *of* the investment. The behavior of the consumer indicates that he has learned this, if he has learned little else about money management.

12

Socioeconomic Implications

> Small reforms are the worst enemies of big reforms.
>
> *French proverb*

Many of the observations and arguments made throughout this book come together now as we take a look at social and institutional implications of present developments.

The United States *is* a Service Economy; it is not just in the process of becoming a service society. This point has been documented and elaborated earlier. But too many economists and political leaders are overlooking this fact and consequently misfocusing on production of goods. This misdirected vision led the Nixon administration, for example, to encourage the production of more automobiles during 1971–1972, as the solution to the economy's sluggishness. The inevitable outcome was to drive up a blind alley.

There is also the prevalent but grave mistake of focusing on the interests of people as producers (especially producers of goods) instead of as consumers. Instead, it must be learned and remembered that *the consumer is the most important person in our society*.

Another fact of our current economic life is what has come to be called consumerism. Buyers of services and goods finally had enough. Shoddy workmanship, glacial-slow repair service, safety hazards in goods, health hazards in foods, ecological disasters on every hand—all these combined to break the compliance of consumers, who rallied in the 1960s and early 1970s to organize against the second-rate treatment they had been getting from government and business.

Inflation and taxes, eating away voraciously at the pocket book, have discouraged the average consumer into both financial and psychological states of gloom. Figures dramatize the simple root of the problem; here is a rough picture of the average consumer's pocketbook.[1]

TABLE 20

WAGE-EARNER SPENDING MONEY EROSION 1967-1971

Each $1.00 of gross wage pay diminished instantly by:	Low estimate	High estimate
Inflation	$ .15	$ .20
Taxes (all)	.20	.30
Debts	—[1]	.25
Economic waste	.20	.40
	$ .55	$ 1.15
This leaves net spending money:	$ .45	$ –.15[2]

[1]Zero debt is surely a myth.
[2]Consumer borrows or cuts back to counteract loss.

Most persons fit around these numbers—some owe more, some less; some pay high taxes, some lower. In the United States almost everyone *owes* someone, though we tend to minimize the fact, as noted earlier, by easy use of such phrases as "I own my house," "I own my car," "I own my TV set." And we are owing more. Consumer loans and installment credit increased remarkably during 1972.

> Through November of this year consumer installment loans at large commercial banks that report weekly increased at an annual rate of 15.4 per cent. This compared with an 11.1 per cent increase a year ago and a 6.5 per cent increase in 1970.
>
> Consumer credit in December rose to a record $2.5 billion, against a $2.1 billion rise in November, which was the previous high. Outstanding consumer installment debt alone rose $1.7 billion in December, and non-installment debt rose to $802 million. Installment and non-installment consumer debt together at December's end totaled $157.56 billion. Non-installment charge-account credit rose in December by $522 million, up from a $146 million increase in November. The increase in consumer debt in 1972 was a record $19.2

billion, up from $11.2 billion for 1971.[2]

The price of this owing has come high in the past few years. The number of persons unable to pay their debts is increasing. During the relative prosperity of the 1960s, the quantity of debtor-relief cases grew so that personal banckruptcies per 1,000 households soared above that for the years during the depths of the Great Depression. In 1955 there were 60,000 bankruptcy petitions filed across the nation; in 1969 there were 185,000, more than triple the earlier figure, and most of these involved individuals. As a matter of fact, personal bankruptcy cases now account for over 90% of the total petitions filed.[3]

In other words, growing rebellion over the quality of services and goods, increasing disillusionment about the erosion of purchasing power, and changing attitudes toward work and its meaning—a phenomenon mentioned earlier—all funnel in to create a psychological context appropriate for social and institutional change. Add to this the significance of the *Service* Economy, plus another objective factor of major import, the cybernetic revolution, and we can see that our economy is ripe for change.

Actually, capitalism is dead. This is not a radical statement. It is, instead, just a recognition of current facts. Basic characteristics of capitalism center around the ideas of profit, competition, and free markets. All three have been on the wane for years.

The only kind of profits that count on Wall Street are those that are called "return on equity," that is, the profits after tax to stockholder's equity, and here is the record from 1950 to 1971:

TABLE 21

PROFIT RATE AFTER TAX TO STOCKHOLDER'S EQUITY

Year	Rate	Year	Rate
1950	15.4%	1961	8.9%
1951	12.1%	1962	9.8%
1952	10.3%	1963	10.3%
1953	10.5%	1964	11.6%
1954	9.9%	1965	13.0%
1955	12.6%	1966	13.4%
1956	12.3%	1967	11.7%
1957	10.9%	1968	12.1%
1958	8.6%	1969	11.5%
1959	10.4%	1970	9.3%
1960	9.2%	1971	9.3% (est.)

SOURCE: Economic Report of the President, January 1972, Table B-38.

Profits peaked in 1950 at 15.4% and have been zigzagging downhill ever since, and most significantly since 1966 in the middle of what economists termed an overheated economy with domestic business booming and with the expenses of fighting the war in Vietnam at the same time.

Declining profits by this drip-drip method indicates that the future has cast its shadow. When large corporations complain of a "profit squeeze" they do not mean that profits have gone to zero, but that their old accustomed high returns on equity are not returning. They are making money but at a decreasing rate. Will profits go to zero? Ultimately, yes. The question, then, is why can't they turn around? Here is one interesting answer:

> The profits of the ABC Company are a function—in the mathematical sense—of the national GNP, varying with its growth rate. This holds true for most American companies, and indeed is fairly obvious without statistical support. A high national growth rate normally means rising profits, and vice versa.
>
> Another statistical conclusion is not so obvious. . . . For nearly every large company there is a *dividing line* in the rate of increase of sales, year by year, above which the rate of profit increases more rapidly than the rate of increase in sales, but below which the rate of profit decreases.
>
> Thus, if the ABC Company's dividing line is found to be at 3.5%, profits will increase faster than the increase in sales above the dividing line. But if sales are increasing at only 2% per year, and thus below the 3.5% dividing line, the rate of profit will decline— even though sales are still going up.[4]

In an affluent society consumers reach saturation levels in the consumption of goods. By 1972, for example, these levels had been reached in the ownership of kitchen ranges and refrigerators as 98.7% and 99.1% of all households owned these durables. In time this will be the case with all the other durable components of the "consumer package." Even replacement and supplementary demand will wane. It can be only a question of time until corporations by the dozens fall below their "dividing lines." Add to this the long-run implications of the consumer's spending for services outweighing his expenditures for goods, and we can recognize that we are witnessing the last days of the New Industrial State, the era when profits disappeared.

While discussing the errors of orthodox economics and the traditional role given to savings and their use, an eminent British economist presents this alternative view of disappearing profits:

> It is impossible to regard this rate of saving as representing the 'will of society' in a sense which gives it authority. The amount of saving must be supposed to be strongly influenced by the distribution of income and wealth between families [as noted earlier], which in this model [orthodox] is completely arbitrary. Moreover savings decisions are made by mortal men whereas 'society' must conceive itself to be perpetual.
>
> If these objections could be met, a worse remains. The model is intended to depict a process of 'deepening' the structure of capital. To take the simplest case, technical knowledge is given and the labour force is constant. Accumulation is improving equipment per man and raising output per head. The capital/output ratio in value terms is rising. Labour is continually being released to man more productive equipment by raising the bread-wage rate to a level that less productive equipment can no longer pay. As time goes by, the rate of return on further investment falls. The faster accumulation takes place, the faster the wage rate rises and the faster the rate of profit falls. It seems that the benefit to 'society' from saving is not properly reflected in the 'reward' to the savers. How then does 'society' secure that the optimum amount of saving takes place?[5]

In either argument the real-life economic forces are inexorable: profits are headed for zero. There is scant evidence that we can stem the tide.

What about competition? This is dear to the heart and tongue of American businessmen, although already today it is a dim memory for most of them. Large industrial corporations learned a long, long time ago that it is economically better to live and let live than to compete, especially with price, in the so-called free marketplace. We evolved, instead, what some call "corporate socialism":

> It is appropriate to note the growth of corporate socialism in America now, after the first full year of Nixon's New

> Economic Policy. Not that it all began August 15, 1971. "One of the most significant signs of the new social era," said Woodrow Wilson in 1913, "is the degree to which government has been associated with business. I speak, for the moment, of the control over the government exercised by big business." The Federal Trade Commission in 1914, the New Deal regulatory agencies and the 1946 Employment Act ended forever any sharp distinction between the public and private sectors. But it was Phases I and II which made a quantum leap away from the theory and practice of competitive capitalism.
>
> It was a paradoxical turnabout, but not without precedent. In the early 1920's, Lenin, facing a severe economic crisis, applied a strong dose of capitalism to get the Soviet economy in gear. He called it his New Economic Policy (NEP).[6]

The end of the free marketplace came on August 15, 1971, when wage and price controls were introduced in peacetime.

Our economy just will not operate the way it is supposed to operate, the way we have been taught that it will operate. The economic theory and techniques—perhaps viable in the 19th century—which we use over and over to bail us out of recurring recessions provide ample evidence that our solutions are merely quasi-solutions creating residual effects that multiply into additional problems. That something is dead wrong is apparent.

Will game plans and new economic plans work? Only if they are genuinely *new*. The old economics is bankrupt. Status Quo economist Arthur Burns, chairman of the Federal Reserve Board, reasoned recently that classic economic policies would have a better chance of working "if life would only quiet down for awhile."[7] We cannot stop the world while we get off. We must deal with the new and boisterous economic world we have. The world we do have and can have and will have is what this book is about.

We are warned against putting too much hope in national economic planning:

> Is there a single country whose economic life, over a period of years, has been guided by an economic plan, so that the targets set out in the plan bear a modest resemblance to events as they actually occur? . . .
>
> For all we know, the few apparent successes (if there are

> any) constitute no more than random occurrences. . . .
> Advocates of plans and planning, naturally enough, do not spend their time demonstrating that it has been successful. Rather they explain why planning is wonderful despite the fact that, as it happens, things have not worked out that way. Planning is defended not in terms of results but as a valuable process.[8]

Fear not. What follows is not a national economic plan. It is rather a brief sketch of hints, speculations, and perhaps inevitabilities about the future. A computer age and a Service Economy will exhibit a redemocratization of certain economic activities and functions. A curious combination of increased decentralization and increased centralization will occur. Consumer sovereignty, as noted, is here. The new consumer, with his new money power, will have more freedom to put his money to work where he thinks it will work best. So much of the handling of his money by others in the past has been so costly for the average person that he developed, especially in the late 1960s, a gun-shy attitude, for example, toward securities: witness the changed behavior of the odd-lotter and the net redemption of mutual funds. The consumer has found these products not favorably consumable, and until he changes his ideas, or institutions change to accommodate him, the search for new capital to finance new ventures will become increasingly difficult in the years to come.

It will be necessary for the people to regain control of their money, and the best place to start is where the money presently is: the banks and the Federal Reserve System.

The function of the Federal Reserve System is all but lost on the average consumer. It was designed as, and remains, a banker's bank, so the average consumer never does business directly with it. The primary focus of the Fed has always been to serve business, not the consumer, and it is still doing this today. The Fed has consistently failed the consumer. In one of the Fed's own studies in 1972, for example, it calculated that the average rate of interest paid by consumers on installment credit was 21%. The average business interest paid during the same time was a third of this, about 7%. Not much financial good trickles down to the consumer from the Fed. The Fed was designed to be business-and-bank oriented, and the consumer is nowhere represented in its hierarchy from the chairman of the Federal

Reserve Board on down. As demonstrated time after time, this note brings into sharp focus again the business orientation of the Fed:

> Within three weeks after [Secretary of Treasury] Connally's Lockheed press conference of May 6, 1971, Arthur Burns of the Federal Reserve Board was seeking $2 billion in federal guarantees for companies whose failures might harm the economy. Ignored were the more than 10,000 small business failures a year that individually don't threaten the economy.[9]

All modern societies need a central bank so that the economics of living can be accomplished, but in the years to come we must consciously redesign the Fed into a different form with a revised focus. This will start with consumers participating in the decision making processes, especially since *only* the Fed has the power to *create new money*. The hows and whys of this should be focused *directly,* not indirectly, on the needs of millions of Americans buying more and more services outside the corporate yard. Among the ignored consumers there is an abundance of talent with the expertise to participate in the technical goings-on at the Fed.

About banks. Obscured from the average consumer is the basic fact that banks need him more than he needs the banks. Once consumers learn this they will be able to cause shifts of money to institutions that will give first priority to *their* needs, not those of Lockheed or General Motors—or like this now common practice, as reported in the newspapers in September 1972:

> The controlling interest in Detroit's Bank of Commonwealth changed hands again Thursday, officially ending its connection with the floundering financial empire of Donald H. Parsons.
>
> Detroit mortgage bankers James T. Barnes, Sr., and James T. Barnes, Jr., announced they had exercised their option to buy 32% of the preferred stock and 39% of the common stock from the Chase Manhattan Bank for an undisclosed sum.
>
> With the bank the Barnes family is assuming $30.5 million debt, money the Federal Deposit Insurance Corporation lent to the bank when the collapse of Parson's empire forced officials to decide the bank "was in danger of closing."
>
> The FDIC actually pledged $60 million, but the younger

> Barnes said he did not think it would be necessary to use any more of it.[!][10]

This sort of thing is and has been much too routine.

A consumer's main contact with his money is through his bank. Banks do little multiplying of the consumer's money and a great deal of dividing it.

In a true service society, however, consumers will not need banks in their present form, but the consumer has to learn this. Many do not know, for example, that under our present fractionalized banking system, banks only keep cash on hand at any time to equal about 20% of the demand if all the customers walked in on the same day to withdraw their demand (checking) deposits and time deposits. The money is not there. It is outside the bank, working. The money is making money for someone else, most generally a corporation, certainly not a consumer-depositor who gets precious little return on his money.

The banks need the small-guy-consumers' money more than they need the banks. This money, together with the new money the banks generate through lending the depositors' money, must be focused now on the needs of consumers. Instead of lowering the boom on them as present practice does, the red carpet should be rolled out, as it is for the banks' "prime" corporate customers. The individual pays far more for a car loan than an auto manufacturer pays for a bank loan; this is the way the system works, and this is construed as being "good"—the best way to resolve the problem.

Banks will come to resemble, in both financial and physical structure, the modern credit unions. Consumers seem to like them a lot; by the middle of 1972, consumers already had $18 billion of their money in these institutions and this just represented the financial action of 24.3 million American wage earners, about one-third of the total.

> Taken altogether, credit unions are larger than all but three U.S. banks and in a class with the biggies, like Chase Manhattan and Bank of America. The biggest single difference is that the commercials [banks] return their profits to the stockholders while credit unions return their surpluses to their depositors and, in some cases, even to their borrowers. Their depositors are their stockholders.[11]

Some difference. Representative Wright Patman recognizes the difference—and its significance. He says "Next to the church, credit unions have done more good for the people than any other institution."[12] He should know. Patman is the long-time chairman of the House Banking and Currency Committee; he is to banks what Ralph Nader is to the automobile manufacturers. Credit unions have their detractors. Guess who? The owner of a finance company stated that "credit unions are an affront to our free enterprise system."[13] Translated into real-life economic English this means it is better *for him* if consumers pay him 38+% for the same money they could get through the credit union for 12%. His money, it should be noted, he obtains from a bank, paying 6%-8%.

Consumers tomorrow will form and own their own banks, which will be a part of a central system with consumer orientation first, not last. In 1972 the *Los Angeles Times* ran an article headlined, "Newest California Fad: Start a Bank."

> And a shortage of banks is not the reason. California already supports 151 banks (96 chartered by the state, 55 by the federal government) and several of the largest branch networks in the world.
>
> The tiny newcomers hope to survive the competition by giving their communities more for their money than the big statewide chains—more civic involvement, better personal relationships and lower service charges, they claim.[14]

Whether these "new" banks will simply look like the old banks and perform the same services at the same prices and reap the same high profits or indeed be *new* banking institutions is a moot question. Likely there will be more old than new. Yet they are harbingers of the change coming. They may well foreshadow a consumer-owned and consumer-oriented institution with new concepts to serve people and not corporations.

The control and operation of the banks and the central system to focus on consumer needs ahead of business needs will be increasingly easy in the years ahead with the increasingly widespread use of "electronic money." This is numbers money transmitted by computers and other electronic data machines. Electronic tellers and electronic change-making machines are already in use, and they will become a large part of our money life in the years to come, but they need not be located in banks per se. They can be in grocery stores or other locations with high traffic counts. This is an area where the National Credit Card idea is relevant. I discuss this later.

Banks in their present form are obsolete. Computer hardware has done this job.

What about loans? In the consumer's bank, lines of credit will be pre-established, so that when a consumer decides to make a big-ticket purchase, like an automobile, the financial signals will mesh electronically and he will drive away in the auto. The same for other types of credit extensions.

Consumers using their own banks and credit sources can easily get together to finance their own apartments or homes, as they do their own churches right now. The same can be done with durables and nondurables.

The need for the rapid transition into electronic money is recognized already today, but it is envisaged under yesterday's guidance and control. In September 1972 Thomas Hal Clarke, a member of the Federal Home Loan Bank Board, told the California State Savings and Loan League convention that today's system of checks, deposit forms, and withdrawal slips is costly, bulky, and incredibly time consuming.

> I believe that the replacement of this procedure by a system of instantaneous electronic transference is absolutely inevitable.
>
> Financial institutions and stores and businesses throughout the nation will eventually be electronically interconnected, so that transfers and account updating will occur at all points in the transaction almost simultaneously.[15]

But again there is that pervasive motif, McLuhan's lament: "trying to do today's job with yesterday's tools—with yesterday's concepts." Or similar: Let's do tomorrow's work with today's tools; we will merely extend present institutions electronically. It will be faster, but the ground rules will be the same: The interest charges will be the same and any savings effected by this network will be passed on to the owners and not the customers who make it all possible and keep it alive and well. A pseudo-solution. No change. Yet change is what the system is crying out for.

Tax monies provide another large source of revenues that can, with consumer direction, be used for direct benefit to consumers. For example, at local levels there is no reason that some present tax collections cannot fund consumer groups of attorneys, economists, and computer experts, who on a full time basis will organize and pursue the consumer's interests while the consumer is himself busy earning his own living. These groups, using cable TV—consumer owned and operated—will hook into regional and national networks for the interchange of data and a variety of information the consumer wants and needs.

An example of the power of diverting small tax payments paid by many people and putting them to work is clearly demonstrated in the hidden subsidy to banks provided by homeowners with mortgages.

> Millions of homeowners make monthly payments for local property taxes along with their regular mortgage payments. Banks and savings and loan associations place these tax payments into escrow accounts and turn them over to local governments once or twice a year, depending on state law. Meantime they loan out their escrow funds at interest, but pay no interest to the depositor-homeowner. To make matters worse, local governments must often borrow from banks—at interest—while waiting for their bank-held taxes to come in.
>
> A recent study by the Citizens Action Group, a community organization in Chicago, calculated that Cook County banks and savings and loans get free use of about $200 million annually from property-tax escrow accounts. At the same time, Cook County in 1970 paid $37.5 million in interest on short-term loans for working cash, called "tax anticipation warrants.". . .
>
> How much does this cost the average homeowner? The House Banking and Currency Committee staff estimates that if banks invest their property-tax escrow funds at four percent, the average family loses about $800 over the life of a 30 year mortgage (the exact amount depends on local property tax rates and the value of the property involved). Actually the loss is probably greater, since many banks comingle their property-tax escrow funds with their general lending funds, which can earn seven percent or more. And the homeowner pays again at the other end of the cycle, when his taxes are raised to pay interest on working cash his local government must borrow.[16]

Money at work works in diverse and curious ways; there is no reason that these channels cannot be turned around 180° and work for the consumers instead of against them.

The computer decentralizes at the same time that it centralizes, and many already foresee the day when a lot of work will be done in the home, like accounting, for example, and the results transmitted to a central gathering area. The same extensions can be found for a variety of our current needs that we are now forced to leave the home to satisfy, such as grocery shopping, for instance.

Today we take tax monies and pay to farmers not to grow cotton; tomorrow we will take tax monies and give them to children to go to schools of their own choice, or take a sabbatical in the form of a foreign trip if that is what the student wants. Today we pay to ride buses; tomorrow we will take highway tax monies and provide free bus service, solving a lot of car congestion problems at the same time. Today we embarrass welfare recipients; tomorrow we will provide guaranteed income for those unable or unwilling to work—and think nothing of this.

Wall Street is just beginning to change and is valiantly trying to alter some of its structure enough to placate the users, but greater change is on the horizon. What about the raising of new capital for new businesses tomorrow? With a stock market now dominated by financial institutions, the old idea of an entrepeneur incorporating and selling shares to individuals who meet in the marketplace is obsolete. The consumer-investor has for a long time been largely out of the market, as a trading place, and it is not likely he will return. Raising of new capital can, however, be done in a grocery store. A computer can in that location print out prospectus-type data to an interested consumer-investor. He can study this output at home, and, if interested, can return, place his order through another machine, and pay for it in yet another machine. These will all be tied into a network that with other computers will show the totals for this financial activity. There is no reason to believe that the consumer's pension funds and bank trust funds cannot be similarly handled. Already today the SEC is suggesting that consumers be given the same type of research data that the mutual funds use and base decisions on, in order to let the informed consumer-investor make his own decisions on equally relevant data.

In other words, the consumer will be able to plan his own personal investment program, e.g., choosing a certain percentage return on his money (the higher the return, the higher the risk, of course), choosing capital gains, selling short, choosing foreign security mixes, choosing stocks alone or stocks and bonds, etc. A variety of these options will be programmed and readily available by the computer. The machine will print out an individual selection; if the consumer does not like it, he will ask for another plan. The portfolios will be prepackaged like meat. He will not need mutual funds or bank trust fund management. In the past he has had this at a frightful cost and the results have added up to something less than fruitful for the average person.

All of the securities in the country will be on one giant computer, and stock holdings will be on data cards. This will wipe out the ability of owners of large blocks of securities to rig the markets, since large orders will be matched on branch terminals designed to accommodate large sizes. A mass of people will buy and sell without ever knowing who did what and at a price eminently more equitable than is now achieved. More with less.

To raise new capital, investment bankers will no longer be needed. Corporations will put the relevant data directly into computers in understandable language and the interested speculator/investor will get them directly from the computer.

Tomorrow's consumer will not be content to channel his savings in accordance with central banker's wishes. He will be able to select from an array of savings-type securities, the ones that best fit his needs and desires.

There will be a lot of financial men looking for new careers in this environment unless they reorient their views.

Now a more extended word about a National Credit Card. Since World War II, the great American industrial machine has surged ever up, with few and mild downturns, and its base has been credit. A quantum growth has taken place in consumer installment credit and home mortgage credit in tandem with corporate borrowing and government borrowing.

Retailers learned a long time ago that a "charge" customer will spend on the average about three times more than a cash customer. Sears has become the sixth largest financial institution in the U.S. "Charge or [long pause . . . more softly] cash?" is the modern sales closer.

It was noted earlier that credit cards have been widely accepted and used during the past few years. It was also noted that the added debt loads have brought in their wake high individual bankruptcies even in our most prosperous times. But such is the behavior of most Americans today and to change this state of affairs would most likely take an economic disaster. That this will happen ultimately is foreordained, since the state will become the ultimate creditor. And in the early 1970s it was seen fullfilling this role explicitly. e.g., Penn Central, Lockheed, etc.

In national economic planning, when efforts are made to get the taxpayer-consumer to save or spend, *tax* increases or decreases have been the historical tool. But, depending on the external economic mix prevailing at the time tax measures are effected, the consumer has often negated their intent and behaved oppositely.

It would be a relatively simple matter, however, for the federal government to develop a National Credit Card. Everyone has a Social Security card and number; this would be the vehicle. Built into the project would be the Internal Revenue Service, which would set credit limits individually and enforce collections (their reputation for this is well known by the consuming masses). The Federal Reserve Board could direct desired spending or savings goals. Every business in America, large and small, would participate.

The entire affair could be run at a profit by the super-manager, the government, using computers. The federal government, under the direction of the Congress, would determine consumer-benefit projects to receive the profits earned: urban rapid transit, pollution control, low income housing, public parks, etc. This seems to end up with a curious twist: The people, in toto, would be allowed, for once, to *participate directly in the profits* of a system they *make profitable*. Gone would be the diverting of at least these monies to fund wars and vested-interest dams and highways.

The hardware to do the job is here now. For example, the Federal Reserve is already transferring sums of money larger than $1,000 from one point to another in the U.S. by using computers.

Naturally, the resistance to such a proposal is also built in: giant banks, giant oil companies, certain retailers, GMAC, not to mention the parasitical collection agencies and credit reporting agencies, whose total costs, when added onto the credit, make the entire system lopsided now. These losers would cry that this spells the end of private enterprise for the profit-competitive system. But that system is gone. As George Romney recently said: "Our economy is no longer predominantly based on a policy of free competitive enterprise."[17] Though this has been recognized by many for a long time, it has taken a much longer time for those in high positions to admit it.

Since the U.S. entered a controlled economy on August 15, 1971 with President Nixon's New Economic Plan, it is certain that other devices will be needed in the years to come to channel the cash flows of the masses of consumers in directions determined by the government.

It is interesting to note that outside this area imaginative private enterprise has already begun expanding the base for credit card plans. For example, in October 1971 Kroger, the nation's third largest food chain, began experimenting with bringing the cashless society to the supermarket and to smaller retail establishments. A Kroger supermarket in Columbus, Ohio installed computer terminals at its check-out counters. These were hooked up to a central computer at the City National Bank & Trust Co. of Columbus for validation of credit card transactions.

All the shopper had to do when he got to the head of the line was present his credit card. The clerk, using a special telephone which linked the terminal unit with City National's computer, placed the card in the terminal and rang up the amount of the purchase on the geared-in register. The computer read information on a magnetic stripe on the back of the card. It then confirmed the amount of the transaction by voice response and authorized the clerk to proceed with the sale. Then, after checking to see if the card had been reported lost or stolen, in which case it would alert the clerk, the computer debited the customer's credit card amount. The computer also transferred an offsetting credit to the supermarket's account and performed reconciling functions at the end of the day.

Other merchants participating in the test—in suburban, affluent Upper Arlington—were a chain discount store, a chain drugstore, a local drugstore, a beauty parlor, a restaurant, and shoe, fabric, jewelry, book, tape, and appliance stores.

Also in 1971 a prearranged auto loan plan was introduced by Security Pacific National Bank in California. Called Ready Auto-

Finance, and seen as an extension of the bank's Master Charge and Ready Reserve Account check guarantee program, the plan provides a preapproved auto loan with a purchase draft valid at any franchised new-car dealer in California. The buyer simply arranges ahead of time for a loan of up to 80% of the price (including tax and insurance) he expects to pay for a new auto. When the deal is ready to be closed, the buyer fills in the bank draft and hands it to the dealer, who turns it in to his own bank.

These smaller beginnings allow us to more easily see the use and implications of a National Credit Card. Its advantages would, of course, be enormously larger—*and* would accrue to all instead of a selected few.

Epilogue

> Growth for the sake of growth is the ideology of the cancer cell.
>
> *Edward Abbey*

Now a few summary statements and additional documentation, along with a brief look ahead.

In the United States the producer-consumer relationship is seen as "a natural order of things." We hardly question it. Despite inflation, rising unemployment, and balance of payments deficits all at the same time, which is labeled "an accident," we are constantly reminded by those in power that the producer-consumer relationship continues to be dominant in our economy. But a Service Economy destroys this dominance. All at once the producer (producer of services) and the consumer are, with few exceptions, one—merged.

We all know that things are not like they used to be, but some of the more subtle changes are tremendously significant. For example, twenty years ago banks urged us to Save!; now they encourage us to overdraw. Consumers used to "go into debt"; now they have a "line of credit." A Louis Harris Survey for the National Retail Merchants Association shows that consumer confidence in retailers plunged from 48% in 1966 to 24% in 1971.[1] This should tell the "producers" something. Prevailing economic thought and practice, wedded to the past, is too treacherous and too wrong for us to tolerate further.

> The justification for subsidizing producers rather than consumers, and among producers, wealthowners rather than workers, is the old trickle-down thesis: if enough benefits are handed out to wealthowners, something will seep through to the workers. Some consequences of this approach can be seen in [the] housing assistance programs of the Department of Housing and Urban Development. . . . HUD's section 235 and 236 programs were intended to stimulate the construction and rehabilitation of inner city homes and apartments. The idea was that if HUD subsidized leaders and developers by paying most of the interest cost on housing loans, more units for low income families would be built. More units *were* built, but so many were overpriced and shoddy, and so many inexperienced buyers were cheated by subsidy-seeking speculators, that HUD has been racked by scandal and saddled with thousands of repossessions. Sadder, wiser and billions of tax dollars later, HUD Secretary George W. Romney now admits it would make a lot more sense to give money directly to poor families to buy or rent shelter in the regular market.[2]
>
> We can no longer afford $100 billion mistakes. [Romney][3]

But we *are* going to be hit with additional Big Mistakes—and not just because of graft, chicanery, or cheap goods—if we fail to recognize the vast importance of our Service Economy. For instance, we noted earlier that one of the major goals of Nixon's New Economic Program of August 1971 was to create jobs in the goods-producing sector, especially automobiles. Table 22 shows what happened in the year after the program was announced.

On a quarterly comparative basis the services-producing sector generated two to five times as many jobs as the goods-producing sector. Surely the strongly held myth among Status Quo Economists about the importance of automobiles to the economic health of the country (they say that one out of six jobs is dependent, directly or indirectly, upon the auto industry) is due for some rethinking. Certainly "what's good for General Motors" is *no longer* "good for the country "—if it ever was. Status Quo Economists, liberal and conservative, roundly applauded most of the New Economic Program. If any of them anticipated the real-life job creation that was bound to take place, it was kept well concealed. Of course, the automobile companies did create *some* jobs nonetheless; they also *sold* a lot of auto-

TABLE 22

CHANGE IN THE NUMBER OF EMPLOYEES IN THE U.S. ON NONAGRICULTURAL PAYROLLS*

Thousands of persons, seasonally adjusted

	1971				1972		
	I	II	III	IV	I	II	III
Total	197	260	82	444	684	743	442
Services-producing industries	248	242	178	370	499	481	381
Transportation and public utilities	7	—12	—46	—3	46	27	—4
Trade	75	75	103	109	154	177	111
Finance, insurance, and real estate	29	35	28	37	29	37	26
Services	57	47	70	106	110	142	152
Federal government	—1	3	1	2	5	—12	—33
State and local government	81	94	22	119	155	110	129
Goods-producing industries	—50	18	—96	75	185	260	61
Mining	—2	—1	—12	—58	62	—11	0
Construction	—35	72	15	71	23	16	—5
Manufacturing	—13	—53	—99	62	100	255	66
Durable	27	—35	—70	41	70	193	88
Nondurable	—41	—17	—29	21	30	62	—21

*Computed from quarterly averages.
Source: *Survey of Current Business,* U.S. Department of Commerce, October 1972 .

TABLE 23

GROSS PRODUCT IN CONSTANT DOLLARS BY INDUSTRY: SELECTED YEARS

Industry	Billion of 1958 dollars			Percent change from previous year			Average annual rate of change[2]
	1971	1961	1959	1971	1961	1959	1960-70
All industries, total (GNP)	741.7	497.2	475.9	2.7	1.9	6.4	4.0
Transportation	35.1	22.5	22.2	2.0	.1	6.1	4.4
Railroads	10.4	8.7	8.9	—2.3	—.8	5.2	2.1
Motor freight & warehousing	13.2	7.5	7.0	6.6	3.3	9.9	5.6
Communication	23.3	10.6	9.5	6.6	5.7	7.1	8.1
Telephone & telegraph	22.0	9.7	8.6	6.5	6.3	7.9	8.5
Electric, gas, & sanitary services	22.5	12.9	11.6	6.6	4.6	8.0	5.5
Wholesale & retail trade	131.9	83.5	80.8	4.0	1.5	7.6	4.4
Wholesale trade	58.1	34.6	32.2	4.0	4.5	9.6	5.4
Retail trade	73.7	48.9	48.6	4.0	—.5	6.3	3.8
Finance, insurance, & real estate	98.8	67.1	61.4	3.4	4.7	3.7	4.1
Finance & insurance	21.0	15.4	14.3	7.7	3.2	.0	2.8
Services	69.5	48.3	45.1	1.1	3.5	5.2	3.9
Government & government enterprises	70.0	50.6	47.9	.0	2.8	1.3	3.6
General government	60.7	44.8	42.5	.0	2.5	1.0	3.3
Agriculture, forestry & fisheries	26.9	23.4	22.3	3.1	1.3	1.1	1.3
Farms	25.5	22.2	21.1	3.3	1.3	1.2	1.3
Mining	16.8	13.3	12.8	—2.6	.9	4.0	2.8
Contract construction	24.0	21.4	22.0	2.0	—1.5	6.6	.9
Manufacturing	221.4	140.4	138.9	1.7	—.3	12.4	4.6
Nondurable goods industries	95.7	60.7	59.0	4.0	1.3	9.2	4.4
Durable goods industries	125.8	79.7	79.9	.0	—1.5	14.8	4.7
Rest of the world	5.6	2.9	2.2				
Residual[1]	—4.3	.1	—.9				
Addenda:							
Private sector	681.0	452.3	433.4	3.0	1.9	7.0	4.2
Private nonfarm business	633.0	414.8	398.4	2.8	1.8	7.4	4.2

[1] Represents the difference between GNP measured as sum of final products and GNP measured as the sum of gross product originating by industries.
[2] Arithmetic average of the 10 annual percent changes.
SOURCE: *Survey of Current Business,* U.S. Department of Commerce, November 1972.

mobiles, thus easing a grievous inventory problem. When that industry looks to Washington for aid, their tunnel vision widens to include their peripheral vision.

When we turn things over to Big Brother, we find that the fixation in Washington on the producer-consumer relationship, the "natural order of things," spells economic disaster for the projects under way, and waste piles on waste for the taxpayer. Witness: housing, education, poverty, etc. And, yet, to have a plan whereby the money would go *directly* to the recipients for them to spend as they see fit for their own good is perceived as contrary to the American Way, as unapple-pieish, and of course as anti-motherhood.

The above statistical evidence released by the government in October 1972 documented the significantly larger increase in service sector jobs as opposed to production sector jobs during the past year. Longer-range data were released in November 1972. Note in Table 23 the services-producing industries—the first seven categories listed in the table (Transportation through Government). For the period 1960-1970, the average annual rate of change for the service industries was 4.86%; for manufacturing, 4.60%. That is, during the decade there was a *6% greater growth of service industries* over manufacturing. Despite this impressive evidence, the *Wall Street Journal* was still peering "ahead" in its rearview mirror in December 1972:

> The average workweek for factory workers, *considered a leading indicator of the demand for labor,* rose 0.2 hour to a seasonally adjusted 40.9 hours, the highest level since October 1968.[4]

In the light of what this book has emphasized about "bad numbers," leading indicators, and where the demand for labor irrefutably exists, one is led to wonder with dismay at the continual reemergence of hackneyed economic phrases and "explanations" heaped upon previous piles of cliches. Moving the bones from one graveyard to another graveyard perhaps describes the process more accurately.

TV and our electric age has, as McLuhan and others tell us, decentralized the structure of our society; in this sense the growth of a Service Economy is a natural result. Services are "tribal," in McLuhan's word, and widely dispersed; though the computer centrally receives all data, the inputs are decentralized. McLuhan notes:

> Subscription TV means audience participation in programming without benefit of ratings or sponsors. Instead of a package deal, the viewer will get service. Service as a matter of course and not a matter of crisis.
>
> Miss America was killed by TV along with the Hollywood star system and the political parties.[5]

I have argued throughout this book that the same processes are at work in our economic life.

Wall Street Money Managers and their in-house business economists, together with the academic economists and the national economists of prominence, spend their time rationalizing the Status Quo; the fact that they have been called "national" *obsoletes* them in a "tribal" environment.

The New York Stock Exchange itself is a victim of this tribalizing process, yet it remains oblivious to the change. In October 1972 NYSE chairman James N. Needham commented on the financial and operational health of the Exchange, saying that "it is basically sound despite a cyclical shrinking of earnings"; he also reported that eighteen firms which reported losses in August were under "special surveillance" and more firms might be put under surveillance because of September losses. He concluded that one of their problems had been the low volume of trading on the NYSE in recent months.[6]

In the last few years regional exchanges, the development of third and fourth markets, crossing of orders, and the like have caused the Exchange and its members to squirm. Being "national" is now a liability, not an asset.

Economic decentralization can be seen in our daily lives, for example, in terms of the rise of specialty magazines and the death of mass-circulation publications such as *Look, Saturday Evening Post, Life;* the rise of the specialty book clubs (Goodbye Book-of-the-Month Club); customizing by the young of mass-produced automobiles; do-it-yourself economics; neighborhood TV. The masses of consumers are out there, "tribalized," so mass-made goods neither fit nor fill needs as they did years ago. (Goodbye Betty Crocker. Goodbye Bank of America.)

At the federal government level, Status Quo Economists strive, with yesterday's economic tools (fiscal and monetary controls, revenue sharing, etc.), to centralize and solve problems in a fragmented Service

Society. Sooner or later we will find macroeconomics (the big picture) returning to microeconomics (the small picture) for its answers; national economic planning will—must—return to the local level. In the meantime we are flirting with catastrophe at many levels. Charles Schultze, Lyndon Johnson's budget director, has concluded:

> In many cases, very little is known about what works and what does not work in the areas of social and industrial behavior that are covered by the newer programs. . . . Indeed, the history of the 1960's makes clear that current federal approaches are not particularly effective.[7]

One problem area is debt. It may take another economic disaster to make it possible for us to "see" again. Note the figures in Table 24.

TABLE 24
DEBT AND GNP GROWTH

	1969 (millions of dollars)	1970 (millions of dollars)	Percentage increase
Gross National Product	$929,095	$974,126	5.01%
Net Public & Private Debt	$ 1,722	$ 1,839	6.79%

SOURCE: *Survey of Current Business,* U.S. Department of Commerce, April 1972.

Others do not perceive this situation as being anything but "good." Martin R. Gainsbrugh, senior vice-president and chief economist of the Conference Board, wrote an advertisement for CIT Financial Corporation in November 1972:

> Public debt in relative terms has thus grown less rapidly than the national economy since 1946, while private debt has grown more rapidly; total debt, as a result of these offsetting trends, remains almost exactly what it was relative to GNP 25 years ago.
>
> Wars and depressions have caused temporary elevations in the relationship of public debt to national output. Still, in relative terms, public debt is no greater now than a generation earlier. Private debt has been trending steadily upward relative to GNP since the end of World War II. But even here the present ratio compares favorably with that prevailing in 1929 and 1939. The record presented in this review suggests that the growth of debt has not been as unbridled as many would believe. The allocation of credit by the vari-

> ous financial mechanisms has been keyed much closer than is generally recognized to the pace of national economic growth.[8]

It is also argued, ever so frequently, that internal debt (debt held in the U.S.) is not important anyway, since "we owe it to each other." What is *not* frequently asked is: Who owns the debt and who receives the interest? Most of the public debt and most of the private debt is owned by corporations (e.g., CIT), banks, and wealthy individuals who receive the interest paid by the masses of consumers and taxpayers. Inevitably, this leads to further concentration of money into fewer hands at a rapid rate—and at the federal government level allows entire sectors, such as housing, to benefit at the expense of other sectors. This ripoff of the benign consumer-taxpayer is reaching the point of no return—in more ways than one. For one thing, he winds up with less each month to spend, and consumer demand, always longed for, slumps.

In addition, when we talk about national economic growth by the debt path, how much of the debt is merely replacing other debt at steadily rising interest rates and consequent economic waste? Public debt is supported by the awesome power to tax (which has limits). Private debt is supported by a viable economic system, not one where assets created, such as those in Vietnam, are "wasted"; where consumers buy money instead of new cars, or, as 44% are doing, borrow simply to pay off other past debts. This says nothing of adding more debt (at incredibly high rates of interest, which engenders *still more debt)* to pay for services at high and accelerating prices, and then incurring more debt (and still more high interest service costs) at still higher prices to pay for the past prices, and endlessly on.

On balance, the debt problem today is *not* the same as that of a generation ago. It is distinctly and more troublesomely different. The nature and the quality of the debt now loom much larger than its relative quantity.

The overall comparison of GNP with debt affords only a *very rough* measure of consuming more than we produce, since it is actually a "bad numbers" comparison (the measurement of GNP is altogether too general and too rough), but it admirably suits the purposes of the Status Quo Economists who give it credence since they and their employers live off the interest.

However, a microeconomics approach provides much more alarming evidence of the excesses. Since the prime focus of this book has been on the economic behavior of the consumer, Table 25 provides some interesting insights into this multiplying of the credit-debt structure:

TABLE 25
FUTURE SHOCK

	1971 Third Quarter	1972 Third Quarter	Percentage Increase or Decrease
Personal Income	137.9	149.4	+8.7%
Personal Taxes	141.6	170.0	+20.5%
Disposable Personal Income	137.4	146.2	+6.5%
Personal Savings	151.0	125.7	—20.8%
Consumer Installment Credit Extended	145.1	160.9	+10.3%
Consumer Installment Credit Repaid	137.4	148.3	+8.0%

NOTE: Figures shown are index numbers compiled by source.
SOURCE: *Finance Facts,* December 1972, p. 2.

One does not need a Ph.D. degree in economics to observe that Credit use by the consumer during this period was reaching runaway proportions, vastly in excess of increases in Disposable Personal Income. The consumer was living further into the future as he used more credit and as he borrowed more than he was repaying. Consumers were approaching bankruptcy en masse. When the consumer's financial future vanishes, so does that for business.

This is what the Status Quo calls "spending ourselves rich." As noted earlier, how can we do this, though, when we spend so much *now* for *services?* when inflation takes an added toll? when the future is continually mortgaged to the hilt? Ability to spend approaches zero for the majority of consumers. In other words, as indicated earlier, consumers, in the main, have been recently buying *money* (at exhorbitant rates), *not goods*. Goods, then, pile up in inventory for some other tomorrow, as automobiles did before the New Economic Program. In sum, then, we are witnessing a gross distortion of the timeworn "spend-ourselves-rich" economic theory, using the consumer as the guinea pig.

A Penny Saved Is a Penny That Hurts the Economy

BY ART BUCHWALD

In order for President Nixon's new economic game plan to work, the United States must increase its gross national product by 9% to $1,065 billion. That is to say, this country must produce that amount of goods and services . . . whether it needs to or not. Now it isn't enough just to produce that amount of goods and services. Someone has to buy them. Unless Mr. John Q. Consumer becomes a big spender, all Mr. Nixon's economic hopes for the country will go down the drain. It is for this reason that the President has set up a Commission on Wild Spending to see that every American does his share to meet the . . . GNP goal. The plan is to swear in several hundred thousand federal marshals to go around the country and persuade people to spend more money than they've ever spent before. This is how it would work:

"Mr. and Mrs. Moore, my name is Coleman and I'm from the UGNP."

"UGNP?"

"Yes, it stands for 'up the gross national product.' Our U.S. Army civilian files on you indicate that you haven't bought a new car this year."

"Oh, that's easy to explain. We have a car already and it's in good condition."

"Mr. Moore, we don't care what condition your car is in. When you don't buy a car, you're stabbing the President's economic blueprint in the back."

"We are?"

"Yes, you are. Do you consider yourselves loyal patriotic Americans?"

"Of course."

"Then why haven't you bought any furniture lately? Or jewelry or luggage or color television sets or snowmobiles or dishwashers or hot pants?"

"Well, you see, Mr. Coleman, we're getting on in years and we try to put away a little money in the savings bank each week . . ."

"Savings bank? I thought so. America is on the brink of financial disaster and you're putting your money in the savings bank. Suppose everyone squirreled his money away in savings accounts. What kind of a free-spending country would we have then?". . .

"But we have everything we need."

"Don't ever say that, Mr. Moore. Don't ever, ever say that. How many vacations have you taken this year?"

"One. You see, we don't . . ."

"No excuses. Do you realize because you've taken only one vacation the Boeing Aircraft Co. is going broke?"

"Please, Mr. Coleman, you're making us feel so bad. What can we do."

"Go down to the savings bank tomorrow morning, withdraw everything and spend, spend, spend. Eat, drink and consume or tomorrow the GNP will die."

"All right, if you say so."

"Thank you, Mr. and Mrs. Moore. President Nixon will be very relieved."

February 11, 1971

In addition, the situation has been aggravated by corporate liquidity falling from a pre-1960 level of +50% to 22% in late 1972, states and cities enjoying just momentary relief after almost two decades of illiquidity, a federal government budget in complete disarray. To compound the troubles, inflation lacked a handle, there was a drastic redistribution of income (away from the consumers and to the producers), and we had a balance of payments deficit by far and away the greatest in U.S. history—with a further weakening of the dollar just down the road. And a Pearl-Harbor type devaluation of the U.S. dollar struck again in February 1973.

When we make money and create debt at a faster rate than we make services and goods. . . . What then?

During the period 1969-1972 the prices of stocks on Wall Street "fluctuated," as the bromide goes, but other more basic changes were going on at the same time, changes we have noted in this book, such as net redemption of mutual funds, the dominance of institutional trading, and a significant fall off in volume on Wall Street.

In October 1972 Howard Stein, president of Dreyfus (a large mutual fund), observed:

> The investing public is simply announcing that it will not participate at the moment in a market that has failed over the past five years to meet their economic expectations. In effect they are not there because the market has not worked for them.[9]

Then Richard Nixon was reelected, then the Dow Jones closing average broke the 1000 barrier, then the Vietnam peace treaty was signed. Did the investing public return? No.

> Throughout the first ten months of 1972 most analysts felt the public would plunge back into the market if and when the Dow pushed above the 1000 on heavy volume. But most measures indicate it hasn't happened yet.[10]
>
> Says Marvin P. Brown, vice president of Heine, Fishbein & Co. stockbrokers: "There is always some story to explain a stock decline, but the real cause at present is the absence of the public."[11]

The Stock Market is another "national" institution that is obsolete. When, in the future, the public can have access to the stock market and can *on their terms* make purchases or sales of individual stocks or mutual fund shares through a computer terminal in their supermarket, *perhaps* then they will return.

The continuing absence (a long-term trend) from Wall Street of the well-heeled private investor and the dominance of institutional trading directed by Money Managers have resulted in institutions (mutual funds, bank trust departments, pension funds, etc.) buying and selling *to each other* in large blocks. When a critical point is reached in the history of any large corporation and the Money Managers decide, as one, to sell, who will buy?

Yesterday won't give up. It continues to hang in there. In October 1972 the Status Quo Economists of the First National City Bank in New York, the nation's second largest bank, were still spelling out the virtues of capital gains tax benefits; they noted:

> It has helped to form and enlarge the great pool of savings that has financed private investment and fueled economic expansion for years. . . . A bigger tax bite out of capital gains is likely to eat up the seed corn of investment.[12]

This came at a time when investment excesses (amply demonstrated by idle plant capacity) were financed with too much credit (debt) and liquidation was staring many in the face. Among other things, we need now to "tribalize" our savings-investment economics, and that presents an *entirely new* Money Game.

Three months later the same bank economists, amidst the economic spectacle of horrors sketched above, carried this headline in their *Monthly Economic Letter* for December 1972: "General Business Conditions: It's Time To Celebrate."

Must we continue to be prisoners of obsolete Status Quo Economists who do us more grievous harm than our generals? For example, the Nixon economists conceived an Economic Game Plan in 1969 which brought on a recession. Strike 1. As the economy deteriorated during 1970 and into August 1971, the economists continued to pitch out their ideas. Then came, among other things, wage and price controls (which John K. Galbraith had urged in a widely noted letter to the *Wall Street Journal*)—Phase 1 for ninety days and Phase 2 as an extension of that. Wall Street, the mass media, and high business and academic economic councils predicted joyous outcomes.

An "index" was stabilized, but not the one people live by, and consumers saw prices moving up, up, up. Strike 2. Then, in January 1973, controls were cast aside, and we were told of Phase 3 (voluntary guidelines). And the economists' applause was still to be heard. Strike 3. You are "out," as any consumer-batter knows. But not true in economics. Milton Friedman, Status Quo professor of economics at the University of Chicago and leader of "monetarist economics," whose ideas were used in the original Game Plan, had this to say on February 18, 1973: "I've been wrong many times. I keep being optimistic."[13] He did not hear the umpire order him out of the game.

If wage and price controls were so good, why did we all begin to "feel" poorer, and why were they thrown out the window? Economic Czar George P. Shultz (a former University of Chicago colleague of Friedman's) had a few words to say about this on February 16, 1973: "Phase 2 would have exploded before long in our face" from built-up inequities, had it been continued.[14] So, we return to chicken-in-every-pot economics—also called pie-in-the-sky economics. By January 1973 the explosion had already started:

> Wholesale prices, paced by farm product prices, soared 1.1% on an adjusted basis last month [January 1973]. That would work out to a yearly rate of 13.2%.
>
> Price of farm products climbed 4.8%, or at an annual rate of 57.6% compared with an annual rate of 68.4% in December—which was a twenty-six year record.
>
> The large December increase in farm prices has begun to show up at the supermarket. The Labor Department said Thursday [February 15, 1973] that the food component of its group, known as consumer finished goods—basically the food purchased by supermarkets—increased 3.3% last month [January 1973], an annual rate of 39.6%[15]

But consumers were still being told that inflation was under control and that it was their state of mind which was not. The GNP Deflator, a price measure which economists look at but which the real world recognizes as being obsolete and useless, had come down. Inflation psychology persisted simply because everytime a consumer went into his supermarket the prices he noted were still going *up*.

Obsolete economics does not die; it does not even fade away, like old generals. It comes back to bat again and can stand endless strike outs with no penalty, promising more than it can ever deliver. It is the consumer who pays.

In a psychological sense, as Gustav Ichheiser has noted, "Nothing evades our attention so persistently as that which is taken for granted."[16] Perhaps we should no longer take Status Quo Economics for granted.

If there is one thing that the Status Quo Economists work overtime at it is reinforcing to the people the economic myth that they are enjoying a "higher standard of living." *Business Week* magazine, for instance, carried an article entitled "Incomes Continue Their Heady Rise" and gave these figures as evidence:

TABLE 26

PERSONAL INCOME

	October 1971	October 1972	Percentage change
	(millions seasonally adjusted)		
U.S. total	$73,035	$81,248	+11.2%

SOURCE: *Business Week,* January 20, 1973, p. 48.

What *Business Week* did *not* mention is what is seen in the next table.

TABLE 27

PERSONAL INSTALLMENT DEBT

	October 1971	October 1972	Percentage change
	(millions)		
U.S. total	$10,718	$12,404	+15.7%

SOURCE: *Federal Reserve Bulletin,* December 1972, Table A-59.

If the consumer's income had increased at such a dramatic rate, why had his borrowing increased even faster? And, as noted earlier, what about the average interest rate on all of this money which the Federal Reserve calculates as averaging 21% (and which, in real life, is higher)? The consumer was simply consuming money while burying himself in debt. And to make matters worse, the net change in credit outstanding on consumer installment loans took a dramatic turn in 1972—for the worse:

TABLE 28

NET CHANGE CREDIT OUTSTANDING
(Credit Extensions less Repayments)

	October 1971	October 1972	Percentage change
	(millions)		
U.S. total	$875	$1,496	+70.9%

SOURCE: *Federal Reserve Bulletin,* December 1972, Table A-58.

While borrowing more, the consumer had cut back sharply on his repayments. Thus, the consumer was *speculating at retail,* as he did in the stock market in 1929. He was gambling that the future would be better. *It had to be,* if he was to survive financially. Never have so many people owed so much money to so few people.

What about the economic future? Does the future cast its shadows? In economics, as in nature, certain affairs must be kept as closely in balance as it is possible to do so. In the economic sense, we look at those affairs with the concept of national income and separate it as follows:

1. Productive investment (e.g., the making of cars)
2. Unproductive investment (e.g., streets, parks, aid to the poor)
3. Consumption (explored in this book)
4. Foreign trade (favorable/unfavorable balance of trade)

When the New Economic Program was announced in August 1971, the central aim was to move a stagnant economy. Therefore, it was necessary in an economic sense to light all burners and to do this as quickly as possible, so the concentration of the government thrust—with the taxpayer's money—was in productive investment: namely, to get the auto industry out of its doldrums (with heavy inventories and potential financial trouble just down the road). And it was easier because of the long love affair between U.S. consumers and their automobiles; so, on this basis and with the high-powered money the Federal Reserve can create, the officials were able to do just exactly that. As 1972 closed, the U.S. Department of Commerce announced that the GNP had grown at a real rate of +6.5% for 1972—a remarkable achievement in light of a historic growth rate in GNP which has averaged close to 3%.

In this seemingly wonderful process, there are *limiting factors,* and a reader is not likely to find them per se in Paul Samuelson's best-selling text on economics. They are:

The higher the rate of growth desired, the higher the relative share of productive investment in the national income. Indeed, the high level of increment of the national income in August 1971 called for an enormous investment to achieve a new, still higher level. It takes a great deal of money-power to move a large economic mass like the U.S. economy. Huge budget deficits (highly visible) coupled with absolutely enormous government agency debts and other federal government credit guarantees (virtually invisible) incurred in late 1971 and 1972 provided the money-power thrust needed. The fuel—money—needed for this rocket was also created at an annual rate of +8% in 1972 (takes a lot now), compared with a 1952-1962 average of +1.7%. There develops as a by-product of this money extension heavy overlays of uncontrollable credit extensions which impart extra impetus to the entire process. Early in 1973, as the Vietnam war ended, Wall Street took its collective eyes off that conflict and became concerned with money and future inflation, and in January the stock market fell from a DJI level near 1050 to 990.

However, the hooker is *ahead,* and it was apparently not perceived, or if it was, then it was not stressed. As surely as night follows day, the higher the relative share of productive investment in the national income, the more unfavorable the effect on consumption (noted in this book) and on unproductive investment (e.g., the cutback in education and O.E.O., with more to come in 1973). Ominously, there emerges also as a result of these general forces difficulties in equilibrating the balance of trade. And 1972 brought a negative balance of payments to the tune of $6.4 billions.

It has happened just as it was supposed *not* to happen. That is why Status Quo Economists cry "Impossible!" Nevertheless, it happened.

And it is *here*—balance of trade payments—that the constraints on GNP growth appear and *guarantee* a lower level of growth in GNP. This means inevitably a sharp slow down from the rapid 1972 GNP growth rate to a rate nearer the long-time average of 3%, but perhaps in the short run a great deal less.

The Status Quo Economists were trying a different approach: seeking to use the world monetary system as the vehicle for turning the deficit in payments around as well as negotiating an end of trade barriers to U.S. goods. This tunnel vision failed to find the light. The game cannot be played that way; the bills fall due.

So, now we have an economy laden with bankrupt consumers. And the American wage earner's gamble at the retail stores and on his own economic future will fail to pay off—just like it did on Wall Street in 1929.

The business cycle emerges again alive and well, but capitalism, as we knew it, expired in the process.

Notes

Introduction

1. New York First National City Bank *Monthly Economic Letter,* January 1971, p. 1 (italics added).
2. As paraphrased by *Saturday Review,* January 23, 1971, p. 56 (italics added).
3. *Los Angeles Times,* March 14, 1971. The *Times* further detailed the Gallup survey:

   To obtain the latest evaluation of the state of business at the grassroots level, this question was asked:

   "How do you size up business conditions in this locality—would you say they are very good, not too good, or bad?"

   Here are the latest national results, compared with figures recorded last August:

   Local Business Conditions
   (Total Sample)

	Aug.	Now	% Point change
Very good	9	5	—4
Good	45	39	—6
Not too good	30	37	+7
Bad	9	12	+3
No opinion	7	7	0

   Following is a comparison by region, based on the combined total of persons saying "very good." The results show an appreciable drop in each region.

   Per Cent Saying
   "Very Good" or "Good"

	Aug.	Now	% Point change
East	49	39	—10
Midwest	53	43	—10
South	62	53	— 9
West	55	40	—15

That the people had been affirming in the market their stated attitudes is shown in the Federal Reserve Board's Indexes of Industrial Production for February 1970 and February 1971:

	Feb. 1970	Feb. 1971
Market Groupings:		
Final Products	169.9	163.0
Consumer Products	162.4	164.2
Business Equipment	196.9	174.0
Materials	171.5	166.7
Industry Groupings:		
Manufacturing	170.3	162.5
Durable Goods	169.6	157.8
Nondurable Goods	171.3	168.2
Utilities	232.7	244.0

(Figures are preliminary and seasonally adjusted)

4. *Los Angeles Times,* March 13, 1971, Part III, p. 9.
5. *Wall Street Journal,* April 15, 1971, p. 1.
6. At the time the Gallup Poll was being taken, the *Los Angeles Times* was reporting on August 31, 1971:

NIXON'S ECONOMIC POLICIES
FAIL TO SPUR BUYING SPREE

As he stood before the network TV cameras August 15, President Nixon may have been hoping his new economic policies would restore consumer confidence and spark an economy-boosting spending spree.

If so, he is in for a disappointment. Retailers both in Southern California and around the nation report no perceptible change, either up or down, as a result of the wage and price controls and import surcharge.

Chapter 1: Consumer Sovereignty

1. Figures for 1970 indicate that of a total U.S. employment of 70,616,000, 67% worked in service-producing industries and 33% in goods-producing industries—manufacturing 27.4%, mining 0.9%, construction 4.7% (Source: Federal Reserve Bank of Cleveland, 1971 Annual Report, p. 3).

   The March 1972 *Manpower Report of the President* stated: "In the fourth quarter [1971] employment in these [service-producing] industries totaled 48.6 million, or more than two-thirds of all payroll jobs." (p. 35).
2. Robert Theobald, *An Alternative Future for America II,* p. 121. See especially chapter 9 in this Theobald volume for more discussion of these issues.
3. Roderic Gorney, *The Human Agenda,* pp. 8–9.
4. *U.S. News and World Report,* March 8, 1971, p. 22.

5. *Newsweek,* February 16, 1970, p. 72.
6. Theobald, *Alternative Future,* pp. 121–22.
7. Walter Lippmann, *Public Opinion,* pp. 54–55.
8. Donald T. Regan, *A View From the Street,* p. 45.

Chapter 2: A Service Economy

1. *Forbes,* August 1, 1972, p. 18.
2. Victor Fuchs, *The Service Economy,* pp. 2, 19, 22, 2. Fuch's summary of changes, listed in terms of percentage of persons employed by sector, reads as follows:

	1929	1965
Agriculture	19.9%	5.7%
Industry	39.7%	39.6%
Service	40.4%	54.8%

3. *Los Angeles Times,* August 13, 1972, Section F, p. 1.
4. Department of Human Resources Development Report, State of California, as reported in *Costa Mesa Daily Pilot,* August 25, 1972, p. 19.
5. *Wall Street Journal,* August 18, 1972, p. 10.
6. Ibid.
7. *Wall Street Journal,* March 6, 1972, p. 1.

Chapter 3: The Service Industries

1. H. S. Houthakker and Lester D. Taylor, *Consumer Demand in the United States,* pp. 101, 102.
2. *Wall Street Journal,* February 10, 1972, p. 4.
3. U. S. Department of Commerce, *Survey of Current Business,* June 1972.
4. *Fortune,* March 1970, p. 89 (italics added).
5. Victor Fuchs, *The Service Economy,* pp. 10, 11.
6. Ibid., pp. 12, 194–95, 12.
7. Ibid., pp. 198–99.
8. Paul Samuelson, "Science and Stocks," *Newsweek,* September 19, 1966, p. 92.

Chapter 5: Bad Numbers

1. The first item is from the New York First National City Bank *Monthly Economic Letter,* August 1972, p. 5; the second and third items from the *Wall Street Journal,* July 24, 1972, p. 3; and the fourth item from the *Wall Street Journal,* May 28, 1971, p. 12.
2. Oskar Morgenstern, *On the Accuracy of Economic Observations,* p. 268.
3. *Wall Street Journal,* March 8, 1971, p. 1.
4. Morgenstern, *Accuracy of Economic Observations,* pp. 58, 59, 60.
5. Ibid., p. 85.

6. W. J. Reichmann, *Use and Abuse of Statistics,* pp. 102, 103.
7. Morgenstern, *Accuracy of Economic Observations,* p. 125.
8. First National City Bank *Letter,* August 1972 (italics added).
9. *Time,* August 2, 1971, p. 58.
10. *Wall Street Journal,* May 24, 1971, p. 1.
11. *Time,* August 2, 1971, p. 59.
12. Ibid., p. 37.
13. Morgenstern, *Accuracy of Economic Observations,* p. 242.
14. Ibid., p. 266.
15. Ibid., p. 272.
16. *Los Angeles Times,* July 7, 1968, Section G, p. 1.
17. Morgenstern, *Accuracy of Economic Observations,* p. 190*n*13.

Chapter 6: Psychology in Business and Consumer Decisions

1. A. C. Pigou, *The Economics of Welfare,* p. 833.
2. Ibid., p. 839–40.
3. Ibid., p. 843.
4. Ibid.
5. Ibid., p. 844.
6. The Schmolders quotations came from an article by him in German, part of which was translated and used in an English-language book, where I read them. Unfortunately, I have lost my reference to the English-language source.
7. James A. Knight, *For the Love of Money: Human Behavior and Money,* pp. 14, 16, 18, 13, 14.
8. R. H. Tawney, *The Aquisitive Society,* p. 4.
9. Harris Trust and Savings Bank, *Barometer of Business,* April 1971, p. 1.
10. Paul Holmos, *The Personal Service Society,* p. 50.
11. Robert Lekachman, *The Age of Keynes,* pp. 99–101.
12. Joan Robinson, *Economic Heresies: Some Old-Fashioned Questions in Economic Theory,* p. 80.
13. *1969 Finance Facts Yearbook,* p. 52.
14. U.S. Savings & Loan League, *S&L Fact Book 1971,* p. 68.
15. Sylvia Porter column, *Costa Mesa Daily Pilot,* July 29, 1971, p. 30.
16. *Wall Street Journal,* July 20, 1972, p. 3.

Chapter 7: "Rich" & "Poor" Stock Ownership

1. Howard Sherman, *Radical Political Economy,* pp. 49–50.
2. Marian Irish and James Prothro, *The Politics of American Democracy,* p. 38.
3. New York Stock Exchange, *Public Transaction Study of 1969.*
4. *Forbes,* November 1, 1970, p. 36 (italics added).
5. *Wall Street Journal,* December 12, 1970, p. 35.
6. *Costa Mesa Globe Herald,* October 15, 1971, p. 9.
7. Ibid., October 1, 1971, p. 11.

8. Robin Barlow, Harvey E. Brazer, and James N. Morgan, *Economic Behavior of the Affluent,* p. 60.
9. Ibid., p. 46.
10. *Wall Street Journal,* January 14, 1971, p. 27.
11. *Newsweek,* May 29, 1967, p. 54.
12. Morgan Guaranty Survey, December 1970, p. 4.

Chapter 8: People-Watching

1. *Business Week,* December 20, 1969, p. 76.
2. Gustave Le Bon, *The Crowd,* p. 8.
3. Survey Research Center, University of Michigan, Ann Arbor, Michigan.
4. *Business Week,* December 20, 1969, p. 76.
5. *U.S. News and World Report,* June 22, 1970, p. 66.
6. *Los Angeles Times,* January 15, 1971, Section C, p. 7.

Chapter 9: The Pulse of the People

1. William James, *Psychology,* p. 61.
2. *Wall Street Journal,* May 28, 1970.
3. Illustrative of the point I often make that the masses basically ignore easily ignored costs (e.g., interest rates) is the fact that from fiscal 1970 to fiscal 1974, payroll taxes have more than tripled, going from $23.4 billion to $78.2 billion. Hidden in payroll deductions, these taxes are less visible to the ordinary consumer than are, for example, personal income taxes or sales taxes. Tax expert Edward J. Harney, partner in the giant accounting firm of Peat, Marwick, Mitchell & Co., says: "I can remember a time when social security tax totaled $30 a year. Now an annual payout of $1,000 is just around the corner. It's unbelievable. *I don't think the ordinary person is really aware of what's happening.*" (italics added)

   The most detailed study of the Social Security tax is the recent (1972) Brookings Institution book, *The Payroll Tax for Social Security,* by John A. Brittain. It concludes that not only is the Social Security tax rising faster than any other federal tax, but it is both increasingly unfair to lower income workers and discriminatory against middle-income families. Then the study significantly suggests:

   > One might have expected a good deal of resistance to a tax of this kind, but little criticism has arisen until recently. That the tax has expanded virtually unchallenged is attributable [in part] to the taxpayer's impression that . . . the rates seem low in comparison with those of the Federal income tax. *Most wage earners don't realize how much they are actually paying. (New York Times,* November 19, 1972, p. 18; italics added)

4. James, *Psychology,* pp. 295, 292.
5. H. J. Leavitt, *Managerial Psychology,* p. 28.
6. Kenneth Boulding, *The Image: Knowledge in Life and Society,* p. 7.

7. James, *Psychology,* p. 299.
8. Daniel Boorstin, *The Image: A Guide to Pseudo-Events in America,* pp. iii, 40.
9. Ibid., pp. 13, 14.

Chapter 10: The Consumer of Stocks

1. Robert Theobald, *Free Men and Free Markets,* pp. 132, 134, 135, 136–37.
2. *Los Angeles Times,* January 31, 1971, Section F, p. 7.
3. Survey Research Center, University of Michigan, Ann Arbor, Michigan.
4. Ibid.
5. *Wall Street Journal,* February 1, 1971, p. 3.
6. Richard T. Gill, *Economics and the Public Interest,* p. 120.
7. Marshall McLuhan and Quentin Fiore, *The Medium is the Massage,* p. 22.
8. Snell and Gail J. Putney, *The Adjusted American: Normal Neuroses in the Individual and Society,* p. 3.
9. Ibid., p. 5.
10. Ibid., p. 8.
11. Ibid., p. 9.
12. Ibid., p. 10.
13. Ibid., p. 27.

Chapter 11: The Black Box Model

1. The dollar amount of these expenditures by those up to twenty-four years old is not very significant in the aggregate; also, with shifting attitudes of the age group twenty-four to thirty-five, their dollar impact should be minimized. Both age groups today do not have the acquisitive instinct of their parents, and when they do, their life styles and "consumer package" ideas are often unlike those of earlier generations. It is the thirty-five to sixty-five age group that has the bulk of the money.
2. I discussed with several competent mathematicians the worthwhileness of quantifying more precisely the numbers in the Black Box model. It was their consensus that yes it could be done but it would not make a significant difference, since large trends up or down were my central concern. Quantifying these more precisely and picking up minute changes might instead prove to be self-defeating. They advised me to settle for simple but effective weighted index numbers.
3. A problem in working with an index number is the necessity to maintain a fairly rigid structure so that the index remains basically the same through time, while still keeping flexible enough to account for important external changes. For example, one development to keep an eye on appeared seriously only in the late 1960s: indicators of social change or of social responsibility—an attempt to get a numerical fix on the hidden costs or social costs of, say, a new factory, as measured by ecological disturbances, etc.

4. As reported in *Business Management,* March 1970, pp. 26, 38. The wide spread in the sixth set of figures (850-924) is explained as follows: "Most brokers divided with an even split between 850-874 and 900-924.
5. James Flanagan's interview appeared as a *Forbes* "The Money Men" article in the September 1, 1970 issue, pp. 43–44.
6. *Los Angeles Times,* AP release, February 9, 1971, Part III, p. 9.
7. *Costa Mesa Daily Pilot,* May 17, 1971, p. 18.
8. *Wall Street Journal,* July 6, 1971, p. 29.
9. *Costa Mesa Daily Pilot,* July 13, 1971, p. 16.
10. *U.S. News and World Report,* July 12, 1971, p. 78.
11. *Finance Facts,* August 1971, p. 4.
12. *Los Angeles Times,* July 24, 1971, p. 1.
13. *Finance Facts,* August 1971, p. 2.
14. *Los Angeles Times,* July 18, 1971, Section G, p. 1.
15. *Tucson Star Citizen,* AP release, July 31, 1971, Section A, p. 16.
16. *Newsweek,* August 2, 1971, p. 68.
17. *The Arizona Republic* (Phoenix), August 1, 1971, p. B-11.
18. *Newsweek,* August 9, 1971, p. 59.
19. *Wall Street Journal,* August 19, 1971, p. 4. The "soon-to-be-published book" referred to is Hurd Baruch's *Wall Street: Security Risk.*
20. *Wall Street Journal,* August 23, 1971, p. 23.
21. *Los Angeles Times.*
22. Ibid., August 22, 1971, Section H, p. 1.

Chapter 12: Socioeconomic Implications

1. "Economic waste" has been defined by Senator Phillip Hart's investigating committee as including, among other variables, poor quality goods and advertising not seen by the consumer but paid for by him in the price of the product.

   Another statistical way to look at the consumer's empty pocketbook is to note the effect inflation and taxes have had on savings, as reported by the United Business Service of Boston. Using the average interest rate paid by savings and loan associations, which is usually higher than rates paid by commercial or savings banks, we see that in 1971, for example, whereas each $100 in a savings account paid $5.33 (in interest), $3.36 of this was lost during the year because of rising prices, and $1.33 went to the federal government for taxes. Therefore, the net return on $100 of savings was $.64; if the saver lived in a state with state income tax, then the net return was even less. United Business Service concluded: "Since 1960 your savings account has produced an annual average real return of a mere ½ of 1 percent a year—after inflation and taxes." (*Parade,* December 24, 1972, p. 4)
2. First paragraph from *New York Times,* December 31, 1972, Section 3, p. 13; second paragraph from *Chicago Sun-Times,* February 6, 1973, p. 40. All figures are from Federal Reserve Board reports and are seasonally adjusted.

3. Federal Reserve Bank of Philadelphia *Monthly Business Review,* August 1971, pp. 3–7.
4. Stuart Chase, *Money to Grow On,* pp. 68–69.
5. Joan Robinson, "Consumer's Sovereignty in a Planned Economy," in *On Political Economy and Econometrics: Essays in Honour of Oskar Lange,* p. 518.
6. Mark Green and Peter Petkas, "Nixon's Industrial State: Creeping Corporatism," *The New Republic,* September 16, 1972, p. 18.
7. *Wall Street Journal,* February 15, 1972, p. 4.
8. Aaron Wildavsky, "Does Planning Work?", *Public Interest,* Summer 1971, pp. 95, 96.
9. Green and Petkas, "Industrial State," *New Republic,* September 16, 1972, p. 19.
10. *Los Angeles Times,* September 22, 1972, Part III, p. 16.
11. *Los Angeles Times,* September 5, 1972, Part III, p. 10.
12. Ibid.
13. Ibid.
14. *Los Angeles Times,* September 24, 1972, Section H, p. 1.
15. Ibid., p. 10.
16. "Banking Your Taxes," *New Republic,* September 16, 1972, p. 10.
17. *Wall Street Journal,* September 2, 1971.

Epilogue

1. *Business Week,* February 10, 1973, p. 90.
2. Peter Barnes, "Earned vs. Unearned Income," *The New Republic,* October 7, 1972, p. 17.
3. *Los Angeles Times,* October 24, 1972, Part III, p. 11.
4. *Wall Street Journal,* December 11, 1972, p. 3 (italics added).
5. Marshall McLuhan, *Culture is Our Business,* p. 104.
6. *Los Angeles Times,* October 25, 1972, Part III, p. 9.
7. New York First National City Bank *Monthly Economic Letter,* October 1972, p. 6.
8. *Wall Street Journal,* November 16, 1972, p. 7.
9. *Los Angeles Times,* October 22, 1972, Section G, p. 1.
10. *Los Angeles Times,* November 26, 1972, Section I, p. 1.
11. *Time,* February 5, 1973, p. 63.
12. First National City Bank *Letter,* October 1972, p. 11.
13. *Los Angeles Times,* February 18, 1973, Part VI, p. 3.
14. *Los Angeles Times,* February 16, 1973, Part I, p. 20.
15. Ibid., Part III, p. 10.

Bibliography

Baran, P. A. and P. M. Sweezy. *Monopoly Capital*. New York: Modern Reader Paperbacks, 1968.

Barber, R. J. *The American Corporation*. New York: E. P. Dutton & Co., 1970.

Barlow, Robin, Harvey E. Brazer, and James N. Morgan. *Economic Behavior of the Affluent*. Washington, D. C.: The Brookings Institution, 1966.

Berelson, B. and G. A. Steiner. *Human Behavior*. New York: Harcourt Brace & World, 1967.

Berle, A. A. *Power Without Property*. New York: Harvest Books, 1959.

Boulding, Kenneth. *Beyond Economics*. Ann Arbor: Ann Arbor Paperbacks, 1970.

———. *The Image: Knowledge in Life and Society*. Ann Arbor: University of Michigan Press, 1961.

———. *The Meaning of the Twentieth Century*. New York: Harper Colophon Books, 1964.

———. *The Organizational Revolution*. Chicago: Quadrangle Books, 1968.

Boorstin, Daniel J. *The Image: A Guide to Pseudo-Events in America*. New York: Harper Colophon Books, 1961.

Brandeis, L. D. *Other People's Money*. New York: Harper Torchbooks, 1967.

Chase, Stuart. *Money to Grow On*. New York: Harper Colophon Books, 1961.

Christoffel, Tom, David Finkelhor, and Dan Gilbarg. *Up Against the American Myth*. New York: Holt, Rinehart & Winston, 1970.

Cootner, P. H. *The Random Character of Stock Market Prices*. Cambridge: M. I. T. Press, 1964.

Dauten, C. A. *Business Cycles and Forecasting*. Cincinnati: Southwestern Publishing Co., 1961.

Davis, Morton D. *Game Theory*. New York: Basic Books, Inc., 1970.
deGrazia, Sebastian. *Of Time, Work and Leisure*. New York: Doubleday, 1964.
Duesenberry, J. S. *Income Saving and The Theory of Consumer Behavior*. New York: Oxford University Press, 1967.
Engel, J. E., D. T. Kollat, and R. D. Blackwell. *Consumer Behavior*. New York: Holt, Rinehart & Winston, 1968.
Fuchs, Victor. *The Service Economy*. New York: National Bureau of Economic Research, 1968.
Fuller, R. Buckminster. *I Seem To Be A Verb*. New York: Bantam Books, 1970.
Galbraith, John Kenneth. *The Affluent Society*. New York: Mentor Books, 1958.
———. *The Great Crash*. Boston: Houghton Mifflin Co., 1961.
Gill, Richard T. *Economics and the Public Interest*. Pacific Palisades, Calif.: Pacific Publishing Co., 1968.
Goffman, E. *Behavior in Public Places*. New York: Free Press, 1963.
Goodman, Paul *Growing Up Absurd*. New York: Vintage Books, 1956.
Gorney, Roderic. *The Human Agenda*. New York: Simon & Schuster, 1972.
Haberler, Gottfried. *Inflation, Its Causes and Cures*. Washington D. C.: American Enterprise Institute for Public Policy Research, 1966.
———. *Prosperity and Depression*. New York: Atheneum, 1963.
Hansen, A. H. *Monetary Theory and Fiscal Policy*. New York: McGraw Hill, 1949.
Hayek, F. A. *The Road to Serfdom*. Chicago: Phoenix Books, 1944.
Heilbroner, Robert L. *Between Capitalism and Socialism*. New York: Vintage Books, 1970.
Holmos, Paul. *The Personal Service Society*. London: Constable and Co. Ltd., 1970.
Houthakker, H. S. and Lester D. Taylor. *Consumer Demand in the United States: Analyses and Projections*. Cambridge: Harvard University Press, 1970.
Ichheiser, Gustav. *Appearances and Realities*. San Francisco: Jossey-Bass, Inc., 1970.
Irish, Marian and James Prothro. *The Politics of American Democracy*. Englewood Cliffs: Prentice-Hall, 1965.
James, William. *Psychology*. New York: Fawcett Publications, 1963.
Katona, G. *The Mass Consumption Society*. New York: McGraw Hill, 1964.
———. *The Powerful Consumer*. New York: McGraw Hill, 1960.
Knight, F. H. *Risk, Uncertainty and Profit*. Chicago: Phoenix Books, 1971.
Knight, James A. *For the Love of Money: Human Behavior and Money*. Philadelphia: J. P. Lippincott Co., 1968.
Leavitt, H. J. *Managerial Psychology*. Chicago: University of Chicago

Press, 1958.
Le Bon, Gustave. *The Crowd: A Study of the Popular Mind.* New York: Ballantine Books, 1969.
———. *The Psychology of Socialism.* Wells, Vermont: Fraser Publishing Co., 1965.
Lekachman, Robert. *The Age of Keynes.* New York: Random House, 1966.
Lewis, J. P. *Business Conditions Analysis.* New York: McGraw Hill, 1959.
Linder, S. B. *The Harried Leisure Class.* New York: Columbia University Press, 1970.
Lippman, Walter. *Public Opinion.* New York: Free Press Paperbacks, 1965.
Lipset, S. M. and Earl Raab. *The Politics of Unreason.* New York: Harper & Row, 1970.
London, Perry, *Behavior Control.* New York: Harper & Row, 1969.
Lowe, Adolph. *On Economic Knowledge.* New York: Harper & Row, 1965.
Matthews, R. C. D. *The Business Cycle.* Chicago: University of Chicago Press, 1965.
McLuhan, Marshall. *Culture Is Our Business.* New York: Ballantine Books, 1972.
McLuhan, Marshall and Quentin Fiore. *The Medium is the Massage.* New York: Bantam Books, 1967.
McNeal, J. U. *Dimensions of Consumer Behavior.* New York: Appleton-Century-Crofts, 1965.
Miller, H. P. *Rich Man, Poor Man.* New York: Thomas Y. Crowell Co., 1964.
Mitchell, W. C. *Business Cycles.* New York: National Bureau of Economic Research, 1963.
Mishan, E. J. *21 Popular Economic Fallacies.* New York: Praeger, 1970.
Morgenstern, Oskar. *On the Accuracy of Economic Observations.* Princeton: Princeton University Press, 1963.
Muller, H. J. *The Uses of the Past.* New York: Mentor Books, 1952.
Myers, J. H. and W. H. Reynolds. *Consumer Behavior and Marketing Management.* Boston: Houghton Mifflin Co., 1967.
Mydral, G. *Beyond the Welfare State.* New York: Bantam Books, 1967.
Neff, Walter S. *Work and Human Behavior.* New York: Atherton Press, 1968.
Nove, Alec and D. M. Nuti (eds.) *Socialist Economics.* London: Penguin Books, 1972.
Pigou, A. C. *The Economics of Welfare.* London: Macmillan & Co., 1920.

Putney, Snell and Gail J. *The Adjusted American: Normal Neuroses in the Individual and Society*. New York: Harper Colophon Books, 1964.

Regan, Donald T. *A View from the Street*. New York: New American Library, 1972.

Reichmann, W. J. *Use and Abuse of Statistics*. New York: Oxford University Press, 1962.

Riesman, David. *Abundance for What?* New York: Doubleday & Co., 1965.

Robinson, Joan. *An Essay on Marxian Economics*. New York: Macmillan, St. Martin's Press, 1969.

———. *Economics, an Awkward Corner*. New York: Pantheon Books, 1967.

———. *Economic Heresies: Some Old-Fashioned Questions in Economic Theory*. New York: Basic Books, 1971.

———. *The Economics of Imperfect Competition*. New York: St. Martin's Press, 1969.

Robinson, R. J. *Money and Capital Markets*. New York: McGraw Hill, 1964.

Sartre, Jean-Paul. *The Psychology of Imagination*. New York: Washington Square Press, 1968.

Sherman, Howard. *Radical Political Economy*. New York: Basic Books, 1972.

Tawney, R. H. *The Aquisitive Society*. New York: Harvest Books, 1948.

Theobald, Robert. *An Alternative Future for America II*. Chicago: Swallow Press, 1970.

———. *Free Men and Free Markets*. New York: Clarkson N. Potter, Inc., 1963.

———. *The Challenge of Abundance*. New York: Mentor Books, 1961.

Acknowledgments

Anyone writing a book owes an enormous debt to the authors of the many books read and listed appropriately in the Bibliography. Beyond this, though, I owe a special debt to James Michaels and James Flanagan of *Forbes* magazine who first published some of my thoughts on the behavior of the masses of the people and its effects on securities prices. New ideas are rarely noticed in our culture, but *Forbes* noticed these, and I am grateful.

I am especially appreciative for Art Buchwald's generous permission to use large excerpts from two of his columns.

Also, let me give acknowledgment and thanks to my daughter, Mrs. Sherri Dougan, for her efforts in trying to make rough typed copy into something more readable. And, lastly, a note of special gratitude to Durrett Wagner of Swallow Press for incisive comments on the contents and for other editorial assistance.

J.L.K.

Index